WiX: A Developer's Guide to Windows Installer XML

Create a hassle-free installer for your Windows
software using WiX

Nick Ramirez

open source
community experience distilled

PUBLISHING

BIRMINGHAM - MUMBAI

WiX: A Developer's Guide to Windows Installer XML

First published: October 2010

Production Reference: 1131010

Published by Packt Publishing Ltd.
32 Lincoln Road
Olton
Birmingham, B27 6PA, UK.

ISBN 978-1-849513-72-2

www.packtpub.com

Cover Image by Asher Wishkerman (a.wishkerman@mpic.de)

Credits

Author
Nick Ramirez

Reviewer
Martin Oberhammer

Acquisition Editor
Eleanor Duffy

Development Editor
Dhiraj Chandiramani

Technical Editors
Vanjeet D'souza
Kavita Iyer
Harshit Shah

Indexer
Tejal Daruwale

Editorial Team Leader
Akshara Aware

Project Team Leader
Priya Mukherji

Project Coordinator
Jovita Pinto

Proofreader
Lynda Sliwoski

Production Coordinator
Melwyn D'sa

Cover Work
Melwyn D'sa

About the Author

Nick Ramirez is a software engineer working at Sophos in Columbus, Ohio. He previously worked with open source solutions like Linux and PHP before moving to C#, WiX, and other Windows technologies. As a member of the engineering team, he has helped to develop install code for the company's enterprise software.

I would like to thank especially my fiancée, Heidi, for her patience while I worked on this book. I'd also like to thank the Packt team for their hard work and guidance along the way. Another big thanks to Martin Oberhammer and Neil Sleightholm for their WiX expertise and help in filling in the gaps

About the Reviewer

Martin Oberhammer was born on December 25, 1975 in Italy. In 1995 he moved to Linz in Austria, where he studied computer science at the Johannes Kepler University and graduated in October 2002.

Martin worked at the Ars Electronica Center in Linz during his study. Together with artists, he created virtual realities for the CAVE. In May 2003 he started working for Utimaco Safeguard AG in Linz and developed advanced authentication techniques, like smart cards, for Microsoft Windows systems. He also made his first experiences in deploying software. The company transferred him to Foxboro, MA in USA in August 2008. Among other things he created setups using WiX technology. He moved to Columbus, OH in October 2009 and started working for Sophos Inc., where he continues creating setups.

Table of Contents

Preface

Since Rob Mensching offered up the WiX toolset as the first open source project from Microsoft in 2004, it has been quietly gaining momentum and followers. Today, thousands use it to build Windows Installer packages from simple XML elements. Gone are the days when you would have had to pay for software to build an installer for you. Now, you can do it yourself for cheap.

Not only that, but WiX has matured into a fairly slick product that's sufficiently easy to use. Best of all, it has all of the bells and whistles you want including the functionality to add user interface wizards, Start Menu shortcuts, control Windows services, and read and write to the Registry.

WiX: A Developer's Guide to Windows Installer XML gives you the knowledge to start building sophisticated installers right away, even if you have no prior experience doing so. Each chapter gets straight to the point, giving you hands on experience, so you'll master the technology quickly.

What this book covers

Chapter 1, Getting Started, explains how after downloading and installing the WiX toolset, you'll start using it right away to create a simple installer. Then, you'll see how to add a basic user interface to it, install it with logging turned on, and view its internal database.

Chapter 2, Creating Files and Directories, gives you deeper understanding of how files are installed and what is the best way to organize them in your project. You'll then use the tool heat.exe to generate WiX markup. Last, you'll learn about copying and moving files, and installing special-case files.

Chapter 3, Putting Properties and AppSearch to Work, gets you introduced to Windows Installer properties as you create your own and use those that are built in. Later, you'll check the end user's computer for specific files, directories, Registry keys, and INI file settings using AppSearch.

Chapter 4, Improving Control with Launch Conditions and Installed States, allows you to leverage conditional statements to set prerequisites for running your installer and to exclude particular features or components from the install. You'll also discover how to check the action and installed state of your features and components.

Chapter 5, Understanding the Install Sequence, allows you to get a clear picture of how the whole installation process works as you examine the order and meaning of installer actions. You will then create custom actions and add them to this built-in sequence to extend the functionality. Then, you'll learn the basics of using the Deployment Tools Foundation library for writing custom action code in C#.

Chapter 6, Adding a User Interface, after giving you a quick introduction to the standard dialog wizards that come with the WiX toolset, allows you to start building your own from scratch. You'll learn all of the required elements to display dialogs and to link them together. You'll also see how to build dialogs for displaying errors and user exits.

Chapter 7, Using UI Controls, gives you hands on experience with each type of UI control including buttons, textboxes, and progress bars.

Chapter 8, Tapping into Control Events, breathes life into your UI controls by having them publish and subscribe to events.

Chapter 9, Working from the Command Line, compiles your code from the command line and then links and binds object files into an MSI. You'll learn to use preprocessor variables and conditional statements and how to create custom preprocessor extensions.

Chapter 10, Accessing the Windows Registry, allows you to read from the Windows Registry and add keys and values to it at install time. You'll also learn how to remove existing keys, copy values, and set permissions.

Chapter 11, Controlling Windows Services, installs Windows services and issues start, stop, and remove commands to them. You'll learn to set the service's user account, add service dependencies, and set failure recovery.

Chapter 12, Localizing Your Installer, creates localized installers for different languages and teaches how light.exe, the WiX linker, plays a role. You'll then learn how to make a single multi-language installer.

Chapter 13, Upgrading and Patching, allows you to learn how to plan for and implement a major upgrade of your product and how to make small updates using patch files.

What you need for this book

In order to both write and run the code demonstrated in this book, you will need the following:

- Visual Studio 2005 or newer (Standard edition or higher)
- The WiX toolset, which can be downloaded from `http://wix.codeplex.com/`

Who this book is for

If you are a developer and want to create installers for software targeting the Windows platform, then this book is for you. You'll be using a lot of XML so that you get accustomed to the basics of writing well-formed documents, using XML namespaces and the dos and don'ts of structuring elements and attributes. You should know your way around Visual Studio, at least enough to compile projects, add project references, and tweak project properties. No prior knowledge of Windows Installer or WiX is assumed.

Conventions

In this book, you will find a number of styles of text that distinguish between different kinds of information. Here are some examples of these styles, and an explanation of their meaning.

Code words in text are shown as follows: "We can include other contexts through the use of the `include` directive."

A block of code is set as follows:

```
<Component Id="CMP_MyProgramEXE"
        Guid="E8A58B7B-F031-4548-9BDD-7A6796C8460D">
  <File Id="FILE_MyProgramEXE"
        Source="MyProgram.exe"
        Name="NewName.exe"
        KeyPath="yes" />
</Component>
```

When we wish to draw your attention to a particular part of a code block, the relevant lines or items are set in bold:

```
File Id="FILE_MyProgramEXE"
        Source="$(var.FilesPath)MyProgram.exe"
        KeyPath="yes" />
```

Any command-line input or output is written as follows:

```
Light.exe -loc en-us.wxl -loc en-us2.wxl -loc de-de.wxl
  -cultures:en-us "*.wixobj" -out myInstaller.msi
```

New terms and **important words** are shown in bold. Words that you see on the screen, in menus or dialog boxes for example, appear in the text like this: "Use the **Add Reference** option in your **Solution Explorer**".

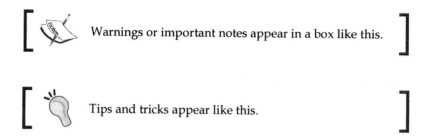

> Warnings or important notes appear in a box like this.

> Tips and tricks appear like this.

Reader feedback

Feedback from our readers is always welcome. Let us know what you think about this book—what you liked or may have disliked. Reader feedback is important for us to develop titles that you really get the most out of.

To send us general feedback, simply send an e-mail to feedback@packtpub.com, and mention the book title via the subject of your message.

If there is a book that you need and would like to see us publish, please send us a note in the **SUGGEST A TITLE** form on www.packtpub.com or e-mail suggest@packtpub.com.

If there is a topic that you have expertise in and you are interested in either writing or contributing to a book, see our author guide on www.packtpub.com/authors.

Customer support

Now that you are the proud owner of a Packt book, we have a number of things to help you to get the most from your purchase.

Downloading the example code for this book

You can download the example code files for all Packt books you have purchased from your account at http://www.PacktPub.com. If you purchased this book elsewhere, you can visit http://www.PacktPub.com/support and register to have the files e-mailed directly to you.

Errata

Although we have taken every care to ensure the accuracy of our content, mistakes do happen. If you find a mistake in one of our books—maybe a mistake in the text or the code—we would be grateful if you would report this to us. By doing so, you can save other readers from frustration and help us improve subsequent versions of this book. If you find any errata, please report them by visiting http://www.packtpub.com/support, selecting your book, clicking on the **errata submission form** link, and entering the details of your errata. Once your errata are verified, your submission will be accepted and the errata will be uploaded on our website, or added to any list of existing errata, under the Errata section of that title. Any existing errata can be viewed by selecting your title from http://www.packtpub.com/support.

Piracy

Piracy of copyrighted material on the Internet is an ongoing problem across all media. At Packt, we take the protection of our copyright and licenses very seriously. If you come across any illegal copies of our works, in any form, on the Internet, please provide us with the location address or website name immediately so that we can pursue a remedy.

Please contact us at copyright@packtpub.com with a link to the suspected pirated material.

We appreciate your help in protecting our authors, and our ability to bring you valuable content.

Questions

You can contact us at questions@packtpub.com if you are having a problem with any aspect of the book, and we will do our best to address it.

1
Getting Started

Windows Installer XML (WiX) is a free XML markup from Microsoft that is used to author installation packages for Windows-based software. The underlying technology is Windows Installer, which is the established standard for installing desktop-based applications to any Windows operating system. It is used by countless companies around the world. Microsoft uses it to deploy its own software including Microsoft Office and Visual Studio. In fact, Microsoft uses WiX for these products.

Windows Installer has many features, but how do you leverage them? How do you even know what they are? This book will help you by making you more familiar with the wide range of capabilities that are available. WiX makes many of the arcane and difficult to understand aspects of Windows Installer technology simple to use. This book will teach you the WiX syntax so that you can create a professional-grade installer that's right for you.

In this chapter, we will cover the following:

- Getting WiX and using it with Visual Studio
- Creating your first WiX installer
- Examining an installer database with Orca
- Logging an installation process
- Adding a simple user interface

Introducing Windows Installer XML

In this section, we'll dive right in and talk about what WiX is, where to get it, and why you'd want to use it when building an installation package for your software. We'll follow up with a quick description of the WiX tools and the new project types made available in Visual Studio.

What is WiX?

Although it's the standard technology and has been around for years, creating a Windows Installer, or **MSI** package, has always been a challenging task. The package is actually a relational database that describes how the various components of an application should be unpacked and copied to the end user's computer.

In the past you had two options:

- You could try to author the database yourself—a path that requires a thorough knowledge of the Windows Installer API.

- You could buy a commercial product like InstallShield to do it for you. These software products will take care of the details, but you'll forever be dependent on them. There will always be parts of the process that are hidden from you.

WiX is relatively new to the scene, offering a route that exists somewhere in the middle. Abstracting away the low-level function calls while still allowing you to write much of the code by hand, WiX is an architecture for building an installer in ways that mere mortals can grasp. Best of all, it's free. As an open source product, it has quickly garnered a wide user base and a dedicated community of developers. Much of this has to do not only with its price tag but also with its simplicity. It can be authored in a simple text editor (such as Notepad) and compiled with the tools provided by WiX. As it's a flavor of XML, it can be read by humans, edited without expensive software, and lends itself to being stored in source control where it can be easily merged and compared.

The examples in this first chapter will show how to create a simple installer with WiX using Visual Studio. However, later chapters will show how you can build your project from the command line using the compiler and linker from the WiX toolset. The WiX source code is available for download, so you can be assured that nothing about the process will be hidden if you truly need to know.

Is WiX for you?

To answer the question "Is WiX for you?" we have to answer "What can WiX *do for you*?" It's fairly simple to copy files to an end user's computer. If that's all your product needs, then the Windows Installer technology might be overkill. However, there are many benefits to creating an installable package for your customers, some of which might be overlooked. Following is a list of features that you get when you author a Windows Installer package with WiX:

- All of your executable files can be packaged into one convenient bundle, simplifying deployment.

- Your software is automatically registered with **Add/Remove Programs**.
- Windows takes care of uninstalling all of the components that make up your product when the user chooses to do so.
- If files for your software are accidently removed, they can be replaced by right-clicking on the MSI file and selecting **Repair**.
- You can create different versions of your installer and detect which version has been installed.
- You can create patches to update only specific areas of your application.
- If something goes wrong while installing your software, the end user's computer can be rolled back to a previous state.
- You can create **Wizard**-style dialogs to guide the user through the installation.

Many people today simply expect that your installer will have these features. Not having them could be seen as a real deficit. For example, what is a user supposed to do when they want to uninstall your product but can't find it in the **Add/Remove Programs** list and there isn't an uninstall shortcut? They're likely to remove files haphazardly and wonder why you didn't make things easy for them.

Maybe you've already figured that Windows Installer is the way to go, but why WiX? One of my favorite reasons is that it gives you greater control over how things work. You get a much finer level of control over the development process. Commercial software that does this for you also produces an MSI file, but hides the details about how it was done. It's analogous to crafting a web site. You get much more control when you write the HTML yourself as opposed to using WYSIWYG software.

Even though WiX gives you more control, it doesn't make things overly complex. You'll find that making a simple installer is very straightforward. For more complex projects, the parts can be split up into multiple XML source files to make it easier to work with. Going further, if your product is made up of multiple products that will be installed together as a suite, you can compile the different chunks into libraries that can be merged together into a single MSI. This allows each team to isolate and manage their part of the installation package.

WiX is a stable technology, having been first released to the public in 2004, so you don't have to worry about it disappearing. It's also had a steady progression of version releases. The most current version is updated for Windows Installer 4.5 and the next release will include changes for Windows Installer 5.0, which is the version that comes preinstalled with Windows 7. These are just some of the reasons why you might choose to use WiX.

Where can I get it?

You can download WiX from the Codeplex site, `http://wix.codeplex.com/`, which has both stable releases and source code. The current release is version 3.0. Once you've downloaded the WiX installer package, double-click it to install it to your local hard drive.

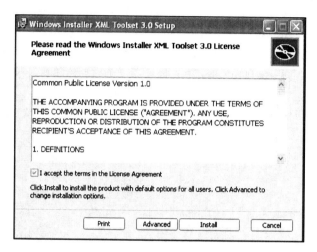

This installs all of the necessary files needed to build WiX projects. You'll also get the WiX SDK documentation and the settings for Visual Studio IntelliSense, highlighting and project templates. Version 3 supports Visual Studio 2005 and Visual Studio 2008, Standard edition or higher.

WiX comes with the following tools:

Tool	What it does
Candle.exe	Compiles WiX source files (`.wxs`) into intermediate object files (`.wixobj`).
Light.exe	Links and binds `.wixobj` files to create final `.msi` file. Also creates cabinet files and embeds streams in MSI database.
Lit.exe	Creates WiX libraries (`.wixlib`) that can be linked together by Light.
Dark.exe	Decompiles an MSI file into WiX code.
Heat.exe	Creates a WiX source file that specifies components from various inputs.
Melt.exe	Converts a "merge module" (`.msm`) into a component group in a WiX source file.
Torch.exe	Generates a transform file used to create a software patch.
Smoke.exe	Runs validation checks on an MSI or MSM file.
Pyro.exe	Creates an patch file (`.msp`) from `.wixmsp` and `.wixmst` files.
WixCop.exe	Converts version 2 WiX files to version 3.

In order to use some of the functionality in WiX, you may need to download a more recent version of Windows Installer. You can check your current version by viewing the help file for `msiexec.exe`, which is the Windows Installer service. Go to your **Start Menu** and select **Run**, type `cmd` and then type `msiexec /?` at the prompt. This should bring up a window like the following:

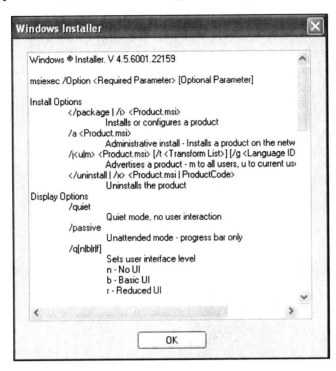

If you'd like to install a newer version of Windows Installer, you can get one from the Microsoft Download Center website. Go to:

`http://www.microsoft.com/downloads/en/default.aspx`

Search for **Windows Installer**. The current version for Windows XP, Vista, Server 2003, and Server 2008 is 4.5. Windows 7 and Windows Server 2008 R2 can support version 5.0. Each new version is backwards compatible and includes the features from earlier editions.

Votive

The WiX toolset provides files that update Visual Studio to provide new WiX IntelliSense, syntax highlighting, and project templates. Together these features, which are installed for you along with the other WiX tools, are called **Votive**. You must have Visual Studio 2005 or 2008 (Standard edition or higher). Votive won't work on the Express versions. If you're using Visual Studio 2005, you may need to install an additional component called **ProjectAggregator2**. Refer to the WiX site for more information:

```
http://wix.sourceforge.net/votive.html
```

After you've installed WiX, you should see a new category of project types in Visual Studio, labeled under the title **WiX**. To test it out, open Visual Studio and go to **File | New | Project**. Select the category **WiX**.

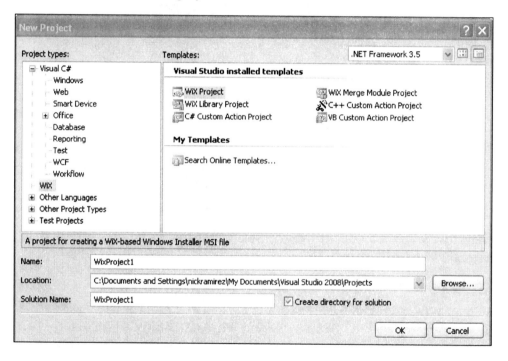

There are six new project templates:

- **WiX Project**: Creates a Windows Installer package from one or more WiX source files

- **WiX Library Project**: Creates a .wixlib library

- **C# Custom Action Project**: Creates a .NET custom action in C#

- **WiX Merge Module Project**: Creates a merge module
- **C++ Custom Action Project**: Creates an unmanaged C++ custom action
- **VB Custom Action Project**: Creates a VB.NET custom action

Using these templates is certainly easier than creating them on your own with a text editor. To start creating your own MSI installer, select the template **WiX Project**. This will create a new .wxs (WiX source file) for you to add XML markup to. Once we've added the necessary markup, you'll be able to build the solution by selecting **Build Solution** from the **Build** menu or by right-clicking on the project in the **Solution Explorer** and selecting **Build**. Visual Studio will take care of calling candle.exe and light.exe to compile and link your project files.

If you right-click on your WiX project in the **Solution Explorer** and select **Properties**, you'll see several screens where you can tweak the build process. One thing you'll want to do is set the amount of information that you'd like to see when compiling and linking the project and how non-critical messages are treated. Refer to the following screenshot:

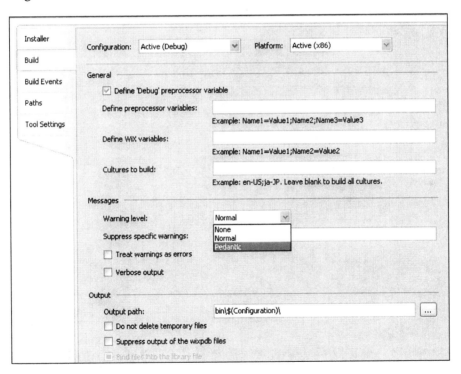

Here, we're selecting the level of messages that we'd like to see. To see all warnings and messages, set the **Warning Level** to **Pedantic**. You can also check the **Verbose output** checkbox to get even more information. Checking **Treat warnings as errors** will cause warning messages that normally would not stop the build to be treated as fatal errors.

You can also choose to suppress certain warnings. You'll need to know the specific warning message number, though. If you get a build-time warning, you'll see the warning message, but not the number. One way to get it is to open the WiX source code (available at `http://wix.codeplex.com/SourceControl/list/changesets`) and view the `messages.xml` file in the `Wix solution`. Search the file for the warning and from there you'll see its number. Note that you can suppress warnings but not errors.

Another feature of WiX is its ability to run validity checks on the MSI package. Windows Installer uses a suite of tests called **Internal Consistency Evaluators** (ICEs) for this. These checks ensure that the database as a whole makes sense and that the keys on each table join correctly. Through Votive, you can choose to suppress specific ICE tests. Use the **Tools Setting** page of the project's properties as shown in the following screenshot:

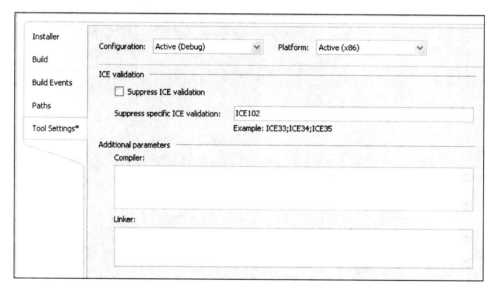

In this example, ICE test 102 is being suppressed. You can specify more than one test by separating them with semicolons. To find a full list of ICE tests, go to MSDN's **ICE Reference** web page at:

`http://msdn.microsoft.com/en-us/library/aa369206%28VS.85%29.aspx`

The **Tool Settings** screen also gives you the ability to add compiler or linker command-line flags. Simply add them to the text boxes at the bottom of the screen. We will discuss command-line arguments for Candle and Light later in the book.

A word about GUIDs

In various places throughout WiX, you'll be asked to provide a **GUID**, which is a **Globally Unique Identifier**. This is so that when your product is installed on the end user's computer, references to it can be stored in the Windows Registry without the chance of having name conflicts. By using GUIDs, Windows Installer can be sure that every software application, and even every component of that software, has a unique identity on the system.

Each GUID that you create on your computer is guaranteed to be different from a GUID that someone else would make. Using this, even if two pieces of software, both called "Amazing Software", are installed on the same computer, Windows will be able to tell them apart.

Visual Studio 2008 provides a way to create a GUID. Go to **Tools | Create GUID** and copy a new GUID using the **Registry Format**. WiX can accept a GUID with or without curly brackets around it as `01234567-89AB-CDEF-0123-456789ABCDEF` or `{01234567-89AB-CDEF-0123-456789ABCDEF}`.

Be sure to only use uppercase letters, though. In this book, I'll display real GUIDs, but you should not reuse them as then your components will not be guaranteed to be unique.

Your first WiX project

To get started, download the WiX Toolset. It can be found at:

`http://wix.codeplex.com/`

Once you've downloaded and installed it, open Visual Studio and select **New Project | WiX | WiX Project**. This will create a solution with a single `.wxs` (WiX source) file. Visual Studio will usually call this file `Product.wxs`, but the name could be anything as long as it ends with `.wxs`.

Even the most minimal installer must have the following XML elements:

- an XML declaration
- a `Wix` element that serves as the root element in your XML document
- a `Product` element that is a child to the `Wix` element, but all other elements are children to it

- a `Package` element
- a `Media` element
- at least one `Directory` element with at least one child `Component` element
- a `Feature` element

XML declaration and Wix element

Every WiX project begins with an XML declaration and a `Wix` element.

```
<?xml version="1.0" encoding="UTF-8"?>
<Wix xmlns="http://schemas.microsoft.com/wix/2006/wi">

</Wix>
```

The `xmlns`, or XML namespace, just brings the core WiX elements into the local scope of your document. At the bottom of the file, you'll have to close the `Wix` element, of course. Otherwise, it's not valid XML. The `Wix` element is the root element of the document. It comes first and last. All other elements will be nested inside of it.

At this point, you could also add the `RequiredVersion` attribute to the `Wix` element. Given a WiX toolset version number, such as "3.0.5419.0", it won't let anyone compile the `.wxs` file unless they have that version or higher installed. If, on the other hand, you're the only one compiling your project, then it's no big deal.

Product element

Next, add a `Product` element.

```
<Wix ... >
  <Product Id="3E786878-358D-43AD-82D1-1435ADF9F6EA"
           Name="Awesome Software"
           Language="1033"
           Version="1.0.0.0"
           Manufacturer="Awesome Company"
           UpgradeCode="B414C827-8D81-4B4A-B3B6-338C06DE3A11">
  </Product>
</Wix>
```

This is where you define the characteristics of the software you're installing: its name, language, version, and manufacturer. The end user will be able to see these properties by right-clicking on your MSI file, selecting **Properties** and viewing the **Summary** tab. Most of the time, these values will stay the same from one build of your project to the next. The exception is when you want to increment the software's version or indicate that it's an upgrade of a previous installation. In that case you need only change the Version, and sometimes Id, attribute. We'll talk more about upgrading previous installations later on in the book.

The Product element's Id attribute represents the so-called ProductCode of your software. It's always a unique number — a GUID — that Windows will use to uniquely identify your software (and tell if it's already installed on the computer). You can either hardcode it, like here, or just put an asterisk. That way, WiX will pick a new GUID for you each time you compile the project.

```
<Wix ... >
  <Product Id="*"
           Name="Awesome Software"
           Language="1033"
           Version="1.0.0.0"
           Manufacturer="Awesome Company"
           UpgradeCode="B414C827-8D81-4B4A-B3B6-338C06DE3A11">
  </Product>
</Wix>
```

The Name attribute defines the name of the software. In addition to being displayed in the MSI file's **Properties** page, it will also be shown in various places throughout the user interface of your installer — that is, once you've added a user interface, which we'll touch on at the end of this chapter.

The Language attribute is used to display error messages and progress information in the specified language to the user. It's a decimal language ID (LCID). A full list can be found on Microsoft's LCID page at:

http://msdn.microsoft.com/en-us/goglobal/bb964664.aspx

The previous example used "1033", which stands for "English-United States". If your installer uses characters not found in the ASCII character set, you'll also need to add a Codepage attribute set to the code page that contains those characters. Don't worry too much about this now. We'll cover languages and code pages later in the book when we talk about localization.

The Version attribute is used to set the version number of your software. It can accept up to four digits separated by periods, although the last digit is ignored by Windows Installer during operations such as detecting previously installed versions of your application. Typically, when you make a big enough change to the existing software, you'll increment the number. Companies often use the *[MajorVersion].[MinorVersion].[Build].[Revision]* format, but you're free to use any numbering system you like.

The `Manufacturer` attribute tells the user who this software is from and usually contains the name of your company. This is another bit of information that's available via the MSI file's **Properties**.

The final attribute to consider is `UpgradeCode`. This should be set to a GUID and will identify your product across version releases. Therefore, it should stay the same even when the Product ID and Version change. Windows will use this number in its efforts to keep track of all the software installed on the machine. WiX has the ability to search for previously installed versions of not only your own software but also those created by others and it uses `UpgradeCode` to do it. Although, technically, this is an optional attribute, you should always supply it.

Package element

Once you've defined your `Product` element, the next step is to nest a `Package` element inside. An example is shown:

```
<Wix ... >
  <Product ... >
    <Package Compressed="yes"
             InstallerVersion="301"
             Manufacturer="Awesome Company"
             Description="Installs Awesome Software"
             Keywords="Practice,Installer,MSI"
             Comments="(c) 2010 Awesome Company"  />
  </Product>
</Wix>
```

Of the attributes shown in this example, only `Compressed` is really required. By setting `Compressed` to `yes`, you're telling the installer to package all of the MSI's resources into CAB files. Later, you'll define these CAB files with `Media` elements.

Technically, an `Id` attribute is also required, but by omitting it, you're letting WiX create one for you. You'd have to create a new one anyway since every time you change your software or the installer in any way, the "package" (the MSI file) has changed and so the ID must change. This really, in itself, emphasizes what the `Package` element is. Unlike the `Product` element, which describes the software that's in the installer, the `Package` element describes the installer itself. Once you've built it, you'll be able to right-click on the MSI and select **Properties** to see the attributes you've set here.

The `InstallerVersion` attribute can be set to require a specific version of `msiexec.exe` (the Windows Installer service that installs the MSI when you double-click on it) to be installed on the end user's computer. If they have an older version, Windows

Installer will display a `MessageBox` telling them that they need to upgrade. It will also prevent you from compiling the project unless you also have this version installed on your own computer. The value can be found by multiplying the major version by 100 and adding the minor version. So, for version 4.5 of `msiexec.exe`, you'd set `InstallerVersion` to "405".

The rest of the attributes shown provide additional information for the MSI file's **Properties** window. `Manufacturer` is displayed in the **Author** text field, `Description` is shown as **Subject**, `Keywords` show up as **Keywords**, and `Comments` show as **Comments**. It's usually a good idea to provide at least some of this information, if just to help *you* distinguish one MSI package from another.

Media element

The files that you intend to install are bundled up into CAB files. You have the option of splitting your package into several parts or keeping it all in one. For each `Media` element that you add to your WiX markup, a new CAB file will be created. Generally, you should limit the number of files you put into a single CAB file to 64 K or less and no single file should be larger than 2 GB. You can find more information about the CAB file format at:

http://msdn.microsoft.com/en-us/library/ee177956(v=EXCHG.80).aspx

`Media` elements come nested inside the `Product` element alongside the `Package` element.

```
<Wix ... >
  <Product ... >
    <Package ... />
    <Media Id="1"
           Cabinet="media1.cab"
           EmbedCab="yes" />
  </Product>
</Wix>
```

Each `Media` element gets a unique `Id` attribute to distinguish it in the MSI **Media** table. It must be a positive integer. If the files that you add to your installation package don't explicitly state which CAB file they wish to be packaged into, they'll default to using a `Media` element with an `Id` of 1. Therefore, your first `Media` element should always use an `Id` of 1.

The Cabinet attribute sets the name of the CAB file. You won't actually see this unless you set EmbedCab to no, in which case the file won't be bundled inside the MSI package. This is atypical, but might be done to split the installation files onto several disks. Even this is becoming rare in the age of 4 GB DVDs and Internet downloads. Setting EmbedCab to no will produce a visible CAB file that must be provided alongside the MSI file during an installation.

If you do choose to split the installation up into several physical disks (or even virtual ISO images), you'll want to add the DiskPrompt and VolumeLabel attributes. In the following example, I've added two Media elements instead of one. I've also added a Property element above them, which defines a variable called DiskPrompt with a value of Amazing Software - [1].

```
<Property Id="DiskPrompt"
        Value="Amazing Software - [1]" />
<Media Id="1"
       Cabinet="media1.cab"
       EmbedCab="no"
       DiskPrompt="Disk 1"
       VolumeLabel="Disk1" />

<Media Id="2"
       Cabinet="media2.cab"
       EmbedCab="no"
       DiskPrompt="Disk 2"
       VolumeLabel="Disk2" />
```

The Property element will be used as the text in the MessageBox the end user sees prompting them to insert the next disk. The text in the DiskPrompt attribute is combined with the text in the property's value, switched with [1], to change the message for each subsequent disk. Make sure you give this property an Id of DiskPrompt.

So that Windows will know when the correct disk is inserted, the VolumeLabel attribute must match the "Volume Label" of the actual disk, which you'll set with whichever CD or DVD burning program you use. Once you've built your project, include the MSI file and first CAB file on the first disk. The second CAB file should then be written to a second disk.

Although we haven't described the `File` element yet, it's used to add a file to the installation package. To include one in a *specific* CAB file, add the `DiskId` attribute, set to the `Id` of the corresponding `Media` element. The following example includes a text file called `myFile.txt` in the `media2.cab` file:

```
<File Id="fileTXT"
      Name="myFile.txt"
      Source="myFile.txt"
      KeyPath="yes"
      DiskId="2" />
```

We'll discuss the `File` element in more detail later on in the chapter. If you're only using one `Media` element, you won't need to specify the `DiskId` attribute on your `File` elements.

Directories

So, now we've defined the identity of the product, set up its package properties, and told the installer to create a CAB file to package up the things we'll eventually install. Then, how do you decide where your product will get installed *to* on the end user's computer? How do we set the default installation path, such as some folder under `Program Files`?

When you want to install to `C:\Program Files`, you can use a sort of shorthand. There are several directory names provided by Windows Installer that will be translated to their true paths at install time. For example, `ProgramFilesFolder` usually translates to `C:\Program Files`. Following is a list of these built-in directory properties:

Directory property	Actual path
AdminToolsFolder	Full path to directory containing administrative tools
AppDataFolder	Full path to Roaming folder for current user
CommonAppDataFolder	Full path to application data for all users
CommonFiles64Folder	Full path to 64-bit Common Files folder
CommonFilesFolder	Full path to Common Files folder for current user
DesktopFolder	Full path to Desktop folder
FavoritesFolder	Full path to Favorites folder for current user
FontsFolder	Full path to Fonts folder
LocalAppDataFolder	Full path to folder containing local (non-roaming) applications
MyPicturesFolder	Full path to Pictures folder
NetHoodFolder	Full path to NetHood folder

Directory property	Actual path
PersonalFolder	Full path to Documents folder for current user
PrintHoodFolder	Full path to PrintHood folder
ProgramFiles64Folder	Full path to 64-bit Program Files folder
ProgramFilesFolder	Full path to 32-bit Program Files folder
ProgramMenuFolder	Full path to Program Menu folder
RecentFolder	Full path to Recent folder
SendToFolder	Full path to SendTo folder for current user
StartMenuFolder	Full path to Start Menu folder
StartupFolder	Full path to Startup folder
System16Folder	Full path to 16-bit system DLLs folder
System64Folder	Full path to System64 folder
SystemFolder	Full path to System folder for current user
TempFolder	Full path to Temp folder
TemplateFolder	Full path to Template folder for current user
WindowsFolder	Full path to Windows folder

The easiest way to add your own directories is to nest them inside one of
the predefined ones. For example, to create a new directory called Install
Practice inside the Program Files folder, you could add it as a child to
ProgramFilesFolder. To define your directory structure in WiX, use
Directory elements:

```
<Wix ... >
  <Product ... >
    <Package ... />
    <Media ... />

    <Directory Id="TARGETDIR"
               Name="SourceDir">
      <Directory Id="ProgramFilesFolder">
        <Directory Id="MyProgramDir"
                   Name="Install Practice" />
      </Directory>
    </Directory>

  </Product>
</Wix>
```

You should place your `Directory` elements inside of the top-level `Product` element. Other than that, there aren't any restrictions about exactly where inside `Product` they have to go. One thing to know is that you must start your `Directory` elements hierarchy with a `Directory` with an `Id` of `TARGETDIR` and a `Name` of `SourceDir`. This sets up the "root" directory of your installation. Therefore, be sure to always create it first and nest all other `Directory` elements inside.

By default, Windows Installer sets `TARGETDIR` to the local hard drive with the most free space — in most cases, the `C:` drive. However, you can set `TARGETDIR` to another drive letter during installation. You might, for example, set it with a `VolumeSelectCombo` user interface control. We'll talk about setting properties and UI controls later in the book.

A `Directory` element always has an `Id` attribute that will serve as a primary key on the `Directory` table. If you're using a predefined name, such as `ProgramFilesFolder`, use that for `Id`. Otherwise, you can make one up yourself. The previous example creates a new directory called `Install Practice` inside the `Program Files` folder. The `Id`, `MyProgramDir`, is an arbitrary value.

When creating your own directory, you must provide the `Name` attribute. This sets the name of the new folder. Without it, the directory won't be created and any files that were meant to go inside it will instead be placed in the parent directory — in this case, `Program Files`. Note that you do not need to provide a `Name` attribute for predefined directories.

You can nest more subdirectories inside your folders by adding more `Directory` elements. Here is an example:

```
<Directory Id="TARGETDIR"
           Name="SourceDir">
  <Directory Id="ProgramFilesFolder">
    <Directory Id="MyProgramDir"
               Name="Install Practice">
      <Directory Id="MyFirstSubDir"
                 Name="Subdirectory 1">
        <Directory Id="MySecondSubDir"
                   Name="Subdirectory 2" />
      </Directory>
    </Directory>
  </Directory>
</Directory>
```

Here, a subdirectory called `Subdirectory 1` is placed inside the `Install Practice` folder. A second subdirectory, called `Subdirectory 2`, is then placed inside `Subdirectory 1`, giving us two levels of nested directories under `Install Practice`.

To put something inside a directory, use a `DirectoryRef` element. `DirectoryRef` takes only a single attribute: `Id`. This is your reference to the `Id` set on the corresponding `Directory` element. `DirectoryRef` elements, like `Directory` elements, are placed as children to the top-level `Product` element.

Using a `DirectoryRef` adds a layer of abstraction between where you define your directory structure and the files that will go into those directories. The following example adds a file (via the `Component` element, which we'll cover next) to the `MyProgramDir` directory.

```
<Directory Id="TARGETDIR"
           Name="SourceDir">
  <Directory Id="ProgramFilesFolder">
    <Directory Id="MyProgramDir"
               Name="Install Practice" />
  </Directory>
</Directory>

<DirectoryRef Id="MyProgramDir">
  <Component ... />
</DirectoryRef>
```

By using a `DirectoryRef`, we're able to separate the markup that adds files to directories from the markup that defines the directories. You can also add a component directly inside a `Directory` element:

```
<Directory Id="TARGETDIR"
           Name="SourceDir">
  <Directory Id="ProgramFilesFolder">
    <Directory Id="MyProgramDir"
               Name="Install Practice">
      <Component ... />
    </Directory>
  </Directory>
</Directory>
```

Placing components directly inside `Directory` elements is more straightforward, but it couples your directory structure more tightly to the files that you're installing. By using `DirectoryRef` elements, you're able to make the two pieces more modular and independent of one another.

Components

Once you've mapped out the directories that you want to target or create during the installation, the next step is to copy files into them. Windows Installer expects every file to be wrapped up in a component before it's installed. It doesn't matter what type of file it is either. Each gets its own `Component` element.

Components, which always have a unique GUID, allow Windows to track every file that gets installed on the end user's computer. During an installation, this information is stored away in the Registry. This lets Windows find every piece of your product during an uninstallation so that your software can be completely removed. It also uses it to replace missing files during a "repair", which you can trigger by right-clicking on an MSI file and selecting **Repair**. You won't get an error by placing more than one file into a single component, but it is considered bad practice.

To really explain components, we'll need something to install. So, let's create a simple text file and add it to our project's directory. We'll call it `InstallMe.txt`. For our purposes, it doesn't really matter what's in the text file. We just need something for testing.

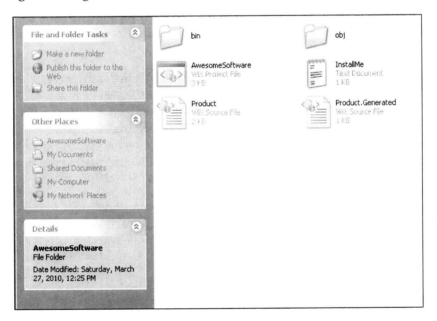

The Component element is used to uniquely identify each file that you plan to install. Each Component element gets a unique GUID via its Guid attribute. To create a GUID in Visual Studio, go to **Tools | Create GUID** and copy a new GUID using the Registry format. Be sure to make all of the letters uppercase. The Id attribute is up to you. It will serve as the primary key for the component in the MSI database, so each one must also be unique.

```
<Component  Id="CMP_InstallMeTXT"
            Guid="E8A58B7B-F031-4548-9BDD-7A6796C8460D">

   <File Id="FILE_InstallMeTXT"
         Source="InstallMe.txt"
         KeyPath="yes" />
</Component>
```

Here, I've created a new component called CMP_InstallMeTXT. I've started it with CMP_ to label it as a component. Although it isn't required, it helps to prefix components in this way so that it's always clear what sort of element it refers to.

The File element inside the component references the file that's going to be installed. Here, it's the InstallMe.txt file located in the current directory (which is the same directory as your WiX source file). You can specify a full or absolute path with the Source attribute.

You should always mark a File element as the KeyPath file and you should only ever include one File inside a Component. A KeyPath file will be replaced if it's missing when the user triggers a repair (Windows Installer documentation calls this *resiliency*). Placing more than one File element inside a single Component is, at least in most cases, not recommended. This is because only one file can be the KeyPath, so the other files wouldn't be covered by a repair. You would really only ever place more than one File in a Component if you *didn't* want the extra files to be resilient.

Once you've created your File and Component elements, you'll need to tell Windows Installer where they should be installed to. To do that, place them inside a DirectoryRef element that references one of your Directory elements—as shown in the following snippet:

```
<DirectoryRef Id="MyProgramDir">
  <Component Id="CMP_InstallMeTXT"
             Guid="E8A58B7B-F031-4548-9BDD-7A6796C8460D">

     <File Id="FILE_InstallMeTXT"
           Source="InstallMe.txt"
           KeyPath="yes" />
  </Component>
</DirectoryRef>
```

To add more files, simply create more `Component` and `File` elements. Of course, they don't all have to be installed to the same place. You might install some to the `MyProgramDir` folder that we're creating and others to a different folder. You always have to create a `Directory` element before you can place components in that directory. For example, you can't use the `AppDataFolder` property to place files in the `Application Data` directory until you've first added a `Directory` element for it.

Files

As you've seen, the actual files inside components are declared with `File` elements. `File` elements can represent everything from simple text files to complex DLLs and executables. Remember, you should only place one file into each component. The following example would add a file called `SomeAssembly.dll` to the installation package:

```
<Component ... >
  <File Id="FILE_SomeAssemblyDLL"
        Name="Some Assembly.dll"
        Source="SomeAssembly.dll"
        KeyPath="yes" />
</Component>
```

A `File` element should always get the `Id`, `Source`, and `KeyPath` attributes. `Name` is optional and gives you a chance to set the name of the file to something user-friendly. Without it, the name will default to whatever it's called in the `Source` attribute. Notice that you should set the value to the file name plus file type extension. In earlier versions of WiX, you'd have to use a separate attribute if the name was longer than eight characters or the extension longer than three. Now, this attribute can handle longer names as well.

Source defines the path to the file during compilation. I've listed a relative path here, but you could also specify an absolute path. The `Id` attribute should be something unique, but you might consider starting it with `FILE` to make it clear that it refers to a `File` element. To mark a file as important (and that it should be replaced if it goes missing), set it as the `KeyPath` for the component. Since you should only ever place one file inside a component, in almost all cases that file should be the `KeyPath`.

There are quite a few optional attributes available for the `File` element. A few useful ones are:

- `Hidden`: Set to `yes` to have the file's `Hidden` flag set. The file won't be visible unless the user sets the directory's options to show hidden files.
- `ReadOnly`: Set to `yes` to have the file's `Read-only` flag set. The user will be able to read the file, but not modify it unless they change the file's properties.
- `Vital`: Set to `yes` to stop the installation if the file isn't installed successfully.

Features

After you've defined your components and the directories that they'll be copied into, your next step is to define features. A **feature** is a group of components that the user can decide to install all at once. You'll often see these in an installation dialog as a list of modules, called a **feature tree**, where each is included or excluded from the installation. Here is an example of such a tree:

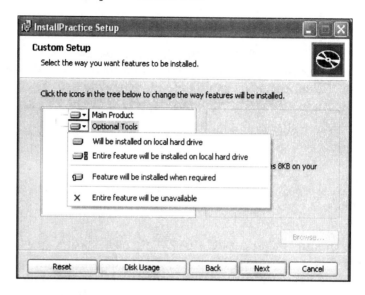

Every component must be included in a feature. Generally, you should group together components that rely on one another or that form a complete, self-sufficient unit. That way, if a feature is disabled, you won't have orphaned files (files that aren't being used) installed onto the computer. In some instances, if your product doesn't have any optional parts, you'll only want to create one feature.

If you've included a feature tree dialog, which we'll explain later in the book, like the one shown, the user can simply click a feature to exclude it. However, even without this, they can select features from the command line. The following command only installs the `Main Product` feature:

```
msiexec /i myInstaller.msi ADDLOCAL="MainProduct"
```

Here, we're using the `msiexec` program to launch an installer. The `/i` flag targets the MSI file to install. The `ADDLOCAL` property is set to the names of the features we want to include. If more than one, use commas to separate the names. To install all available features set `ADDLOCAL="ALL"`, as shown:

```
msiexec /i myInstaller.msi ADDLOCAL=ALL
```

To create a new feature in your WiX file, add a `Feature` element inside the `Product` element. The following example installs three components under the feature `Main Product`. Another feature called `Optional Tools` installs another component. Components are included in a feature with the `ComponentRef` element. The `Id` attribute of `ComponentRef` targets the `Id` attribute from the corresponding `Component` element.

```
<Feature Id="MainProduct"
         Title="Main Product"
         Level="1">
  <ComponentRef Id="CMP_MyAppEXE" />
  <ComponentRef Id="CMP_ReadMeTXT" />
  <ComponentRef Id="CMP_StartMenuShortcuts" />
</Feature>

<Feature Id="OptionalTools"
         Title="Optional Tools"
         Level="1">
  <ComponentRef Id="CMP_ToolsEXE" />
</Feature>
```

The `Feature` element's `Id` attribute uniquely identifies the feature and is what you'll reference when using the `ADDLOCAL` property on the command line. The `Title` attribute is used to set a user-friendly name that can be displayed on dialogs. Setting the `Feature` element's `Level` attribute to 1 means that feature will be included in the installation by default. The end user will still be able to remove it through the user interface or via the command line. If, on the other hand, `Level` is set to 0, that feature will be removed from the feature tree and the user won't be able to install it.

If you wanted to, you could create a more complex tree with features nested inside features. You could use this to create more categories for the elements in your product and give the user more options concerning what gets installed. You would want to make sure that all possible configurations function correctly. Windows Installer makes this somewhat manageable in that if a parent feature is excluded, its children features will be too. Here's an example of a more complex feature setup:

```
<Feature Id="MainProduct"
         Title="Main Product"
         Level="1">
  <ComponentRef Id="CMP_MyAppEXE" />
  <ComponentRef Id="CMP_StartMenuShortcuts" />

  <Feature Id="SubFeature1"
           Title="Documentation"
           Level="1">
```

```
            <ComponentRef Id="CMP_ReadMeTXT" />
       </Feature>
   </Feature>


   <Feature Id="OptionalTools"
            Title="Optional Tools"
            Level="1">
      <ComponentRef Id="CMP_ToolsEXE" />
   </Feature>
```

Here, I've moved the `ReadMe.txt` file into its own feature called `Documentation` that's nested inside the `Main Product` feature. Disabling its parent feature (`Main Product`), will also disable it. However, you could enable `Main Product` and disable `Documentation`.

If you're going to use a feature tree, you have the ability to prevent the user from excluding a particular feature. Just set the `Absent` attribute to `disallow`. You might do this for the main part of your product where excluding it wouldn't make sense.

You might also consider adding the `Description` attribute, which can be set to a string that describes the feature. This could be displayed in your dialog alongside the feature tree, if you decide to use one. It would look something like this:

```
   <Feature Id="ProductFeature"
            Title="Main Product"
            Description="Installs the Main Feature"
            Level="1">

      <ComponentRef Id="cmp_MyAppEXE" />
      <ComponentRef Id="cmp_ReadMeTXT" />
      <ComponentRef Id="cmp_StartMenuShortcuts" />
   </Feature>
```

Start Menu shortcuts

Having a working installer is good, but wouldn't it be nice to add some shortcuts for the application to the Start Menu? To do so, create a new component with a nested `Shortcut` element. Shortcuts are stored in their own table in the MSI database. First, add another `Directory` element that references the Start Menu via the built-in `ProgramMenuFolder` name:

```
   <Directory Id="TARGETDIR"
             Name="SourceDir">
     <Directory Id="ProgramFilesFolder">
       <Directory Id="MyProgramDir"
```

```
              Name="Awesome Software" />
  </Directory>
  <Directory Id="ProgramMenuFolder">
    <Directory Id="MyShortcutsDir"
              Name="Awesome Software" />
  </Directory>
</Directory>
```

Here, I've added a reference to the Start Menu folder with the `ProgramMenuFolder` `Directory` element Id. I've then told the installer to create a new subfolder inside it called `Awesome Software`. Now, you can use a `DirectoryRef` element to reference your new shortcuts folder, as in the following code snippet:

```
<DirectoryRef Id="MyShortcutsDir">
  <Component Id="CMP_DocumentationShortcut"
            Guid="33741C82-30BF-41AF-8246-44A5DCFCF953">

    <Shortcut Id="DocumentationStartMenuShortcut"
            Name="Awesome Software Documentation"
            Description="Read Awesome Software Documentation"
            Target="[MyProgramDir]InstallMe.txt" />
  </Component>
</DirectoryRef>
```

Each `Shortcut` element has a unique identifier set with the `Id` attribute. The `Name` attribute defines the user-friendly name that gets displayed. `Description` is set to a string that describes the shortcut and will appear when the user moves their mouse over the shortcut link.

The `Target` attribute defines the path on the end user's machine to the actual file being linked to. For that reason, you'll often want to use properties that update as they're changed instead of hardcoded values. In the previous example, the main installation directory is referenced by placing the `Id` of its corresponding `Directory` element in square brackets, which is then followed by the name of the file. Even if the path of `MyProgramDir` changes, it will still lead us to the `InstallMe.txt` file.

Two things that should accompany a shortcut are a `RemoveFolder` element and a `RegistryValue` element. `RemoveFolder` ensures that the new Start Menu subdirectory will be removed during an uninstall. It uses an `Id` attribute to uniquely identify a row in the MSI `RemoveFile` table and an `On` attribute to specify when to remove the folder. You can set `On` to `install`, `uninstall`, or `both`. You can specify a `Directory` attribute as well to set to the `Id` of a `Directory` element to remove. Without one, though, the element will remove the directory defined by the parent `DirectoryRef` element.

Let's add the `RemoveFolder` and `RegistryValue` elements to our component:

```
<DirectoryRef Id="MyShortcutsDir">
  <Component Id="CMP_DocumentationShortcut"
             Guid="33741C82-30BF-41AF-8246-44A5DCFCF953">

    <Shortcut Id="DocumentationStartMenuShortcut"
              Name="Awesome Software Documentation"
              Description="Read Awesome Software Documentation"
              Target="[MyProgramDir]InstallMe.txt" />

    <RemoveFolder Id="RemoveMyShortcutsDir"
                  On="uninstall" />

    <RegistryValue Root="HKCU"
                   Key="Software\Microsoft\AwesomeSoftware"
                   Name="installed"
                   Type="integer"
                   Value="1"
                   KeyPath="yes" />
  </Component>
</DirectoryRef>
```

The `RegistryValue` element is needed simply because every component must have a KeyPath item. Shortcuts aren't allowed to be KeyPath items as they aren't technically files. By adding a `RegistryValue`, a new item is added to the Registry and this is marked as the KeyPath. The actual value itself serves no other purpose. We will cover writing to the Registry in more detail later.

There's actually another reason for using a `RegistryValue` as the `KeyPath`. The shortcut we're creating is being installed to a directory specific to the current user. Windows Installer requires that you always use a registry value as the `KeyPath` item when doing this in order to simplify uninstalling the product when multiple users have installed it.

Another type of shortcut to add is one that uninstalls the product. For this, add a second `Shortcut` element to the same component. This shortcut will be different in that it will have its `Target` set to the `msiexec.exe` program, which is located in the `System` folder. The following example uses the predefined `System64Folder` directory name because it will automatically map to either the 64-bit or 32-bit `System` folder, depending on the end user's operating system.

By setting `Target` to the path of an executable, you're telling Windows to launch that program when the user clicks the shortcut. The `msiexec` program can remove software by using the `/x` argument followed by the `ProductCode` of the product you want to uninstall. The `ProductCode` is the `Id` specified in the `Product` element.

```xml
<DirectoryRef Id="MyShortcutsDir">
  <Component Id="CMP_DocumentationShortcut"
             Guid="33741C82-30BF-41AF-8246-44A5DCFCF953">

    <Shortcut Id="DocumentationStartMenuShortcut"
              Name="Awesome Software Documentation"
              Description="Read Awesome Software Documentation"
              Target="[MyProgramDir]InstallMe.txt" />

    <Shortcut Id="UninstallShortcut"
              Name="Uninstall Awesome Software"
              Description=
              "Uninstalls Awesome Software and all of its components"
              Target="[System64Folder]msiexec.exe"
              Arguments="/x [ProductCode]" />

    <RemoveFolder Id="RemoveMyShortcutsDir"
                  On="uninstall" />

    <RegistryValue Root="HKCU"
                   Key="Software\Microsoft\AwesomeSoftware"
                   Name="installed"
                   Type="integer"
                   Value="1"
                   KeyPath="yes" />
  </Component>
</DirectoryRef>
```

Notice that we don't have to use the exact GUID from the Product element to get the ProductCode. We can reference it using the built-in property called ProductCode surrounded by square brackets. If you'd like to add an icon to your shortcut, first add an Icon element as another child to the Product element. Then, reference that icon with the Icon attribute on the Shortcut element.

```xml
<Icon Id="icon.ico" SourceFile="myIcon.ico"/>
<DirectoryRef ... >
  <Component ... >
    <Shortcut Id="DocumentationStartMenuShortcut"
              Name="Awesome Software Documentation"
              Description="Read Awesome Software Documentation"
              Target="[MyProgramDir]InstallMe.txt"
              Icon="icon.ico" />

    <RemoveFolder ... />
    <RegistryValue ... />
  </Component>
</DirectoryRef>
```

Be sure to add the new component that contains the shortcuts to one of your features:

```
<Feature Id="ProductFeature"
         Title="Main Product"
         Level="1">
  <ComponentRef Id=" CMP_InstallMeTXT" />
  <ComponentRef Id="CMP_DocumentationShortcut" />
</Feature>
```

Putting it all together

Now that you've seen the different elements used to author an MSI package, here is the entire `.wxs` file:

```
<?xml version="1.0" encoding="UTF-8"?>
<Wix xmlns="http://schemas.microsoft.com/wix/2006/wi">

  <Product Id="3E786878-358D-43AD-82D1-1435ADF9F6EA"
           Name="Awesome Software"
           Language="1033"
           Version="1.0.0.0"
           Manufacturer="Awesome Company"
           UpgradeCode="B414C827-8D81-4B4A-B3B6-338C06DE3A11">

    <Package InstallerVersion="301"
             Compressed="yes" />
    <Media Id="1"
           Cabinet="media1.cab"
           EmbedCab="yes" />

    <!--Directory structure-->
    <Directory Id="TARGETDIR"
               Name="SourceDir">
      <Directory Id="ProgramFilesFolder">
        <Directory Id="MyProgramDir"
                   Name="Awesome Software" />
        <Directory Id="ProgramMenuFolder">
          <Directory Id="MyShortcutsDir"
                     Name="Awesome Software" />
        </Directory>
      </Directory>
    </Directory>

    <!--Components-->
```

```xml
    <DirectoryRef Id="MyProgramDir">
      <Component Id="CMP_InstallMeTXT"
                 Guid="E8A58B7B-F031-4548-9BDD-7A6796C8460D">
        <File Id="FILE_InstallMeTXT"
              Source="InstallMe.txt"
              KeyPath="yes" />
      </Component>
    </DirectoryRef>

    <!--Start Menu Shortcuts-->
    <DirectoryRef Id="MyShortcutsDir">
      <Component Id="CMP_DocumentationShortcut"
                 Guid="33741C82-30BF-41AF-8246-44A5DCFCF953">

        <Shortcut Id="DocumentationStartMenuShortcut"
                  Name="Awesome Software Documentation"
                  Description="Read Awesome Software Documentation"
                  Target="[MyProgramDir]InstallMe.txt" />

        <Shortcut Id="UninstallShortcut"
                  Name="Uninstall InstallPractice"
                  Description="Uninstalls Awesome Software"
                  Target="[System64Folder]msiexec.exe"
                  Arguments="/x [ProductCode]" />

        <RemoveFolder Id="RemoveMyShortcutsDir"
                      On="uninstall" />

        <RegistryValue Root="HKCU"
                       Key="Software\Microsoft\AwesomeSoftware"
                       Name="installed"
                       Type="integer"
                       Value="1"
                       KeyPath="yes" />
      </Component>
    </DirectoryRef>

    <!--Features-->
    <Feature Id="ProductFeature"
             Title="Main Product"
             Level="1">
      <ComponentRef Id="CMP_InstallMeTXT" />
      <ComponentRef Id="CMP_DocumentationShortcut" />
    </Feature>
  </Product>
</Wix>
```

Compile the project in Visual Studio and you should get a new MSI file.

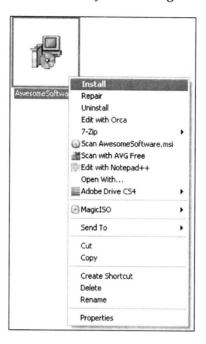

You can double-click it or right-click and select **Install** to install the software. Doing so should create a subfolder for your program in the Start Menu.

You should also find a new folder under Program Files.

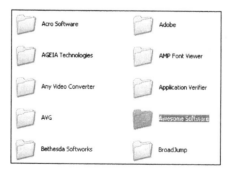

To uninstall the software, you have several options:

- Use the uninstall shortcut from the Start Menu
- Right-click on the MSI file and select **Uninstall**
- Uninstall it from Add/Remove Programs
- From a command prompt, navigate to the directory where the MSI file is and use the command:

```
msiexec /x AwesomeSoftware.msi
```

Adding a User Interface

Although you'll eventually want to add your own dialogs to gather information from the user that's important for your own application, you may want to use one of WiX's built-in dialog sequences in the meantime. All of them are stored in an assembly called `WixUIExtension.dll`. You can add a reference to this file with Visual Studio's **Add a Reference** screen. The file exists in WiX's `Program Files` folder. You may have to navigate to `C:\Program Files\Windows Installer XML v3\bin`.

Once you've added the new reference, add the following line to your WiX source file. It doesn't matter exactly where, as long as it's a child to the `Product` element:

```
<UIRef Id="WixUI_Minimal" />
```

This will insert the `Minimal` dialog set into your installation sequence. It shows a single dialog screen containing a license agreement and **Install** button. Feel free to try any of the other dialog sets. Just replace `WixUI_Minimal`, with one of the other names in the `UIRef` element. `WixUI_Advanced` and `WixUI_InstallDir` require some further setup to really work properly. You can try out the following attributes:

- `WixUI_Advanced`
- `WixUI_FeatureTree`
- `WixUI_InstallDir`
- `WixUI_Mondo`

We will explore these standard dialogs in more detail later and also explain how to create your own.

Viewing the MSI database

I mentioned before that an MSI file is really a sort of relational database. WiX does all the work of creating tables, inserting rows, and matching up keys in this database. However, as we progress through the rest of the book, I encourage you to explore how it looks behind the scenes. For example, we discussed the `File` and `Component` elements. Sure enough, there are two tables called `File` and `Component` in the MSI that contain the definitions you've set with your XML markup. To get inside the installer, you'll need a tool called Orca.

Orca.exe

Once you've compiled your project in Visual Studio, you'll have a working MSI package that can be installed by double-clicking it. If you'd like to see the database inside, install the MSI viewer, **Orca.exe.** Orca is provided as part of the Windows SDK and despite the icon of a whale on the shortcut, stands for **One Really Cool App.** You can find versions of the SDK at Microsoft's Windows Development Center website:

`http://msdn.microsoft.com/en-us/windows/bb980924.aspx`

After you've installed the SDK (specifically, the .NET tools that are included), you can find the installer for Orca—`Orca.msi`—in the `Microsoft SDKs` folder in `Program Files`. On my machine, it can be found in `C:\Program Files\Microsoft SDKs\Windows\v7.0\Bin`.

Install Orca and then right-click on your MSI file and select **Edit with Orca.**

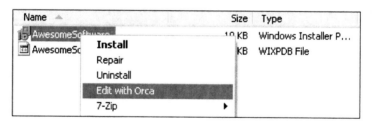

Orca lets you view the database structure of your installer. This can be a big help in troubleshooting problems or just to get a better idea about how different elements work together. Following is a screenshot of the `Component` database:

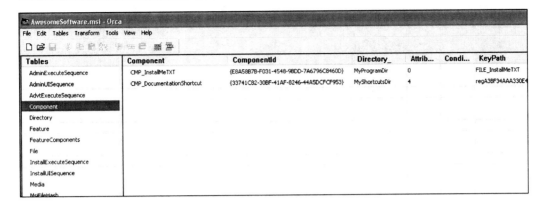

If you wanted to, you could edit your MSI package directly with Orca. This is helpful when learning or trying out different concepts. You'll need to know exactly which tables and rows to modify. Sometimes, though, you'll be able to just change a single value and check its effect.

Turning logging on during installation

If you get into trouble with your installer, it may help to run it with logging turned on. To do so, install your package from a command prompt using `msiexec` with the arguments `/l*v` and the name of a file to write the log to. For example, if you had an installer called `myInstaller.msi`, you could use this command to write a log during the installation to a file called `myLog.txt`:

```
msiexec /i myInstaller.msi /l*v myLog.txt
```

Every event that occurs during installation will be recorded here. It works for uninstalls too. Simply use the `/x` argument instead of `/i`. The log can be pretty helpful, but also very verbose. If your installer fails midway through, you might try searching the log for the text `return value 3`. This indicates that an action returned a status of failure. Often, you'll also see a specific MSI error code. You can find its meaning by searching for that number in the **MSI SDK Documentation** help file that comes with WiX.

Other resources

If you have specific questions about WiX, you'll find additional resources at the following websites:

- WiX users Mailing List:

  `http://sourceforge.net/mailarchive/forum.php?forum_name=wix-users`

- Microsoft Windows Installer documentation:

  `http://msdn.microsoft.com/en-us/library/cc185688(VS.85).aspx`

Summary

In this chapter, we discussed downloading the WiX toolset and its various features. Creating a simple MSI package is relatively easy. There are only a handful of XML elements needed to get started. As we explore more complex setups, you'll be introduced to elements that are more specialized.

Throughout the rest of this book, I'll make references to the structure of the MSI database. Orca is an excellent tool for seeing this structure yourself. Although this book focuses on WiX and not the underlying Windows Installer technology, it helps sometimes to see how the mechanics of it work. You may find it useful to consult Microsoft's MSI documentation too, which can be found online or in a help file provided by WiX, to get a deeper understanding of the properties and constructs we will discuss.

2
Creating Files and Directories

In the previous chapter, we saw that creating a WiX installer isn't so tough. Less than seventy lines of code and you've got a professional-looking deployment solution. One of the things we covered was how to copy files and create directories on the end user's computer. We've covered the basics, but now it's time to dig deeper.

In this chapter you will learn how to:

- Organize your `File` and `Directory` elements using `DirectoryRef` and `ComponentGroup` elements
- Split your WiX markup using `Fragment` elements to keep it manageable
- Use `heat.exe` to create `Component` markup
- Install special case files such as installing to the GAC

File element

The `File` element, as you've seen, is used to designate each file that you plan to copy to the end user's computer. Its `Source` attribute tells WiX where to find the file on your local machine. The `Name` attribute tells the installer what the file will be called after it's installed. Each `File` element also needs an `Id`. This uniquely identifies it in the MSI database's *File* table.

```
<Component Id="CMP_MyProgramEXE"
        Guid="E8A58B7B-F031-4548-9BDD-7A6796C8460D">
  <File Id="FILE_MyProgramEXE"
        Source="MyProgram.exe"
        Name="NewName.exe"
        KeyPath="yes" />
</Component>

<Component Id="CMP_AnotherFileDLL"
```

```
              Guid="E9D74961-DF9B-4130-8FBC-1669A6DD288E">
    <File Id="FILE_AnotherFileDLL"
          Source="..\..\AnotherFile.dll"
          KeyPath="yes" />
</Component>
```

This example includes two files, `MyProgram.exe` and `AnotherFile.dll`, in the installation package. Both use relative paths for their `Source` attributes. The first file is located in the current directory while the second is two directories up. Another option is to use a **preprocessor variable** to store the location of your files.

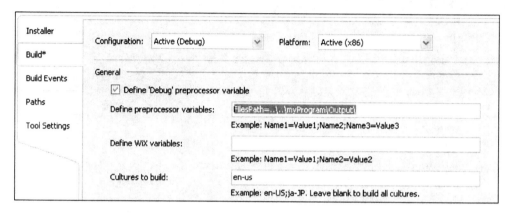

Preprocessor variables are evaluated at compile time and replaced with the strings that they've been set to. Here, we've added a variable called `FilesPath` on the **Build** page of my WiX project's **Properties** and set it to `..\..\myProgram\Output\`. In this case, the `Output` directory is where the files we plan to install are located on the computer. We can insert this variable in the markup by using `$(var.FilesPath)`, as in the following snippet:

```
<Component Id="CMP_MyProgramEXE"
           Guid="E8A58B7B-F031-4548-9BDD-7A6796C8460D">
    <File Id="FILE_MyProgramEXE"
          Source="$(var.FilesPath)MyProgram.exe"
          KeyPath="yes" />
</Component>
```

At compile time, the variable will be replaced with the path that we've defined. You can define more than one preprocessor variable on the **Build** page by separating them with semicolons. You might do this if you wanted to define several directories to use in your markup.

Going back to the previous example, notice that the `Name` attribute wasn't used for `AnotherFile.dll`. Omitting the `Name` attribute like this tells the installer to keep the original file name as it appears in the `Source` attribute. So, `MyProgram.exe` will be renamed to `NewName.exe` on the end user's computer, but `AnotherFile.dll` will still be called `AnotherFile.dll`.

Something else to notice is that each file is wrapped in its own `Component` element. Doing so will allow you to mark every file that you're installing as a **KeyPath** file. This allows them to be replaced if they're accidentally deleted. The process of replacing missing files is known as a **repair**. Repairs are triggered automatically when the end user clicks on a program shortcut or by right-clicking on the finished MSI file and selecting **Repair**. A component can have only one KeyPath file, but every component should have one. Set a `File` element's `KeyPath` attribute to `yes` to mark that file as the KeyPath. Although it's possible to put more than one file in the same component, it's considered bad practice.

DirectoryRef element

In the previous chapter, you saw that to define which directories to copy your files into, you use `Directory` elements. These take an `Id` and, if it's a new directory that you're creating, a `Name` attribute. You can use any of the built-in IDs to reference one of the common Windows directories. For example, suppose we wanted to add a file to the `C:\Windows\system32` folder. We'd add a reference to it using the built-in `SystemFolder` property for its `Id`:

```
<Directory Id="TARGETDIR"
           Name="SourceDir">
  <Directory Id="SystemFolder" />
</Directory>
```

If, on the other hand, it's a directory that you're creating, you can set the `Id` to anything you like. The `Name` attribute will set the name of the new folder. After you've defined the directories that you want to use (or create) with `Directory` elements, you'll use `DirectoryRef` elements to add components to them.

```
<DirectoryRef Id="SystemFolder">
  <Component Id="CMP_AnotherFileDLL"
             Guid="E9D74961-DF9B-4130-8FBC-1669A6DD288E">
    <File Id="FILE_AnotherFileDLL"
          Source="AnotherFile.dll"
          KeyPath="yes" />
  </Component>
</DirectoryRef>
```

Here, we're placing one `Component` inside the `system32` folder by referencing it with a `DirectoryRef` that matches the `Directory` element we used before. If you wanted to, you could use a new `DirectoryRef` for each file.

```
<DirectoryRef Id="SystemFolder">
  <Component Id="CMP_AnotherFileDLL"
            Guid="E9D74961-DF9B-4130-8FBC-1669A6DD288E">
    <File Id="FILE_AnotherFileDLL"
          Source="AnotherFile.dll"
          KeyPath="yes" />
  </Component>
</DirectoryRef>

<DirectoryRef Id="SystemFolder">
  <Component Id="CMP_MyProgramEXE"
            Guid="E8A58B7B-F031-4548-9BDD-7A6796C8460D">
    <File Id="FILE_MyProgramEXE"
          Source="MyProgram.exe"
          KeyPath="yes" />
  </Component>
</DirectoryRef>
```

However, it's easier to use one `DirectoryRef` and place multiple `Component` elements inside of it:

```
<DirectoryRef Id="SystemFolder">
  <Component Id="CMP_AnotherFileDLL"
            Guid="E9D74961-DF9B-4130-8FBC-1669A6DD288E">
    <File Id="FILE_AnotherFileDLL"
          Source="AnotherFile.dll"
          KeyPath="yes" />
  </Component>

  <Component Id="CMP_MyProgramEXE"
            Guid="E8A58B7B-F031-4548-9BDD-7A6796C8460D">
    <File Id="FILE_MyProgramEXE"
          Source="MyProgram.exe"
          KeyPath="yes" />
  </Component>
</DirectoryRef>
```

You could, for example, place hundreds of files inside the `system32` folder using only one `DirectoryRef` element.

ComponentGroup element

The ComponentGroup element can be used to group Component elements, which is helpful as it offers a way to reference all of your components with a single element. For example, when adding components to a Feature (which you must always do), you *could* use ComponentRef elements directly. This is the technique we used in the previous chapter.

```
<Feature Id="ProductFeature"
        Title="Main Product"
        Level="1">
  <ComponentRef Id="CMP_MyProgramEXE" />
  <ComponentRef Id="CMP_AnotherFileDLL" />
</Feature>
```

However, by creating a ComponentGroup, you can reference multiple components with a single ComponentGroupRef element. This is shown in the snippet:

```
<Feature Id="ProductFeature"
        Title="Main Product"
        Level="1">
  <ComponentGroupRef Id="MyComponentGroup" />
</Feature>
```

To create a ComponentGroup, add a new ComponentGroup element to your .wxs file. It can go anywhere inside the Product element. Then, you have a choice. You can either nest Component elements inside it or use ComponentRefs to reference your components indirectly. For example, here we use Component elements inside a ComponentGroup.

```
<ComponentGroup Id="MyComponentGroup">
  <Component Id="CMP_MyProgramEXE"
          Guid="E8A58B7B-F031-4548-9BDD-7A6796C8460D"
          Directory="SystemFolder">
    <File Id="FILE_MyProgramEXE"
          Source="MyProgram.exe"
          KeyPath="yes" />
  </Component>

  <Component Id="CMP_AnotherFileDLL"
          Guid="E9D74961-DF9B-4130-8FBC-1669A6DD288E"
          Directory="SystemFolder">
    <File Id="FILE_AnotherFileDLL"
          Source="AnotherFile.dll"
          KeyPath="yes" />
  </Component>
</ComponentGroup>
```

We've added `Directory` attributes to the `Component` elements, as we've moved them out of a `DirectoryRef` element and into a `ComponentGroup`. This has the same effect, though. It will tell the installer where to copy these files to. The other option is to continue to nest `Component` elements inside `DirectoryRef` elements and then use `ComponentRef` elements to include them in a group.

```
<DirectoryRef Id="SystemFolder">
  <Component Id="CMP_MyProgramEXE"
             Guid="E8A58B7B-F031-4548-9BDD-7A6796C8460D">
    <File Id="FILE_MyProgramEXE"
          Source="MyProgram.exe"
          KeyPath="yes" />
  </Component>

  <Component Id="CMP_AnotherFileDLL"
             Guid="E9D74961-DF9B-4130-8FBC-1669A6DD288E">
    <File Id="FILE_AnotherFileDLL"
          Source="AnotherFile.dll"
          KeyPath="yes" />
  </Component>
</DirectoryRef>

<ComponentGroup Id="MyComponentGroup">
  <ComponentRef Id="CMP_MyProgramEXE" />
  <ComponentRef Id="CMP_AnotherFileDLL" />
</ComponentGroup>
```

The usefulness of a `ComponentGroup` becomes more obvious when your program needs to copy more than a few files to the end user's machine. You'll be able to include, remove or move entire sets of components from a feature simply by moving the `ComponentGroupRef` element.

Fragment element

Up to this point, we've been adding all of our WiX elements to the `Product.wxs` file. When your installer packages hundreds of files, you'll find that having all of your code in one place makes reading it difficult. You can split your elements up into multiple `.wxs` files for better organization and readability. Whereas your main source file, `Product.wxs`, nests everything inside a `Product` element, your additional `.wxs` files will use `Fragment` elements as their roots.

The `Fragment` element doesn't need any attributes. It's simply a container. You can place just about anything inside of it, such as all of your `Directory` elements or all of your `Component` elements. For the next example, add a new WiX source file to your project and place the following markup inside it. Here, we're using the same `ComponentGroup` that we discussed earlier. You can call the file `Components.wxs`, and it would look something like this:

```xml
<?xml version="1.0" encoding="UTF-8"?>
<Wix xmlns="http://schemas.microsoft.com/wix/2006/wi">
  <Fragment>
    <ComponentGroup Id="MyComponentGroup">
      <Component Id="CMP_MyProgramEXE"
                 Guid="E8A58B7B-F031-4548-9BDD-7A6796C8460D"
                 Directory="MyProgramDir">
        <File Id="FILE_MyProgramEXE"
              Source="MyProgram.exe"
              KeyPath="yes"  />
      </Component>

      <Component Id="CMP_AnotherFileDLL"
                 Guid="E9D74961-DF9B-4130-8FBC-1669A6DD288E"
                 Directory="MyProgramDir">
        <File Id="FILE_AnotherFileDLL"
              Source="AnotherFile.dll"
              KeyPath="yes" />
      </Component>
    </ComponentGroup>
  </Fragment>
</Wix>
```

Here, the markup for the components is contained within a separate file. We've used a `ComponentGroup` to group them, but, of course, that's optional. To include this group in `Product.wxs` reference it with a `ComponentGroupRef` element in one of your `Feature` elements, as shown:

```xml
<Feature Id="ProductFeature"
         Title="Main Product"
         Level="1">
  <ComponentGroupRef Id="MyComponentGroup" />
</Feature>
```

Like before, you'll use a `ComponentGroupRef` element to add this group to a feature. Referencing any single element like this will pull all of the elements in the fragment into the scope of your project. For components, this doesn't make much difference since you still have to reference all of them — or at least a `ComponentGroup` of them — inside a `Feature` element. However, it makes more of a difference for other elements.

For example, **properties**, which are variables that you can use to store data, are represented by `Property` elements and could be stored in a separate file within a `Fragment`. Then, by referencing just one of them in your main source file with a `PropertyRef` element, you'd pull all of them into your project. With fragments, it's all or nothing. Referencing one element in the fragment references them all. You might use this to your advantage, pulling in elements that don't have reference elements to use. For example, there's no reference element for the `Media` element. There's no such thing as a "MediaRef". However, if you included a `Property` element in the same fragment as your `Media` elements, you could pull them in too by referencing that property with a `PropertyRef`. The `Media.wxs` file would look like this:

```
<?xml version="1.0" encoding="UTF-8"?>
<Wix xmlns="http://schemas.microsoft.com/wix/2006/wi">
  <Fragment>
    <Property Id="MediaProperty"
              Value="1" />
    <Media Id="1" Cabinet="media1.cab" EmbedCab="yes" />
    <Media Id="2" Cabinet="media2.cab" EmbedCab="yes" />
    <Media Id="3" Cabinet="media3.cab" EmbedCab="yes" />
  </Fragment>
</Wix>
```

To reference the `Media` elements in your project, reference the property that's with them. This is done by adding the following code to `Product.wxs`:

```
<?xml version="1.0" encoding="UTF-8"?>
<Wix xmlns="http://schemas.microsoft.com/wix/2006/wi">
  <Product  Id="3E786878-358D-43AD-82D1-1435ADF9F6EA"
            Name="Awesome Software"
            Language="1033"
            Version="1.0.0.0"
            Manufacturer="Awesome Company"
            UpgradeCode="B414C827-8D81-4B4A-B3B6-338C06DE3A11">
    <Package InstallerVersion="301"
             Compressed="yes" />
    <PropertyRef Id="MediaProperty" />

    <Directory Id="TARGETDIR"
               Name="SourceDir">
      <Directory Id="ProgramFilesFolder">
        <Directory Id="MyProgramDir"
                   Name="Awesome Software" />
      </Directory>
    </Directory>
```

```xml
        <DirectoryRef Id="MyProgramDir">
          <Component Id="CMP_InstallMeTXT"
                     Guid="E8A58B7B-F031-4548-9BDD-7A6796C8460D">
            <File Id="FILE_InstallMeTXT"
                  Source="InstallMe.txt"
                  KeyPath="yes" />
          </Component>
        </DirectoryRef>

        <Feature Id="ProductFeature"
                 Title="Main Product"
                 Level="1">
          <ComponentRef Id="CMP_InstallMeTXT" />
        </Feature>
      </Product>
    </Wix>
```

Fragments are a great way of splitting up your code to make it more manageable.
As we've seen, it's easy to pull them into the scope of your project. You could even
pull one fragment into another and then pull that one into your main source file.
WiX will take care of running the validity checks to make sure that everything links
together properly.

Note that it's possible to have more than one Fragment element in the same source
file. In that case, you must use a reference element for each one. They're sort of like
islands. They're isolated from one another. However, it's often simpler to stick to
one fragment per file. The following file defines two fragments:

```xml
    <?xml version="1.0" encoding="UTF-8"?>
    <Wix xmlns="http://schemas.microsoft.com/wix/2006/wi">
      <Fragment>
        <Property Id="MediaProperty"
                  Value="1" />
        <Media Id="1"
               Cabinet="media1.cab"
               EmbedCab="yes" />
      </Fragment>

      <Fragment>
        <Property Id="MediaProperty2"
                  Value="1" />
        <Media Id="2"
               Cabinet="media2.cab"
               EmbedCab="yes" />
      </Fragment>
    </Wix>
```

Referencing the `MediaProperty` property with a `PropertyRef` will only pull in the elements in the first fragment. To get those in the second fragment, you'd have to also reference the `MediaProperty2` property.

The `Fragment` element is so helpful that the WiX team has employed its use for an even bigger type of project organization: `.wixlib`. You can create separate projects that only contain a single fragment and compile it into a **WiX library** (`.wixlib`) that can be added as a reference in your main WiX project. This allows other teams to handle their own WiX code and send it to you already compiled. To try it out, create a new project in your solution using the **Setup Library Project** template.

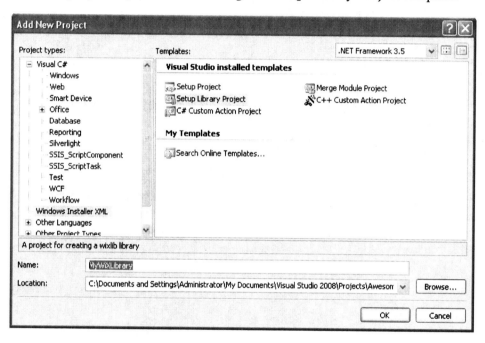

The contents of this type of project aren't anything you haven't seen before. It's simply a fragment. You'll start off with the following markup:

```xml
<?xml version="1.0" encoding="UTF-8"?>
<Wix xmlns="http://schemas.microsoft.com/wix/2006/wi">
  <Fragment>
    <!-- TODO: Put your code here. -->
  </Fragment>
</Wix>
```

You can add properties, components, and anything else you'd ordinarily be able to add to a fragment to this project. When it's compiled, you'll have a .wixlib file that can be added as a reference in your main WiX project. Use the **Add Reference** option in your **Solution Explorer**. Like other fragments, you'll be able to reference the .wixlib file's contents by using a reference element like PropertyRef. This is a great tool that allows multiple teams to work on the installer without stepping on one another's toes.

In the past, installation developers often used **merge modules** (.msm) to separate installation code. Merge modules, like WiX libraries, contain compiled installer code and offer a way of splitting up large projects. WiX libraries, which are easier to author, can serve as a replacement for merge modules. Although we won't cover it in this book, WiX does provide an XML element called Merge for importing a merge module into your project.

Harvesting files with heat.exe

When your project contains many files to install, it can be a chore to create File and Component elements for all of them. Instead, WiX can do it for you. One of the tools that ships with the toolset is called **heat.exe**. You can find it in the bin directory of the WiX program files. Navigate to WiX's bin directory from a command prompt and type heat.exe -? to see information about its usage.

To make things easy, consider adding the path to the WiX bin directory to your computer's PATH environment variable so that you won't have to reference the full path to the executable each time you use it. You can do this by right-clicking on **My Computer** in your Start Menu and then going to **Properties | Advanced | Environment Variables**. From there, you can add the WiX bin path, C:\Program Files\Windows Installer XML v3\bin, to PATH by finding PATH in the list of System variables and clicking **Edit**.

 Note that WiX, during its installation, adds an environment variable called WIX, but this references the bin folder's parent directory.

Following is a list of the arguments available to Heat:

Heat command syntax:

```
heat.exe harvestType harvestSource <harvester arguments>
  -o[ut] sourceFile.wxs
```

Argument	What it does
`-ag`	Autogenerate component GUIDs at compile time
`-cg <ComponentGroupName>`	Component group name (cannot contain spaces)
`-dr <DirectoryName>`	Directory reference to root directories
`-ext <extension>`	Extension assembly or "cass assembly"
`-gl`	Generated GUIDs are not in brackets
`-gg`	Generate GUIDs now
`-indent <N>`	Indentation multiple (overrides default of 4)
`-ke`	Keep empty directories
`-nologo`	Skip printing heat logo information
`-out`	Specify output file
`-pog:<group>`	Specify output group of VS project, one of: `Binaries`, `Symbols`, `Documents`, `Satellites`, `Sources`, `Content`
`-scom`	Suppress COM elements
`-sfrag`	Suppress fragments
`-srd`	Suppress harvesting the root directory as an element
`-suid`	Suppress unique identifiers for files, components, and directories
`-svb6`	Suppress VB6 COM elements
`-sw<N>`	Suppress all warnings or a specify message ID
`-t:<xsl>`	Transform harvested output with XSL file
`-template`	Use template, one of: fragment, module, product
`-v`	Verbose output
`-var`	Substitute `File/@Source="SourceDir"` with a preprocessor variable
`-wx[N]`	Treat all warnings or a specific message ID as an error
`-?	-help`	View help

Heat can look at a directory, evaluate all of the files in it, and create a `.wxs` file defining the components you'd need to install all of those files. First, let's add a new directory with a few text files in it. You can create it anywhere you like. Once you have it, add two or three files to it. You can either create new text files or use some that you already have.

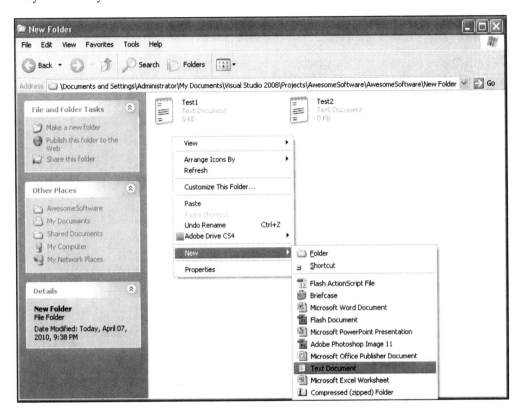

Now, open a command prompt and navigate to this directory. I'll assume that the WiX `bin` directory has been added to your PATH environment variable and won't reference the full path to `heat.exe`. The first argument that you have to give to Heat is a `harvestType`, which can be one of the following:

- `dir`: Harvest a directory
- `file`: Harvest a file
- `perf`: Harvest performance counters
- `project`: Harvest output of a VS project
- `website`: Harvest an IIS website

We'll be harvesting the files from the directory we've created, so we'll use `dir`. The second argument is the path to the directory. It must be an absolute path and should not end in a backslash. I'll truncate it in this example for the sake of clarity. The last argument, which is preceded by the `-out` flag, is the name of a source file for Heat to create. This will contain the WiX markup needed to install the files it finds. So, our Heat command looks like this so far:

```
heat.exe dir "C:\New Folder" -out ".\HeatFile.wxs"
```

We've asked it to create a file called `HeatFile.wxs` in the current directory. Here's what we get:

```
<?xml version="1.0" encoding="utf-8"?>
<Wix xmlns="http://schemas.microsoft.com/wix/2006/wi">
  <Fragment>
    <DirectoryRef Id="TARGETDIR">
      <Directory Id="dirB81CE037F36D241058F8A43AAFDFE612"
                 Name="New Folder" />
    </DirectoryRef>
  </Fragment>

  <Fragment>
    <DirectoryRef Id="dirB81CE037F36D241058F8A43AAFDFE612">
      <Component Id="cmp154B5D55534D51EA6679BF67168C1D72"
                 Guid="PUT-GUID-HERE">
        <File Id="filB2F0330A7280060ACCD0CFAF56B40DA8"
              KeyPath="yes"
              Source="SourceDir\Test1.txt" />
      </Component>
    </DirectoryRef>
  </Fragment>

  <Fragment>
    <DirectoryRef Id="dirB81CE037F36D241058F8A43AAFDFE612">
      <Component Id="cmp735C6BDA70156318193CB4A6C649FC6A"
                 Guid="PUT-GUID-HERE">
        <File Id="fil0719BEF9518EFD5FC8C9C75E5A670F00"
              KeyPath="yes"
              Source="SourceDir\Test2.txt" />
      </Component>
    </DirectoryRef>
  </Fragment>

  <Fragment>
    <DirectoryRef Id="dirB81CE037F36D241058F8A43AAFDFE612">
```

```
        <Component Id="cmpC9439409E8A1642355A4FDF410CC7EFD"
                Guid="PUT-GUID-HERE">
            <File Id="filE46FE85CD981AEB0AD645246FCB018B3"
                KeyPath="yes"
                Source="SourceDir\Test3.txt" />
        </Component>
    </DirectoryRef>
  </Fragment>
</Wix>
```

It created WiX markup for us. However, things aren't quite as good as they could be. For one thing, it has created a `Directory` element with a `Name` attribute of `New Folder`, the same as my impromptu folder. This will create a directory called "New Folder" on the end user's computer. That's not what I wanted. Also, it has set the `Guid` attribute on each `Component` to `PUT-GUID-HERE`. Although this could be useful in some circumstances, I'd much rather it created the GUIDs for me.

It has also set the `Source` attribute on each `File` element to `SourceDir\FILENAME`. When we build the project, the compiler will expect to find the text files in the directory where the `HeatFile.wxs` file is, as we didn't tell it otherwise. Finally, it hasn't made it easy for us to reference the components that it created. It would have been nice to see all of these components grouped into a `ComponentGroup` element.

To fix these problems, we'll just add some more arguments to our call to Heat:

Argument	What it does
`-cg <ComponentGroup>`	Add the `-cg` flag with a name to use for a new `ComponentGroup`. Heat will then group the components.
`-dr <DirectoryName>`	Use the `-dr` flag with the name of one of the directories you actually wanted to create. That way, the components will be copied into that directory during the installation. For some reason, you have to specify `-dr` before `-cg` for this to work.
`-gg`	To have Heat create GUIDs for us, add the `-gg` flag.
`-g1`	To have the GUIDs not have curly brackets, use the `-g1` flag. This is just a preference.
`-sfrag`	By default, Heat puts each component and your directory structure in separate Fragment elements. Adding `-sfrag` puts these elements into the same Fragment.
`-srd`	There's not really any reason to harvest the folder where the files are, so add the `-srd` flag.
`-var <VarName>`	We can use the `-var` flag with the name of a preprocessor variable (preceded by `var.`) to insert in place of `SourceDir`. Later on, we can set the variable from within the project's **Properties** or on the command line.

Now, our call to Heat will look something like this:

```
heat.exe dir "C:\New Folder" -dr MyProgramDir -cg NewFilesGroup
 -gg -g1 -sf -srd -var "var.MyDir" -out ".\HeatFile.wxs"
```

The new `HeatFile.wxs` looks like this:

```xml
<?xml version="1.0" encoding="utf-8"?>
<Wix xmlns="http://schemas.microsoft.com/wix/2006/wi">
  <Fragment>
    <ComponentGroup Id="NewFilesGroup">
      <ComponentRef Id="cmp6E6E0088162FB06CBCEA9A4AA7CBC603" />
      <ComponentRef Id="cmpC3D97EF2ADF77EB61AEF04285A25C2D2" />
      <ComponentRef Id="cmp5B1A530DE50F4D3437F2171E2CAB91A6" />
    </ComponentGroup>
  </Fragment>

  <Fragment>
    <DirectoryRef Id="MyProgramDir">
      <Component Id="cmp6E6E0088162FB06CBCEA9A4AA7CBC603"
               Guid="25AC35F2-7D3B-4DE5-8C03-79AA7897D991">
        <File Id="filCA67D5B125E878518FEA8F7FB62EF550"
            KeyPath="yes"
            Source="$(var.MyDir)\Test1.txt" />
      </Component>
      <Component Id="cmpC3D97EF2ADF77EB61AEF04285A25C2D2"
               Guid="6F103D35-F1B0-4640-AAB4-373F92DBD808">
        <File Id="filA2FD0B78B439D62B0C28A829A9508C01"
            KeyPath="yes"
            Source="$(var.MyDir)\Test2.txt" />
      </Component>
      <Component Id="cmp5B1A530DE50F4D3437F2171E2CAB91A6"
               Guid="3ED7AAC8-13B3-4CBA-8224-FC78EBA939BB">
        <File Id="fil3C980C5A1D26D4B12D481104B14E98D2"
            KeyPath="yes"
            Source="$(var.MyDir)\Test3.txt" />
      </Component>
    </DirectoryRef>
  </Fragment>
</Wix>
```

This looks a lot better. Now, the components are grouped, each `Component` has a GUID and is being installed into the `MyProgramDir` folder that I'm creating, and the `File` elements are using the `$(var.MyDir)` variable in their `Source` attributes. To include these new components in `Product.wxs`, add a reference to the `ComponentGroup` with a `ComponentGroupRef` in one of the features:

```
<Feature Id="ProductFeature"
         Title="Main Product"
         Level="1">
  <ComponentRef Id="CMP_InstallMeTXT" />
  <ComponentGroupRef Id="NewFilesGroup" />
</Feature>
```

Also, be sure to add a value for the `MyDir` variable. Here, we set it to the **New Folder** path:

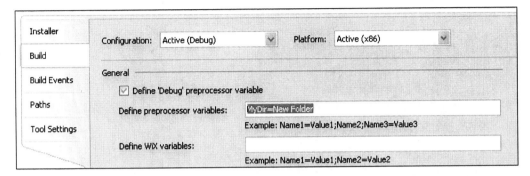

After you've compiled the project, you can use Orca to look at the MSI data that this produces. The *Component* table will show the new components and the *File* table will show the new files.

Tables	Component	ComponentId	Directory
AdminExecuteSequence	cmp6E6E0088162FB06CBCEA9A4AA7CBC603	{25AC35F2-7D3B-4DE5-8C0...	MyProgramDir
AdminUISequence	cmpC3D97EF2ADF77EB61AEF04285A25C2D2	{6F103D35-F1B0-4640-AAB...	MyProgramDir
AdvtExecuteSequence	cmp5B1A530DE50F4D3437F2171E2CAB91A6	{3ED7AAC8-13B3-4CBA-822...	MyProgramDir
Component			
Directory			
Feature			
FeatureComponents			
File			

Remember that every time you run Heat on a directory, and you've set the `-gg` flag, it will create new GUIDs for your components. If you've already shipped a version of your software to customers, then these GUIDs should not be changed. To do so would prevent Windows from accurately keeping track of them. Heat will also create new `Id` attributes for `File` and `Component` elements each time you use it. This is just something to keep in mind, especially if other parts of your installer expect the `Id` to stay the same from one day to the next.

Copying and moving files

File and Component elements allow you to add new files to the end user's computer. However, WiX also provides ways to copy and move files. For these tasks, you'll use the CopyFile element. We'll discuss how to use it in the following sections.

Copying files you install

The CopyFile element can copy a file that you're installing and place it in another directory. You'll nest it inside the File element of the file you want to duplicate. First, we'll add a subdirectory to the MyProgramDir folder that we're already creating under Program Files. The new directory will be called Copied Files.

```
<Directory Id="TARGETDIR"
           Name="SourceDir">
  <Directory Id="ProgramFilesFolder">
    <Directory Id="MyProgramDir"
               Name="Awesome Software">
      <Directory Id="CopiedFiles"
                 Name="Copied Files" />
    </Directory>
  </Directory>
</Directory>
```

Now, we can nest a CopyFile element inside the File element of the file we want to copy. Here, we're copying the InstallMe.txt file to the Copied Files folder and renaming it to InstallMeCOPY.txt. Notice that we use the DestinationDirectory attribute to specify the Id of the Copied Files element. We use the DestinationName attribute to specify the new file name. Every CopyFile element has to have a unique Id, so we set that too.

```
<!--Components-->
<DirectoryRef Id="MyProgramDir">
  <Component Id="CMP_InstallMeTXT"
             Guid="E8A58B7B-F031-4548-9BDD-7A6796C8460D">
    <File Id="FILE_InstallMeTXT"
          Source="InstallMe.txt"
          KeyPath="yes">
      <CopyFile Id="Copy_InstallMeTXT"
                DestinationDirectory="CopiedFiles"
                DestinationName="InstallMeCOPY.txt" />
    </File>
  </Component>
</DirectoryRef>
```

That's all you need. During installation, the `InstallMe.txt` file will be copied to the `Copied Files` folder and named `InstallMeCOPY.txt`. If you wanted to, you could nest multiple `CopyFile` elements under the same `File` element and copy that file to several places. Just be sure to give each `CopyFile` element a unique `Id`.

If you don't want to hardcode the destination directory, you can use the `DestinationProperty` attribute instead of `DestinationDirectory` to reference a directory at install time. `DestinationProperty` accepts the name of a property that's set to a directory path. Here is an example:

```
<Property Id="CopiedFilesFolder"
          Value="C:\CopiedFiles" />
<DirectoryRef Id="MyProgramDir">
  <Component Id="CMP_InstallMeTXT"
             Guid="E8A58B7B-F031-4548-9BDD-7A6796C8460D">
    <File Id="FILE_InstallMeTXT"
          Source="InstallMe.txt"
          KeyPath="yes">
      <CopyFile Id="Copy_InstallMeTXT"
                DestinationProperty="CopiedFilesFolder"
                DestinationName="InstallMeCOPY.txt" />
    </File>
  </Component>
</DirectoryRef>
```

So here we've hardcoded the path again. It's just that this time we used a property to do it instead of a `Directory` element. The `DestinationProperty` attribute is most useful when you can set the property dynamically. There are various ways that you can do this:

- Ask the user for it on a UI dialog and then set the property with the result. We'll talk about setting properties from dialogs later in the book.
- Set the property from a custom action. This is something else we'll cover later. The action that you create must be executed before the `DuplicateFiles` action in the `InstallExecuteSequence`.
- Set the property from the command line. We'll cover this in the next chapter.
- Use AppSearch, which we'll cover, to find the directory you want and set the property with it.

Copying existing files

In addition to being able to copy files that you're installing, you can also copy files that already exist on the end user's computer. For this, you'll nest the CopyFile element inside its own Component element and not inside a File element. Here's an example that copies a file called TEST.txt that's on the Desktop to a folder called Copied Files.

```
<!--Directory structure-->
<Directory Id="TARGETDIR"
           Name="SourceDir">
  <Directory Id="ProgramFilesFolder">
    <Directory Id="MyProgramDir"
               Name="Awesome Software">
      <Directory Id="CopiedFiles"
                 Name="Copied Files" />
    </Directory>
  </Directory>
  <Directory Id="DesktopFolder" />
</Directory>

<!--Components-->
<DirectoryRef Id="MyProgramDir">
  <Component Id="CMP_CopyTestTXT"
             Guid="E25E8584-D009-43bE-99E9-A46D58105DD0"
             KeyPath="yes">
    <CopyFile Id="CopyTest"
              DestinationDirectory="CopiedFiles"
              DestinationName="TESTCopy.txt"
              SourceDirectory="DesktopFolder"
              SourceName="TEST.txt" />
  </Component>
</DirectoryRef>
```

We've added a Directory element to reference the Desktop folder so that we can reference it later in the CopyFile element. The Component element that holds the CopyFile has its KeyPath attribute set to yes. We did this because we're not installing anything with this component and *something* has to be the KeyPath. In cases like this, when there's nothing else to serve the purpose, it's fine to mark the component itself as the KeyPath.

The `CopyFile` element here has the `DestinationDirectory` and `DestinationName` attributes like before, but it also has the `SourceDirectory` and `SourceName` attributes. `SourceDirectory` is set to the `Id` of a `Directory` element where the file you want to copy is. `SourceName` is the name of the file you want to copy. If you wanted to, you could use the `DestinationProperty` attribute instead of `DestinationDirectory` and `SourceProperty` instead of `SourceDirectory`. These are used to set the directory paths at installation time, as discussed before.

Moving existing files

Suppose you didn't want to copy a file that already existed, but rather move it to some other folder. All you need to do is add the `Delete` attribute to your `CopyFile` element. This will delete the file from its current location and copy it to the new location. So, that's another way of saying "move". Here's an example:

```
<DirectoryRef Id="MyProgramDir">
  <Component Id="CMP_MoveTestTXT"
             Guid="E25E8584-D009-43bE-99E9-A46D58105DD0"
             KeyPath="yes">
    <CopyFile Id="MoveTest"
             DestinationDirectory="CopiedFiles"
             DestinationName="TESTCopy.txt"
             SourceDirectory="DesktopFolder"
             SourceName="TEST.txt"
             Delete="yes" />
  </Component>
</DirectoryRef>
```

Unfortunately, when you uninstall the software, it doesn't move the file back. It just removes it completely from its current location.

Installing special-case files

In the following sections, we'll take a look at installing files that are different from other types that we've talked about so far. Specifically, we'll cover how to install an assembly file (`.dll`) to the Global Assembly Cache and how to install a TrueType font file.

Adding assembly files to the GAC

The **Global Assembly Cache (GAC)** is a central repository in Windows where you can store .NET assembly files so that they can be shared by multiple applications. You can add a .NET assembly to it with WiX by setting the `File` element's `Assembly` attribute to `.net`. The following example installs an assembly file to the GAC:

```
<DirectoryRef Id="MyProgramDir">
  <Component Id="CMP_MyAssembly"
            Guid="4D98D593-F4E0-479B-A7DA-80BBB78B54CB">
    <File Id="File_MyAssembly"
          Assembly=".net"
          Source="MyAssembly.dll"
          KeyPath="yes" />
  </Component>
</DirectoryRef>
```

Even though we've placed this component inside a `DirectoryRef` that references the `MyProgramDir` directory, it won't really be copied there since we're installing it to the GAC. Another approach is to create a dummy folder called GAC that's used solely for this purpose. In that case, you wouldn't give that `Directory` a `Name` attribute, which would prevent it from truly being created.

I'm using an assembly called `MyAssembly.dll` in this example that I created with a separate Visual Studio project. Any DLL that you want to install to the GAC must be strongly signed. You can do this by opening the **Properties** for that project in Visual Studio, viewing the **Signing** page, checking the box that says **Sign the assembly**, and creating a new `.snk` file.

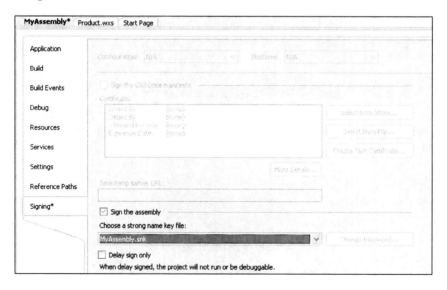

Once you've installed the package that now contains the strongly-signed assembly, you'll be able to check if the DLL file actually made it into the GAC. Navigate to the `C:\WINDOWS\assembly` folder to see a list of installed assemblies.

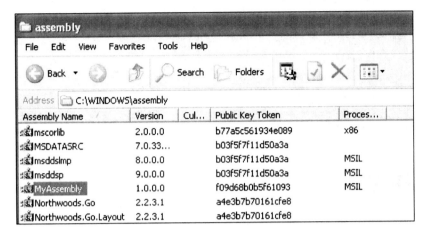

The nice thing is that when the user uninstalls the software, the assembly will be removed from the GAC—that is, unless another software product is still using it. Windows keeps a count of products using each assembly and deletes your `.dll` only when the count reaches zero.

Installing a TrueType font

To install a TrueType font onto the system, set the `File` element's `Source` attribute to the location of a TTF file on your build machine and the `TrueType` attribute to `yes`. This will include the font file in your package and install it to the end user's computer. The `File` element is nested inside a `Component` element, which is placed in the built-in `FontsFolder` directory. In the following example, we add a `Directory` element with an `Id` of `FontsFolder` and reference it with a `DirectoryRef`:

```
<Directory Id="TARGETDIR"
           Name="SourceDir">
  <Directory Id="ProgramFilesFolder">
    <Directory Id="MyProgramDir"
               Name="Awesome Software" />
  </Directory>
  <Directory Id="FontsFolder" />
</Directory>

<DirectoryRef Id="FontsFolder">
```

```
     <Component Id="CMP_MyFont"
               Guid="CFF27814-D7A8-4054-B3B1-F5DB44CD5AB9">
       <File Id="myFontFile"
             Source="myFont.TTF"
             TrueType="yes"
             KeyPath="yes" />
     </Component>
   </DirectoryRef>
```

Here, the `File` element is using the `TrueType` attribute to signify that this file is a font file. It will include `myFont.TTF`, from the current build directory, in the install package and copy it to the end user's `C:\WINDOWS\Fonts` folder.

Creating an empty folder

Ordinarily, Windows Installer won't let you create empty folders. However, there is a way: Use the `CreateFolder` element inside an otherwise empty `Component` element. First, you'll define the name of your empty directory with a `Directory` element. Follow this example:

```
<Directory Id="TARGETDIR"
           Name="SourceDir">
  <Directory Id="ProgramFilesFolder">
    <Directory Id="MyProgramDir"
               Name="Awesome Software">
      <Directory Id="MyEmptyDir"
                 Name="Empty Directory" />
    </Directory>
  </Directory>
</Directory>
```

Here, we've added a new `Directory` element named `Empty Directory` inside our main application folder. The next step is to add a component to this directory by using a `DirectoryRef` element. Notice that we've set the `KeyPath` attribute on the component to `yes`, as there will be no file to serve this purpose.

```
<DirectoryRef Id="MyEmptyDir">
  <Component Id="CMP_MyEmptyDir"
             Guid="85DAD4AE-6404-4A40-B713-43538091B9D3"
             KeyPath="yes">
    <CreateFolder />
  </Component>
</DirectoryRef>
```

The only thing inside the component is a `CreateFolder` element. This tells Windows Installer that the folder will be empty, but that it should still create it during the install. As always, be sure to add this new component to a `Feature`, as so:

```
<Feature Id="ProductFeature"
         Title="Main Product"
         Level="1">
  <ComponentRef Id="CMP_InstallMeTXT" />
  <ComponentRef Id="CMP_MyEmptyDir" />
</Feature>
```

Setting file permissions

WiX allows you to set the permissions that Windows users and groups have to the files that you install. You can see these permissions by right-clicking on a file and selecting the **Security** tab. On Windows XP, you may have to configure your system so that this tab is visible. In Windows Explorer, open the folder that you want to configure and go to **Tools | Folder Options | View**. Then, uncheck the box that says **Use simple file sharing**. Here's an example of the **Security** tab on a file:

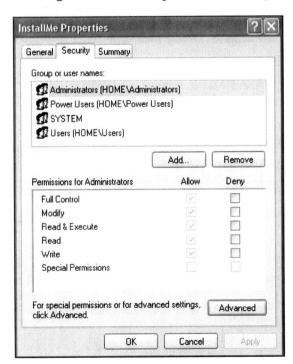

To set the permissions for a file that you're installing, nest a `PermissionEx` element inside the corresponding `File` element. This element, which is available from the `WixUtilExtension`, has various attributes that can be used to define file permissions. Before you can use it, you'll need to add a reference to `WixUtilExtension.dll` in your project. Go to **Add Reference** in the **Solution Explorer**, navigate to the WiX `bin` directory, and select the assembly. Next, add the following namespace to your `Wix` element:

```
<Wix xmlns="http://schemas.microsoft.com/wix/2006/wi"
     xmlns:util="http://schemas.microsoft.com/wix/UtilExtension">
```

The following attributes are available to the `PermissionEx` element. Each can be set to either `yes` or `no`.

Attribute	What it does
GenericAll	Gives the user all permissions.
GenericRead	Must have at least one other permission specified. Grants all Read privileges: "Read Data", "Read Attributes", "Read Extended Attributes", and "Read Permissions".
GenericWrite	Grants "Write Data, "Append Data", "Write Attributes", and "Read Permissions".
GenericExecute	Grants "Execute File", "Read Attributes", and "Read Permissions".
Read	Grants "Read Data".
Write	Grants "Write Data".
Execute	Grants "Execute File" permission.
Append	Grants "Append Data".
Delete	Grants "Delete".
ChangePermission	Grants "Change Permissions".
ReadPermission	Grants "Read Permissions".
TakeOwnership	Grants "Take Ownership".
Synchronize	If "yes", then threads must wait their turn before accessing the file.

The following example references the `util` namespace from the `Wix` element and uses its `PermissionEx` element to set file permissions on the `InstallMe.txt` file. Notice that I'm also using another element from `WixUtilExtension` called `User`. This can be used to create a new Windows user on the target computer. The `Product.wxs` file would look something like this:

```
<?xml version="1.0" encoding="UTF-8"?>
<Wix xmlns="http://schemas.microsoft.com/wix/2006/wi"
     xmlns:util="http://schemas.microsoft.com/wix/UtilExtension">
```

```xml
<Product Id="3E786878-358D-43AD-82D1-1435ADF9F6EA"
         Name="Awesome Software"
         Language="1033"
         Version="1.0.0.0"
         Manufacturer="Awesome Company"
         UpgradeCode="B414C827-8D81-4B4A-B3B6-338C06DE3A11">
  <Package InstallerVersion="301"
           Compressed="yes" />

  <!--Directory structure-->
  <Directory Id="TARGETDIR"
             Name="SourceDir">
    <Directory Id="ProgramFilesFolder">
      <Directory Id="MyProgramDir"
                 Name="Awesome Software" />
    </Directory>
  </Directory>

  <!--Components-->
  <DirectoryRef Id="MyProgramDir">
    <Component Id="CMP_InstallMeTXT"
               Guid="E8A58B7B-F031-4548-9BDD-7A6796C8460D">

      <!--Creates new user-->
      <util:User Id="MyNewUser"
                 CreateUser="yes"
                 Name="nickramirez"
                 Password="password"
                 PasswordNeverExpires="yes"
                 RemoveOnUninstall="yes"
                 UpdateIfExists="yes" />
      <File Id="FILE_InstallMeTXT"
            Source="InstallMe.txt" KeyPath="yes">

        <!--Sets file permissions for user-->
        <util:PermissionEx User="nickramirez"
                           GenericAll="yes" />
      </File>
    </Component>
  </DirectoryRef>

  <!--Features-->
  <Feature Id="ProductFeature"
           Title="Main Product"
           Level="1">
    <ComponentRef Id="CMP_InstallMeTXT" />
  </Feature>
</Product>
</Wix>
```

Here, we've given all privileges to the user nickramirez, whom we've just created. You can see all of the users for a computer by going to your Start Menu, right-clicking on **My Computer**, selecting **Manage**, and viewing the **Local Users and Groups** node. The PermissionEx element's GenericAll attribute gives the user all possible privileges. Just so you know, any users that you create during an installation will be removed during an uninstallation if you set the User element's RemoveOnUninstall attribute to yes.

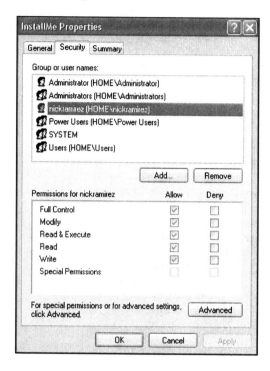

Speeding up file installations

We haven't talked too much about how the files and directories that you author in your WiX source files are stored in the MSI database's tables. The files are stored in a table called *File*, the directories in a table called *Directory*, and the components in a table called *Component*. You can see this by opening the MSI package with Orca.exe.

In the following example, I have four files that are being installed. I've used the convention of prefixing my file IDs with "FILE_", giving me FILE_InstallMeTXT, for example.

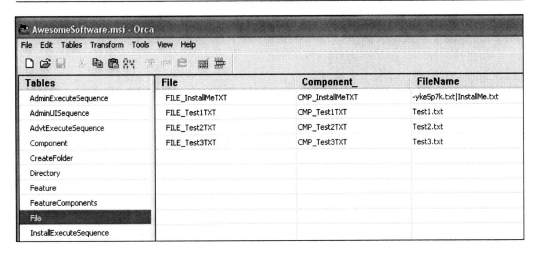

Each file in the *File* table is sorted alphabetically by the `Id` you gave to it via the `File` element. This is the order in which the files are copied to the end user's computer. So, how can you make things faster? You can give your files IDs that will cause WiX to sort them more efficiently.

The file copy process takes longer when Windows has to write to one directory and then switch to another and then another and so on. If it could copy all of the files that belong to a certain directory at the same time and then move to another location, the process would be more efficient. As it is, Windows may leave and return to the same directory several times as it goes through the alphabetical list.

To speed things up, we should add the name of the directory where the file is set to go to the `Id` of the file. To be effective, this should come at the beginning of the `Id`. That way, files going to the same place will appear next to each other in the list. So, in addition to prefixing our file IDs with "FILE_", we could also indicate the directory that each is being copied to. For example, `FILE_MyProgramDir_InstallMeTXT` signifies that this file is being copied to the `MyProgramDir` directory. Any other files being copied to the same place should also get `MyProgramDir` in their IDs.

The following example displays a list that is better organized. It uses the name of the destination directory as part of the files' Ids. Files going to the same place will be grouped together in the alphabetical list.

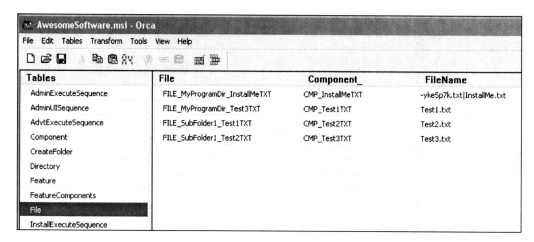

I've used underscores to separate the prefixes, but it's also common to use periods. So, I could have named the first file `FILE.MyProgramDir.InstallMe.Txt` instead of `FILE_MyProgramDir_InstallMeTXT`. It's really just a matter of preference.

Summary

In this chapter, we discussed the elements used to install files and create directories. The `File`, `Directory` and `Component` elements play vital roles here, but you may also benefit from using `ComponentGroup` to group your components. This allows you to better organize your markup and even to separate it into multiple WiX source files.

The `heat.exe` tool can create `Component` elements for you. You simply need to point it at a certain directory. However, it's best to fine-tune its arguments so that the output that you get is optimal. We discussed a few other topics such as how to copy a file, how to set file permissions and how to organize your `File` element `Id` attributes for maximum installation speed.

In the next chapter, we'll move on to discuss WiX properties and the various ways of searching the end user's system for files, directories, and settings.

3

Putting Properties and AppSearch to Work

WiX uses variables, called **properties**, to store data during the course of the installation. It's a temporary storage, so it won't persist once the installation is complete. However, it's the only way to pass information from one action during the install to another. For example, to collect a username and password from the end user you'll need to store them in properties. Then, you might pass them to another part of the install, use them in an outside executable or assembly, or save them to the Registry. You can also use properties in conditional statements that can alter the flow of the install or stop it if some piece of data isn't right.

In this chapter, you will learn:

- The syntax for declaring and setting properties
- How to reference properties in other parts of your markup
- The built-in properties that Windows Installer sets for you
- What AppSearch is and how to use it to search the end user's computer for installed components, Registry keys, and so on

Custom properties

You'll often need to define and set custom properties to hold your install time data. In the following sections, we will explore the meaning of WiX properties and how best to use them.

Declaring and setting properties

To declare a property, add a `Property` element to your WiX markup anywhere inside the `Product` element. A `Property` element only needs two attributes: `Id` and `Value`. The `Id` sets the name of the property, used later to reference it, and `Value` sets the data contained inside. The following example creates a new property called `myProperty` and sets its value to the string `my value`:

```
<Property Id="myProperty"
          Value="my value" />
```

`Id` should begin with either a letter or underscore and consist of only lower and uppercase letters, numbers, underscores, and periods. When referencing it, it's case sensitive. So, `MyPropertyId` is not the same as `MyPropertyID`.

The data in `Value` can be almost any string. If you need to use double quotes in the value, you can either surround it with single quotes, as in the next example:

```
<Property Id="myProperty"
          Value='Do you see the "quotes"?' />
```

Or you can use the XML entity `&quot;` in place of the double quotes:

```
<Property Id="myProperty"
          Value="Do you see the &quot;quotes&quot;?" />
```

If you omit the `Value` attribute, the property will be set to `null`. During compilation, properties with null values are left out of the MSI package. It will be as if you hadn't declared them at all. However, you're allowed to declare a property and set it later. One way to do this is to create a second `Property` element that sets the value, which is allowed as long as you didn't set it in the first place:

```
<Property Id="myProperty" />
<Property Id="myProperty"
          Value="my value" />
```

This works because the property wasn't set in the first `Property` element. If it had been, the project build would have failed with an error regarding duplicate properties. You can also set the value of a `Property` element by adding inner text to it, as in the following example:

```
<Property Id="myProperty">my value</Property>
```

Properties can also be declared and set from the command line. If you do, you're not required to declare the property in your WiX markup first. Declaring them on the command line creates them dynamically. When defining properties on the command line, their `Id`s must be uppercase. This is to make them "public", which we'll discuss later in the chapter. To add a property in this way add the name and value of your property, separated by an equals sign, after the `msiexec` command.

```
msiexec /i myInstaller.msi PROPERTY1=100 PROPERTY2="my value"
```

Here, we're declaring two properties, `PROPERTY1` and `PROPERTY2`, and setting their respective values. If these properties don't exist in our WiX markup, they will be created on the fly. You can add more than one property by separating them with spaces, as we've done here. Literal string values should be surrounded by double quotes. If your value has double quotes in it, you can escape them by using two double quotes instead of one:

```
msiexec /i myInstaller.msi PROPERTY1="Game title: ""Starcraft""."
```

You can clear a property by setting its value to an empty string, such as:

```
msiexec /i myInstaller.msi PROPERTY1=""
```

Properties declared on the command line override those set in your WiX markup. So, you could declare a WiX `Property` element in your XML to give it a default value, then override that value from the command line.

Referencing properties

To make use of a property, you'll usually reference it in one of the attributes of another WiX element. You'll put square brackets around its name. For example, to refer to a property called `USERNAME`, you'd use `[USERNAME]`.

Not all element attributes will interpret this square bracket notation back into its original literal value. The MSI SDK calls these special fields "formatted" string fields. You should consult the MSI documentation to find a full list. Generally, any attribute on an element that becomes something the end user will see in the UI (text on dialogs, buttons, lists, and so on) or the names of shortcuts and registry keys will have the ability to interpret it. Here is a list of elements that have attributes you're likely to use property values (with square brackets) in:

- `Control`: `Text` attribute
- `ListItem`: `Text` attribute
- `Dialog`: `Title` attribute
- `Shortcut`: `Target`, `Arguments`, and `Description` attributes
- `Condition`: `Message` attribute
- `RegistryValue`: `Name` and `Value` attributes

In the next example, we'll create a property called `myProperty` that has a value of `0`. A conditional statement that follows checks the value to see if it's equal to `1`. When this evaluates to false, you'll see the message. Notice that I'm using the square bracket notation in the `Message` attribute to reference `myProperty`:

```
<Property Id="myProperty"
          Value="0" />

<Condition Message=
               "Value of myProperty is [myProperty]. Should be 1">

  <![CDATA[Installed OR myProperty = "1"]]>
</Condition>
```

When you use a property in the child text of an element, the syntax is different. In that situation, you reference the `Id` of the property but leave off the square brackets. Conditional statements, such as those found inside the `Condition` element, are a good example. Look back at the previous example to see that `myProperty` is referenced in the inner text of the `Condition` element without using square brackets. The `Installed` keyword is another property set by WiX that tells the installer to only check this condition during an install.

Declaring properties in your main `.wxs` file is fine if you only have a few, but once you've got a good number it's easier to move them into their own `.wxs` file using the `Fragment` element. To access these in your in your main `.wxs` file, add a `PropertyRef` element with the name of one of the properties. A `PropertyRef` element brings that property into the scope of your project. Remember, if there are multiple properties defined inside a `Fragment` element in a separate source file, you only need to reference one of them to pull them all in. Here's an example that references one of the properties defined by WiX:

```
<PropertyRef Id="NETFRAMEWORK30" />

<Condition Message=
           "You must install Microsoft .NET Framework 3.0 or higher.">

  <![CDATA[Installed OR NETFRAMEWORK30]]>
</Condition>
```

This example is one that's used pretty often and utilizes the `NetFXExtension`. After you've added a reference to the `WixNetFxExtension.dll` to your project, which can be found in the WiX bin directory, you add a `PropertyRef` to the `NETFRAMEWORK30` property that's defined in a `Fragment` in that library. You can use this to test if .NET 3.0 is installed on the computer, like in the `Condition` element shown earlier.

In case you're interested, here's how the `WixNetFxExtension` defined the `NETFRAMEWORK30` property:

```
<Fragment>
  <Property Id="NETFRAMEWORK30"
            Secure="yes">

    <RegistrySearch Id="NetFramework30"
                    Root="HKLM"
                    Key="SOFTWARE\Microsoft\NET Framework
                    Setup\NDP\v3.0\Setup"
                    Name="InstallSuccess"
                    Type="raw" />

  </Property>
</Fragment>
```

Instead of setting the `NETFRAMEWORK30` property with a `Value` attribute, it's been set with a `RegistrySearch` element. `RegistrySearch` is a type of `AppSearch` and we'll cover it later in this chapter.

Property visibility and scope

Two things to consider when working with properties are *visibility* and *scope*. In regards to visibility, when you install an MSI package it's possible to get a log of the process. You can see this log by installing from the command line with logging turned on. The following command installs a package called `myInstaller.msi` and writes a verbose log using the `/l*v` flag:

`msiexec /i myInstaller.msi /l*v log.log`

When you submit this command, it will log every event during the install to a text file called `log.log`. At the end of the log, all properties will be listed in plain text. This isn't a good thing if one of your properties contains a password or other sensitive data. To prevent a specific property from showing in the install log, mark it as `Hidden`:

```
<Property Id="MY_PASSWORD"
          Value="some value"
          Hidden="yes" />
```

Set the `Hidden` attribute to `yes` if you don't want to show the property as an entry in the log. Marking a property as hidden does not, however, prevent it from displaying its value in the MSI database's *Property* table. Therefore, you probably shouldn't set the literal value of a password directly in a property, as in the above example. Instead, set the value from the command line or collect it from the user via the UI. That way, it is defined dynamically and the end user can not see it by opening the MSI package with `Orca.exe`.

Scope is also a consideration. By default, properties are not **public**, meaning that they are not available when the installer runs through its execution phase (when changes are made to the end user's system). We'll talk more about this phase later on. For now, just know that if you plan on using your properties when writing to the Registry, laying down files, or during any other act that changes the user's computer, then those properties must be made public.

Making a property public is just a matter of making its `Id` all uppercase. The property `MY_PASSWORD` is public, while `my_Password` is not. One example of when to do this is when you collect information from the user with a dialog and then want to take some action on it during the execution phase such as store it in the Registry.

The following property, because it's uppercase, will persist throughout the entire installation.

```
<Property Id="MY_PROPERTY"
        Value="my string" />
```

However, this will not:

```
<Property Id="My_Property"
        Value="my string" />
```

You could consider this a **private** property. It will only last during the current session. We will discuss the install phases in detail in *Chapter 5*.

Secure properties

The `Secure` attribute is used so that you can pass public properties to the Execute phase when doing a managed installation with elevated privileges. What does that mean? It applies to computers that use **UAC** (User Account Control), such as Windows Vista, Server 2008, and Windows 7. Usually, an installer will prompt the user to elevate their privileges, or in other words enter the password of the built-in Administrator account, before performing tasks that change directories and Registry keys outside the logged-in user's permissions zone.

However, sometimes system administrators that oversee large networks might store the installer in a central location, such as in a file share, and allow non-administrators to use it without being prompted to elevate (this is known as a **managed software deployment**). Whenever this happens, the installer, marking that actions are being done by a non-administrator, labels the whole process as restricted. In that case, only a small list of properties are allowed to be passed around. To add more properties to that list, you'll need to mark them as secure.

So, to sum up, the following conditions would produce a situation where a property would need to be public *and* secure:

- The user performing the install is not the built-in Administrator
- The install is a per-machine install (the ALLUSERS property is set to 1 in your markup) instead of per-user
- Through some UAC wrangling, such as placing the installer in a file share with the appropriate permissions so that users don't need to elevate to use it (setting the Registry key AlwaysInstallElevated also does this)
- The install needs to access the property during the **Execute** phase, which is the phase during which the installer makes changes to the computer

If these conditions are met, Windows Installer restricts the properties that can be passed to only those that are secure. Use the Property element's Secure attribute in that case:

```
<Property Id="MY_PROPERTY"
          Value="my string"
          Secure="yes" />
```

You can tell when you need to use the Secure attribute if, in the install log, you see that the RestrictedUserControl property has been set by Windows Installer. You'll also see some of your properties, if they're used in the Execute sequence, being ignored. Here is a sample log of that happening:

```
MSI (s) (C8:BC) [23:49:58:906]:
        Machine policy value 'EnableUserControl' is 0
MSI (s) (C8:BC) [23:49:58:906]: PROPERTY CHANGE:
        Adding RestrictedUserControl property. Its value is '1'.
MSI (s) (C8:BC) [23:49:58:906]:
        Ignoring disallowed property MYPROPERTY
```

Notice that there's another property called EnableUserControl. If you set it to 1 in your markup, all properties will be marked as Secure.

Property datatypes

The properties in WiX are not strongly typed, meaning that you don't need to specify whether a property is an integer, string, or boolean. Most of the time, you'll be setting properties by using the WiX `Property` element. The alternative is to set them from the command line or to set them dynamically with a UI control or custom action. Using a `Property` element always implicitly casts the property as a string. Therefore, you can always treat these properties as string values. However, depending on how you reference it, it's possible for WiX to interpret your property as an integer.

If, in a conditional statement, you compare your property to an integer (a whole number without quotes around it), WiX will assume that your property is an integer too. For example, here I compare a property to the number 3 without quotes around it. WiX will cast my property to an integer and then perform the comparison.

```
<Property Id="MyProperty"
        Value="5" />

<Condition Message="Some message if condition is false." >
   <![CDATA[MyProperty > 3]]>
</Condition>
```

The same is true when comparing a property to a string. WiX will assume your property is a string and perform the comparison.

```
<Property Id="MyProperty"
        Value="5" />

<Condition Message="Some message if condition is false.">
   <![CDATA[MyProperty = "5"]]>
</Condition>
```

Both strings and integers can use any of the following comparison operators. With the "greater than" and "less than" signs, a string is considered less than another if, from left to right, one of its characters comes before the character in the other string. For example, the string "abc" is less than "abd" because "c" comes before "d". The table below shows the comparison operators and examples for integers and strings that evaluate to true.

Operator	Meaning	Integer example	String example
<	Less than	1 < 2	"abc" < "def"
>	Greater than	2 > 1	"b" > "a"
<=	Less than or equal to	2 <= 3	"a" <= "b"

Operator	Meaning	Integer example	String example
>=	Greater than or equal to	3 >= 2	"b" >= "a"
=	Equal to	2 = 2	"a" = "a"
<>	Not equal to	2 <> 1	"a" <> "b"

Note that if the property is a decimal, such as 2.0, then you can't compare it to a numeric value unless you put quotes around that value. This is because WiX has no concept of decimals and so must evaluate them as strings. For example, the following statement, unexpectedly, evaluates to false:

```
<Property Id="myNum"
          Value="2.0" />

<Condition Message="myNum must be > 1.">
   <![CDATA[myNum > 1]]>
</Condition>
```

However, by putting quotes around 1, it evaluates to true as it should:

```
<Property Id="myNum"
          Value="2.0" />

<Condition Message="myNum must be > 1.">
   <![CDATA[myNum > "1"]]>
</Condition>
```

Normally, when you compare two string values, case counts. However, if you prefix the comparison operator with a tilde (~), case will be ignored. For example:

```
<Property Id="MyProperty"
          Value="sample string" />

<Condition Message="Some message if condition is false.">
   <![CDATA[MyProperty ~= "SAMPLE STRING"]]>
</Condition>
```

Something else you can do is check if a property is defined at all. Evaluating a property by itself checks that it has been set, as in this example:

```
<Condition Message="Some message if condition is false">
   <![CDATA[MY_PROPERTY]]>
</Condition>
```

Placing the NOT keyword in front of the property checks that the property is not defined:

```
<Condition Message="Some message if condition is false">
  <![CDATA[NOT MY_PROPERTY]]>
</Condition>
```

WiX datatypes are very simplistic. After all, if you were to look at the MSI's *Property* table, you'd see only two columns: property and value. There's no extra column to tell what type of data it is. Take this into account when planning the conditional statements that you write.

Predefined Windows Installer properties

You've seen that you can define your own properties, but there are also a number that come predefined for you. Quite a few are created automatically as part of the install process. For example, there's the property called Installed that's set if the product is already installed locally. Looking through the install log will uncover many more.

In this section, you'll be introduced to some of these automatic properties. You'll also see that some properties, although their Id attributes are defined for you, only come to life when you instantiate them with Property elements.

Implied properties

There are certain properties that don't need to be set with a Property element. They're implied. They're set for you. First, there are those that are created when you set attributes on the Product element. The following properties are automatically created:

- Manufacturer
- ProductCode
- ProductLanguage
- ProductName
- ProductVersion
- UpgradeCode

You can use these properties just as you would those you create yourself. They're available to you in all phases of the install. They can be accessed in the attributes and inner text of other elements just like normal.

Another set of implied properties are directories. We discussed the built-in directory properties in *Chapter 1*. They're given names like `ProgramFilesFolder`. In addition to using them in your `Directory` elements, you can use them anywhere that other properties are used. Also, any directories that you create with `Directory` elements are also available as properties, referenced by the `Directory` element's `Id` attribute.

Another set of implied properties are those that guide how Windows Installer does its job. For example, there's the `Installed` property, which tells you that the product is already installed. You'll usually see it during an uninstall or if the product is in maintenance mode. Another is the `Privileged` property, which is set when the install is performed by an administrator. Another example is the `REMOVE` property, which is only set during an uninstall. Taking a look at the install log will reveal many of these.

Cited properties

Most of the properties that are built into Windows Installer *aren't* implied. You have to set them explicitly with a `Property` element. They're different from the properties that you'll create yourself in that the `Id` must match the predefined name. There is a fairly long list of these available. Check the *Property Reference* in the *MSI SDK* help file that comes with WiX by searching in it for the phrase "Property Reference". You can also find them at:

```
http://msdn.microsoft.com/en-us/library/aa370905%28v=VS.85%29.aspx
```

I won't list them all here, but to give you an idea, here are properties that affect what gets shown in Add/Remove Programs once your product has been installed. Your product will automatically show up in the list without the use of properties, but these provide extra information or disable the default functionality.

Property	Description
ARPAUTHORIZEDCDPREFIX	URL of the update channel for the application
ARPCOMMENTS	Provides Comments for Add/Remove Programs
ARPCONTACT	Provides the Contact for Add/Remove Programs
ARPINSTALLLOCATION	Fully qualified path to the application's primary folder
ARPHELPLINK	URL for technical support
ARPHELPTELEPHONE	Technical support phone numbers
ARPNOMODIFY	Prevents displaying a Change button for the product in Add/Remove Programs
ARPNOREMOVE	Prevents displaying a Remove button for the product in Add/Remove Programs

Property	Description
ARPNOREPAIR	Disables the Repair button in Add/Remove Programs
ARPPRODUCTICON	Identifies the icon to display for the product in Add/Remove Programs
ARPREADME	Provides the ReadMe for Add/Remove Programs
ARPSIZE	Estimated size of the application in kilobytes
ARPSYSTEMCOMPONENT	Prevents the application from displaying at all in Add/Remove Programs
ARPURLINFOABOUT	URL for the application's home page
ARPURLUPDATEINFO	URL for the application's update information

Here are a few examples of how these properties would be set.

```
<Icon Id="myIcon"
      SourceFile="..\myIcon.ico" />

<Property Id="ARPPRODUCTICON"
          Value="myIcon" />
<Property Id="ARPCOMMENTS"
          Value="(c) Amazing Software" />
<Property Id="ARPNOREPAIR"
          Value="1" />
<Property Id="ARPCONTACT"
          Value="Nick Ramirez" />
<Property Id="ARPHELPLINK"
          Value="http://www.MYURL.com/AmazingSoftware/support.html"/>
<Property Id="ARPREADME"
          Value="http://www.MYURL.com/AmazingSoftware/readme.html" />
```

As you can see, setting a built-in property is just like setting your own custom properties except that the Id must use the predefined name.

One other built-in property that you should know about is ALLUSERS. You can set it to a 1, 2, or an empty string (""). A 1 means that the install will be performed in the per-machine context, meaning that its components will be installed to folders accessible to anyone that uses the system. Setting ALLUSERS to an empty string tells the installer to use the per-user context, meaning that its components will be installed only for the current user. A value of 2 means that the installer will sometimes be in the user context and sometimes in the machine context, depending upon whether or not the user who initiated it has administrator rights. However, even this rule varies based upon the operating system.

In general, you should set ALLUSERS to 1, the per-machine context. Setting it to the per-user context can only be done if you're certain that no Registry keys or files will be installed to machine-level locations. This is rarely the case. A value of 2 usually causes scenarios that are too complex to plan for. So, it's best to avoid it. The following example sets the ALLUSERS property to 1:

```
<Property Id="ALLUSERS"
          Value="1" />
```

The reason that this property is important is that during an upgrade, you'll want to find out if a previous version of the software is already installed. For that, the ALLUSERS property must be set to the same value as it was originally. Otherwise, the installer may look in the wrong place and fail to detect the software, even if it's there. So, keep it consistent. Always set it to the same value, preferably 1.

One thing to note is that you can also set the InstallScope attribute on the Package element to either perMachine or perUser. This will have the same effect as setting the ALLUSERS property directly. If you do, you should remove any Property elements that set it.

AppSearch

Windows Installer lets you search the computer during an install for specific files, directories and settings. Collectively, these fall under the category of AppSearch, which is the name of the MSI database table where search tasks are stored.

There are five types of searches:

- **DirectorySearch**: Search for the existence or path of a directory
- **FileSearch**: Search for a specific file
- **ComponentSearch**: Search for a file by its component GUID
- **RegistrySearch**: Search the Windows Registry for a key
- **IniFileSearch**: Search inside INI files for configuration settings

Each of these types refers to the WiX element that you'd use to perform the search. Each is the child element of a Property element. So, you'll start off with a Property element whose value will be filled with the result of the search.

There's an attribute of the Property element, ComplianceCheck, that can be used with all of the types. When set to yes, an error dialog will be shown if the search isn't successful. It will then end the installation.

The error message you get is very generic though. You're better off detecting whether or not a certain file exists, setting a property based on the result, and crafting a targeted message if it isn't found (using a launch condition, discussed later). That way, users will know *what* wasn't found. Although there's nothing stopping you from creating a custom launch condition *and* setting ComplianceCheck to yes, it isn't necessary since the install will end if the launch condition fails and launch conditions always come before the compliance check is performed.

DirectorySearch

You may want to check if a directory exists on a computer and, if it exists, get its path. You can do this by using the DirectorySearch element. First, create a Property element to hold the search result and then add a DirectorySearch element with the parameters of the search. The Id attribute of the Property must be public, so be sure to capitalize it. The DirectorySearch element accepts three parameters: Id, Depth, and Path. Here's an example:

```
<Property Id="DESKTOP_PATH">
  <DirectorySearch Path="C:\Documents and Settings\All Users\Desktop"
                   Depth="0"
                   AssignToProperty="yes"
                   Id="DoesDesktopExist" />
</Property>
```

Here, we're searching for the *Desktop* folder under the *All Users* account. You're more likely to be searching for more specialized folders, but this works for demonstration purposes. If the search is successful, the full path to the Desktop will be stored in the property DESKTOP_PATH (the name could be anything). If not, then the property won't be set. The AssignToProperty attribute tells the installer to use this DirectorySearch element to set the property. This will become more useful later when we start nesting DirectorySearch elements inside one another.

Notice that this search is pretty specific about where this directory should be: We've given an *absolute* path to the directory we're looking for. The Depth attribute is set to zero to signify that we don't want WiX to search in any subfolders.

What if I didn't know exactly where this directory was, though? We could be more generic with the search criteria. We could, for example, use a relative path instead:

```
<Property Id="DESKTOP_PATH">
  <DirectorySearch Path="Desktop"
                   Depth="5"
                   AssignToProperty="yes"
                   Id="DoesDesktopExist" />
</Property>
```

Here we've set the `Path` attribute to just `Desktop` and the `Depth` attribute to five. Now we're telling the installer to search for a folder called `Desktop` and that we're willing to go five directories deep to find it. Because we haven't explicitly told it where to start the search from, it will search all attached drives starting at their root directories (such as `C:\`, `D:\`, and others).

Because our search is so generic, you might be in for a wait. We also run into another problem: It's going to find the wrong `Desktop`. The search will stop as soon as it has found a match, which in this case is:

`C:\Documents and Settings\Administrator\Desktop`

Yet we'd wanted to find the `All Users` desktop. `Administrator` comes before `All Users` alphabetically.

In cases like this, you should tell Windows Installer where to start searching by nesting `DirectorySearch` elements inside one another. Then, the parent element becomes the starting point and the child the directory you're searching for. As in the following example:

```
<Property Id="DESKTOP_PATH">
  <DirectorySearch Path="C:\Documents and Settings\All Users"
                   Depth="0"
                   Id="CDrive">

    <DirectorySearch Path="Desktop"
                     Depth="3"
                     Id="DesktopPath"
                     AssignToProperty="yes" />
  </DirectorySearch>
</Property>
```

In this example, we've set the parent `DirectorySearch` to have a path of:

`C:\Documents and Settings\All Users`

This will be our starting point. From here, we can tell the installer to search to a certain depth, in this example three, for a specific folder by setting the `Path` and `Depth` on the child `DirectorySearch` element. Now, the search will find the correct Desktop folder. Notice that we only set the `AssignToProperty` on the innermost `DirectorySearch`. That's the one that holds the end destination, so we want it to be the only one to set the property's value.

The `Path` attribute actually gives you quite a few options. It can accept any of the following:

- A Windows share, such as `\\myshare\myFolder`
- A path relative to the top-level directory for any attached drives, such as `\temp`
- An absolute path, such as `C:\temp`
- The name of a folder, such as `temp`
- an environment variable (using WiX preprocessor syntax), such as `$(env.ALLUSERSPROFILE)`

You should know that if the installer can't find the path you set in the parent element, it will skip it and use its default: every attached drive's root directory.

In the previous example, we were still pretty specific about where to look. If we wanted to be truly generic, we could nest more `DirectorySearch` elements. For example, we could start with the C drive, look for the "All Users" folder, and then find the `Desktop` beneath that, as in the following example:

```
<Property Id="DESKTOP_PATH">
   <DirectorySearch Path="C:\"
                    Depth="0"
                    Id="CDrive">

     <DirectorySearch Path="All Users"
                      Depth="3"
                      Id="AllUsersFolder">

       <DirectorySearch Path="Desktop"
                        Depth="3"
                        Id="DesktopFolder"
                        AssignToProperty="yes" />
     </DirectorySearch>
   </DirectorySearch>
</Property>
```

In this example, there are three `DirectorySearch` elements. The first is the starting point: `C:\`. The `Depth` is set to zero because we don't need to go any deeper to find this directory. The second element is looking for the `All Users` folder and it will go as far as three levels down from `C:\` to find it. The third `DirectorySearch` is looking for a folder called `Desktop` inside the `All Users` folder. We wait until this last element to set the `AssignToProperty` to `yes`. That's pretty generic, but not so generic that we'll lose our way. We've given the installer enough information to find what we want, but we didn't have to hardcode an absolute path.

Note that although it seems superfluous, each `DirectorySearch` element must get its own `Id`. Windows Installer uses these `Id` attributes to tie all of the elements together into one cohesive search. It's interesting to look inside the MSI package and see how all of this is stored. Directory searches are found in the *DrLocator* table. Here's what you'd find for the previous search:

Signature	Parent	Path	Depth
DesktopFolder	AllUsersFolder	Desktop	3
AllUsersFolder	CDrive	All Users	3
CDrive		C:\	0

The table structure mirrors the parent-child relationship seen in WiX. In the `AppSearch` table, you'd see a row with the property `DESKTOP_PATH` mapped to the Signature `DesktopFolder`.

FileSearch

There may be times when you want to find a specific file instead of just a directory. For this, you'll still use a `DirectorySearch` element, but you'll nest a `FileSearch` element inside it. This tells the installer that you're looking for a file inside that directory:

```
<Property Id="MY_FILE">
    <DirectorySearch Path="C:\Documents and Settings\All Users\Desktop"
                     Depth="0"
                     Id="DesktopPath"
                     AssignToProperty="no">

        <FileSearch Name="myFile.txt"
                    Id="myFileSearch" />
    </DirectorySearch>
</Property>
```

In this example, there's one `DirectorySearch` element with an absolute path to the desired directory. The nested `FileSearch` element names the file you're looking for there. If it's found, the `MY_FILE` property will be populated with the absolute path to the file. You can use any of the various definitions for the `DirectorySearch` element's `Path` attribute discussed in the last section. Or if you omit the `Path` attribute altogether, you'll be telling the installer to look at all attached drives for the file you specify.

The `FileSearch` element can't do recursive searches through subfolders. So, its parent `DirectorySearch` element must name the exact folder where the file is supposed to be, if it specifies a path with the `Path` attribute. For example, you can't name the `All Users` folder if the file you're looking for is really in the `Desktop` folder. You may have to nest `DirectorySearch` elements to make this work. Here's an example that uses several `DirectorySearch` elements, but ultimately names the `Desktop` folder as the direct parent to the `FileSearch`:

```
<Property Id="MY_FILE">
  <DirectorySearch Path="C:\"
                   Depth="0"
                   Id="DesktopPath"
                   AssignToProperty="no">

    <DirectorySearch Path="All Users"
                     Depth="3"
                     AssignToProperty="no"
                     Id="AllUsersFolder">

    <DirectorySearch Path="Desktop"
                     Depth="0"
                     AssignToProperty="no"
                     Id="DesktopFolder">

      <FileSearch Name="myFile.txt" Id="myFileSearch" />
    </DirectorySearch>
   </DirectorySearch>
  </DirectorySearch>
 </Property>
```

Here, the direct parent to the `FileSearch` element is a `DirectorySearch` that names the folder where the file is. In this case, it's the `All Users\Desktop` folder. When you add a `FileSearch`, set the `DirectorySearch` element's `AssignToProperty` attribute to no so that the installer knows that it's the `FileSearch` that should define the property. The `FileSearch` element's `Name` attribute is the name of the file you're looking for.

In the previous example, if the file `myFile.txt` is found in the `All Users\Desktop` folder, the `MY_FILE` property will be populated with the full path:

```
C:\Documents and Settings\All Users\Desktop\myFile.txt
```

If not, the property will be set to null.

You can add other attributes to the `FileSearch` element to refine your search, such as the `MinSize` and `MaxSize` attributes for a range of file sizes (in bytes), `MinDate` and `MaxDate` for range of modification dates, and `MinVersion` and `MaxVersion` for a range of file versions. As shown in the snippet:

```
<FileSearch Name="myFile.txt"
            MinSize="100"
            MaxSize="200"
            MinVersion="1.5.0.0"
            MaxVersion="2.0.0.0"
            MinDate="2009-12-20T12:30:00"
            MaxDate="2009-12-25T12:30:00" />
```

Note that `MinDate` and `MaxDate` must use the format, "YYYY-MM-DDTHH:mm:ss", where "YYYY" is the year, "MM" the month, "DD" the day, "HH" the hour, "mm" the minute, and "ss" the second. "T" is actually the letter "T". You can also add a `Language` attribute to limit the search to files with a specific language ID. For example, "1033" is "English, United States". To specify more than one language, separate them by commas.

You can see the searches you've set up in the MSI database under the *Signature* table. There, the filename, version, size, date, and language are listed. An `Id` on that table is joined to the *DrLocator* table where the directory structure is defined. The entire search is referenced on the *AppSearch* table, where it is linked with a property. You can probably see how defining the structure and data of the MSI is greatly simplified by using WiX markup.

ComponentSearch

A second way to search for files installed on the end user's computer is to use a `ComponentSearch` element. Like other search elements, `ComponentSearch` is nested inside a `Property` element. If the file you're looking for is found, the path of its parent directory will be saved to the property. Note that it won't be the full path to the file itself, but close enough.

To understand `ComponentSearch` you have to remember that Windows Installer uses components with unique GUIDs as containers for the files that get copied to a computer. `ComponentSearch` looks for the GUID that was set on a component or more specifically, the file that was marked as the KeyPath in that component. So, as long as you know the GUID, you can find the file. In fact, you can even look for files installed by other programs, as long as you know the GUID.

Use `Orca.exe` to open an MSI installer and check the *Component* table for a file's GUID. It's marked as *ComponentId*. The actual filename is available on the *File* table and is mapped to the *Component* table via the *Component* column. To set the GUID in the `ComponentSearch` element, use the `Guid` attribute. Here's an example:

```
<Property Id="CANDLE_PATH">
  <ComponentSearch Id="candlePath"
                   Guid="{FBD4BCFB-F1B7-4B6D-B07C-E999A24521CF}" />
</Property>
```

Here, we are looking for the `candle.exe` file that's installed with the WiX toolset. You can open the WiX MSI installer to find the GUID, which is specified here in the `Guid` attribute. On my system, this search sets the property CANDLE_PATH to the directory `C:\Program Files\Windows Installer XML v3\bin\`. This tells me that `candle.exe` is installed and where I can find it. (Candle, by the way, is the WiX compiler.)

`ComponentSearch` has several uses. You might use it to find out where the user installed your software, as it returns the absolute path to the directory where the specified file is. You could also use it to check if someone else's software is installed. To make such a check reliable, be sure to look for a file that's definitely going to be there. The downside to `ComponentSearch` is that you're relying on the GUIDs staying the same. This is pretty safe when it's your own software, but can be risky with anyone else's.

There's one other optional attribute of the `ComponentSearch` element: `Type`. The `Type` attribute can be set to either `file`, its default, or `directory`. Setting it to file causes it to do what it normally does — look for the KeyPath file of the component and return its parent directory. You would set `Type` to `directory` only when your search involves a component that did not specify a file as its KeyPath. Take this example:

```
<DirectoryRef Id="INSTALLLOCATION">
  <Directory Id="newDir" Name="New Directory">
    <Component Id="newDirComp"
               Guid="EA8062E0-E9C2-49E7-B76D-32161923F9F9"
               KeyPath="yes">

      <CreateFolder />
    </Component>
  </Directory>
</DirectoryRef>
```

Here, we've created a component that is tasked with creating an empty folder called New Directory in the install directory. There are no files in the component to make a KeyPath out of. So, we've set the `KeyPath` attribute to `yes` on the `Component` element itself. If we don't specify a KeyPath at all, the component will be assumed to be the KeyPath by default.

When there's no file specified as the KeyPath, you can set the `ComponentSearch` element's `Type` attribute to `directory` and it will return the path to the component's parent directory—just like normal. Otherwise, we get the strange behavior of `ComponentSearch` returning the directory above the parent directory. For example, if we set the `Type` to `file` (or leave it out), we get the install directory, `INSTALLLOCATION`, back. If we set `Type` to `directory`, we get the component's parent directory, `newDir`. So, it's basically something you have to do just to get the expected behavior.

```
<!--Returns INSTALLLOCATION: C:\Program Files\mySoftware\-->
<Property Id="MY_DIRECTORY_PATH ">
  <ComponentSearch Id="myCompSearch"
                Guid="{EA8062E0-E9C2-49E7-B76D-32161923F9F9}"
                Type="file" />
</Property>

<!--Returns newDir: C:\Program Files\mySoftware\New Directory-->
<Property Id="MY_DIRECTORY_PATH ">
  <ComponentSearch Id="myCompSearch"
                Guid="{EA8062E0-E9C2-49E7-B76D-32161923F9F9}"
                Type="directory" />
</Property>
```

Of course, if there *is* a KeyPath file, setting the `ComponentSearch` element's `Type` attribute to `directory` will cause the search to return `null`. In general, the applications for this confusing logic are so few that you'll rarely have to worry about using the `Type` attribute.

RegistrySearch

WiX lets you read values from the Windows Registry with its `RegistrySearch` element. Like the previous search types, `RegistrySearch` has a `Property` element as its parent. If the Registry value you're looking for is found, its value will be saved to the property. Here's an example:

```
<Property Id="DIRECTX_VERSION">
  <RegistrySearch Id="DirectX_Version"
                Root="HKLM"
                Key="SOFTWARE\Microsoft\DirectX"
                Name="Version"
                Type="raw" />
</Property>
```

This searches for the version of DirectX installed on the user's computer. The version number is located in the Registry as a value called `Version` in the `HKEY_LOCAL_MACHINE\SOFTWARE\Microsoft\DirectX` key. If the search finds it, it saves the value to the property `DIRECTX_VERSION`, which is an arbitrary name.

To get there with `RegistrySearch`, set the `Root` attribute to the abbreviated version of `HKEY_LOCAL_MACHINE`, which is `HKLM`. Your possible values for `Root` are:

- `HKLM`: For `HKEY_LOCAL_MACHINE`
- `HKCR`: For `HKEY_CLASSES_ROOT`
- `HKCU`: For `HKEY_CURRENT_USER`
- `HKU`: For `HKEY_USERS`

The `Key` attribute is the Registry path beneath `Root` to the item you're looking for. In this example, it's set to `SOFTWARE\Microsoft\DirectX`. This path is not case sensitive. The `Name` attribute is the value in the key that you want to read. This is also not case sensitive.

The `Type` attribute tells the installer what sort of data it can expect to find in this Registry item. You have three options here: `directory`, `file`, or `raw`. Using `directory` or `file` lets you combine a `RegistrySearch` with either a `FileSearch` or `DirectorySearch`. It's used as a way to search the computer's directory structure for a file or directory after it gets the location of it from the Registry.

Suppose you want to read a value from the Registry and that value is the path to a file. You then want to check that the file is truly where it says it is on the filesystem. As an example, assume that there's a Registry item `HKLM\SOFTWARE\WIXTEST\PathToFile` that's set to the value `C:\Program Files\mySoftware\myFile.txt`. You can get this value from the Registry by using the `RegistrySearch` element, as in the following example:

```
<Property Id="MY_PROPERTY">
  <RegistrySearch Id="myRegSearch"
                  Root="HKLM"
                  Key="SOFTWARE\WIXTEST"
                  Name="PathToFile"
                  Type="file">

    <FileSearch Id="myFileSearch" Name="[MY_PROPERTY]" />
  </RegistrySearch>
</Property>
```

Here, the `RegistrySearch` element finds the item in the Registry and sets the value of `MY_PROPERTY`. Next, the nested `FileSearch` element can now read that property and use it to find the file on the computer. If it finds it, it replaces the value of `MY_PROPERTY` with the location of the file—which should be the same. If it doesn't find it, it sets the value to `null`.

In order for this to work, you have to set the `RegistrySearch` element's `Type` attribute to `file`. This tells the installer that it should expect to find the path to a file in the Registry and that you intend to nest a `FileSearch` element inside the `RegistrySearch`.

You can do something similar with `DirectorySearch`. Take this example, assuming there is another Registry item called `PathToDirectory` where the value is the path to the directory `C:\Program Files\mySoftware\myDirectory\`.

```
<Property Id="MY_PROPERTY">
   <RegistrySearch Id="myRegSearch"
                   Root="HKLM"
                   Key="SOFTWARE\WIXTEST"
                   Name="PathToDirectory"
                   Type="directory">

      <DirectorySearch Id="myDirSearch"
                       Path="[MY_PROPERTY]" />
   </RegistrySearch>
</Property>
```

Here, `Type` is set to `directory` allowing you to nest a `DirectorySearch` element inside `RegistrySearch`. This type also tells the installer that it should expect the Registry value to hold the path to a directory. Like the `FileSearch` example, this one uses the `RegistrySearch` result to set a property and then uses that property to search the filesystem. This time, it's looking for a directory instead of a file. If it finds it, it will set the property to the path. If not, the property will be set to `null`.

Setting `Type` to `raw` lets you read the Registry value and set a property, but nothing more. In many cases, this will be all you want. Be aware that Windows Installer will add special characters to the value to distinguish different datatypes. The following table explains what it will add to different kinds of values. This only applies when `Type` is set to `raw`.

Type of data	Characters added
DWORD	Starts with '#' optionally followed by '+' or '-'
REG_BINARY	Starts with '#x' and the installer converts and saves each hexadecimal digit as an ASCII character prefixed by '#x'
REG_EXPAND_SZ	Starts with '#%'
REG_MULTI_SZ	Starts with '[~]' and ends with '[~]'
REG_SZ	No prefix, but if the first character of the registry value is '#', the installer escapes the character by prefixing it with another '#'

All of the attributes mentioned so far—Id, Key, Root, Name, and Type—are required. There is one optional attribute though called Win64. When set to yes, it will search the 64-bit portion of the Registry instead of the 32-bit one. Of course, this only applies to 64-bit operating systems. Here is an example:

```
<Property Id="MY_PROPERTY">
  <RegistrySearch Id="myRegSearch"
               Root="HKLM"
               Key="SOFTWARE\WIXTEST"
               Name="myRegistryItem"
               Type="raw"
               Win64="yes" />
</Property>
```

Registry searches are represented in the MSI database on the *RegLocator* table. There you'll find a column for the Root, Key, Name, and Type. The Id is listed under the *Signature* column and is referenced by various other tables including *AppSearch*, *DrLocator*, and *Signature*. For complex searches where FileSearch or DirectorySearch elements are nested inside RegistrySearch, these tables are joined together by this Id.

IniFileSearch

The last type of search in the WiX arsenal is IniFileSearch, which lets you search INI configuration files for settings. An INI file is a text file with an .ini extension that uses a simple syntax to list configuration settings. Here is a sample INI file:

```
; Test INI file
[section1]
name=Nick Ramirez
occupation=software developer

[section2]
car=Mazda3
miles=70000

[section3]
breakfast=yogurt
```

WiX always searches the %windir% directory, which is usually C:\Windows for INI files. So, save this code as myConfigFile.ini in that directory.

In an INI file, you can comment out text by putting a semicolon at the beginning of the line. Mark different sections by putting brackets around the name. In each section, create key-value pairs separated by equal signs. And there you have it, pretty simple stuff.

An `IniFileSearch` uses four attributes: `Id`, `Name`, `Section`, and `Key`. Let's look at an example:

```
<Property Id="MY_PROPERTY">
  <IniFileSearch Id="myIniSearch"
                 Name="myConfigFile.ini"
                 Section="section1"
                 Key="name"
                 Type="raw" />
</Property>
```

The `Id` specifies the primary key of the item in the MSI database *IniLocator* table. It's also referenced on the *AppSearch* table where it's tied to the `MY_PROPERTY` property. The `Name` attribute is the name of the INI file. `Section` refers to the bracketed section name and `Key` is the left-hand side of one of the key-value pairs under that section. This particular search will set the property to "Nick Ramirez". That's the value of the `name` key in the `section1` section.

The `Type` attribute can be `file`, `directory`, or `raw`. Raw is the simplest as it just returns the literal value of the key. Unlike `RegistrySearch`, there won't be any special characters added to it. This is what you'll use in most cases.

If you set `Type` to `file`, Windows Installer will expect the INI value to be the path to a file. Once it finds this value, it will use it to set the parent property. After that, you're free to use that property in a nested `FileSearch` element to confirm that the file exists. If it doesn't, the property will be set to `null`.

```
[section1]
filePath=C:\Program Files\mySoftware\myFile.txt
```

Product.wxs

```
<Property Id="MY_PROPERTY">
  <IniFileSearch Id="myIniSearch"
                 Name="myConfigFile.ini"
                 Section="section1"
                 Key="filePath"
                 Type="file">

    <FileSearch Id="myFileSearch"
                Name="[MY_PROPERTY]" />
  </IniFileSearch>
</Property>
```

Here, the installer searches for the INI file, finds it, and uses the specified key to set the value of the property. It then uses that property in the `FileSearch` element's `Name` attribute to check that the file is where `MY_PROPERTY` says it is.

Setting the `Type` attribute to `directory` works the same way except that you nest a `DirectorySearch` element instead. In this case, the `DirectorySearch` checks that the directory in the property exists.

myConfigFile.ini

```
[section1]
directoryPath=C:\Program Files\mySoftware\
```

Product.wxs

```
<Property Id="MY_PROPERTY">
  <IniFileSearch Id="myIniSearch"
                 Name="myConfigFile.ini"
                 Section="section1"
                 Key="dirPath"
                 Type="directory">

    <DirectorySearch Id="myDirSearch"
                     Path="[MY_PROPERTY]" />
  </IniFileSearch>
</Property>
```

In this example, the `directoryPath` key in the INI file is set to `C:\Program Files\mySoftware\`. The `DirectorySearch` element checks that this directory really exists once it has been set as the property value. If it does, the property will keep the path as its value. Otherwise, it will be set to `null`.

Summary

In this section, we discussed WiX properties and the AppSearch feature. Properties allow you to store information during the course of the installation. Properties are referenced with square brackets when used in the attribute of another element. Be sure to look up whether or not a particular element attribute can interpret the square bracket notation. When used in the inner text of another element, the square brackets aren't needed.

We talked about some of the built-in Windows Installer properties. There are actually quite a few of these and we'll probably cover many more as we continue on. You've seen some that affect things like the Add/Remove Programs list, but there are also less flashy ones that Windows Installer uses just to do its job. However, knowing about them can be to your advantage when it comes to debugging or even creating conditional statements based upon them.

Windows Installer can do a variety of searches with its AppSearch feature: file, directory, registry, component, and INI file searches. These go hand-in-hand with properties as the result of the searches are saved to properties. Probably one of the handiest uses for AppSearch is to find out if a particular bit of software is installed. You can use this as part of a prerequisite check before installing your own software. You can also use them to find if directories or files exist, and if so, where they are. In the next chapter, we'll cover conditional statements and how to read the install state of features and components.

4

Improving Control with Launch Conditions and Installed States

We've covered how to store data in properties and how to search the target computer for files, directories, and settings using AppSearch. All by itself that makes WiX an attractive solution for deploying software. However, things are about to get more interesting. We're going to discuss how to use the information you've collected to control *what* gets installed and *if* the installer will continue past its initial start up.

WiX gives you a powerful tool that allows you to make these decisions—conditions. In this chapter, you will learn to:

- Set launch conditions to require prerequisites for your install
- Utilize feature and component conditions to prevent a portion of your software from being installed
- Read the action state and installed state of your features and components

Conditions

The conditions in this chapter use the Condition element to house their logic. The meaning of this element changes depending on where it's placed relative to other elements and which attributes it uses. We'll discuss three types: *launch conditions, feature conditions,* and *component conditions.*

Launch conditions check for prerequisites at the beginning of the installation and prevent it from continuing if their requirements aren't met. They're placed anywhere inside either the `Product` element in your main `.wxs` file or a `Fragment` element in a separate file. **Feature conditions** and **component conditions** are child elements to `Feature` and `Component` elements, respectively. Both prevent a specific feature or component from being installed if a condition isn't satisfied.

First, we'll take a look at the generic syntax of conditional statements and then move on to discussing each of the three types.

Condition syntax

Conditions contain statements that evaluate to either true or false. In most cases you'll be comparing a property to some value. We discussed the logical operators that you can use for comparisons in the previous chapter. Here's a table that summarizes each one:

Operator	Meaning
<	Less than
>	Greater than
<=	Less than or equal to
>=	Greater than or equal to
=	Equal to
<>	Not equal to
NOT	Negates the condition
AND	Combines two conditions, if both are true, the condition passes
OR	Combines two conditions, if either is true, the condition passes

You can use a single property as a condition to check that that property has been defined. Use the NOT keyword before it to check that it has *not* been defined. Or, getting more complex, you can use the AND and OR operators to string several conditional statements together. The following examples should give you an idea about the different statements you can make:

- `PropertyA`: true if PropertyA is defined
- `NOT PropertyA`: true if PropertyA is not defined
- `PropertyA < PropertyB`: true if PropertyA is less than PropertyB
- `PropertyA <> "1"`: true if PropertyA is not equal to "1"

- `PropertyA = "1" AND PropertyB = "2"`: true if PropertyA equals "1" and PropertyB equals "2"

- `PropertyA = "1" OR PropertyB = "2"`: true if PropertyA equals "1" or PropertyB equals "2"

These statements are the inner text of the `Condition` element. It's a good idea to always place them inside CDATA tags so that the XML parser won't mistake them for XML elements. Here's an example that uses CDATA tags:

```
<Condition ... >
  <![CDATA[PropertyA < PropertyB]]>
</Condition>
```

As you can see, the conditional statement is placed inside a `Condition` element. As we cover different types of conditions, we'll look at the attributes that are used in each case.

Launch conditions

The MSI database for an installer has a table called *LaunchCondition* that lists rules that the end user must comply with in order to install the software. Each rule is called a **launch condition**. To add one, place a `Condition` element inside your `Product` element. You'll find that this table is evaluated early on, right after AppSearch is performed. This makes it the second thing to happen during the installation process. This is good in two ways. It lets you inform the user that they're missing something before they get too far along and it allows you to use the results from AppSearch in your conditions.

Examples of launch conditions include requiring that a version of .NET is installed, that the computer has a certain operating system, or that the user is an administrator. You should know that although WiX allows you to create a long list of conditions, you cannot control the order in which they're evaluated. Therefore, you should try to think of each one as having equal weight. If any one of them fails the installation will abort. The order should be thought of as inconsequential. You can add more conditions by adding more `Condition` elements.

The following example shows a launch condition that checks the value of a property. In a real-world scenario this property would contain something useful like the result of a component or file search. It shows the basic structure though.

```xml
<?xml version="1.0" encoding="UTF-8"?>
<Wix ... >
  <Product ... >
    <Package ... />
    <Media ... />
    <Property Id="myVar"
              Value="3" />
    <Condition Message="myVar must be set to 2">
      <![CDATA[Installed OR myVar = 2]]>
    </Condition>
  </Product>
</Wix>
```

Here, we're setting a property called `myVar` that has a value of 3. The condition checks that the variable is set to 2. When it fails, a message box will pop up and display the text we've set in the `Condition` element's `Message` attribute.

Notice that we've used the `Installed` keyword to say that we only want to evaluate this condition if the software has not already been installed. Otherwise, it will be evaluated during both install and uninstall. The last thing you want is to prevent the user from uninstalling the software because they're missing a prerequisite. Here's what the user will see when the condition fails:

In real-world conditional statements, you'll use properties from AppSearch or set dynamically with a custom action. We'll talk about using custom actions in the next chapter.

A great thing about WiX is that there are already a lot of properties defined for you that you could use in your launch conditions. Some of these, as you've seen, are available from the get-go. Others become available after you've added a reference to one of the WiX extensions, such as `WixNetFxExtension`. The next example checks that .NET 3.5 has been installed by using the `NETFRAMEWORK35` property from `WixNetFxExtension`. It simply checks that the property has been defined:

```
<PropertyRef Id="NETFRAMEWORK35" />

<Condition Message="You must install Microsoft .NET 3.5">
  <![CDATA[Installed OR NETFRAMEWORK35]]>
</Condition>
```

You'll have to add a reference in your project to `WixNetFxExtension.dll`, found in the WiX `bin` directory. This extension defines several other properties as well, explained in this table:

Property name	Meaning
NETFRAMEWORK10	.NET Framework 1.0 is installed
NETFRAMEWORK20	.NET Framework 2.0 is installed
NETFRAMEWORK30	.NET Framework 3.0 is installed
NETFRAMEWORK35	.NET Framework 3.5 is installed
NETFRAMEWORK35_CLIENT_SP_LEVEL	Indicates the service pack level for the .NET Framework 3.5 client profile
WINDOWSSDKCURRENTVERSION	The Windows SDK current active version

There's also the `WixPSExtension`, also found in the WiX `bin` directory, that defines the `POWERSHELLVERSION` property. You can use it to check the version of Windows Powershell that's installed.

```
<PropertyRef Id="POWERSHELLVERSION" />
<Condition Message="You must have PowerShell 1.0 or higher.">
  <![CDATA[Installed OR POWERSHELLVERSION >= "1.0"]]>
</Condition>
```

Notice here that I had to put quotes around `1.0` in the condition because `POWERSHELLVERSION` returns a decimal number. In that case, you must quote the value you compare it to.

In addition to the WiX extension files, such as `WixNetFxExtension` and `WixPSExtension`, Windows Installer also provides many built-in properties. For these, you don't have to reference any additional files or use `PropertyRefs` to gain access to them. A useful one is `VersionNT`, which can be used to check the operating system. Its value is an integer that corresponds to a particular OS. Refer to the following table:

Operating system	VersionNT value
Windows 2000	500
Windows XP	501
Windows Server 2003	502
Windows Vista	600
Windows Server 2008	600
Windows Server 2008 R2	601
Windows 7	601

With `VersionNT`, the numbers get higher with each new OS, so you can use "greater than or equal to" comparisons to make sure that an OS is later than or equal to a certain product. Here's an example that checks that the system is running Windows Vista or newer:

```
<Condition Message=
        "OS must be Windows Vista, Server 2008, or higher.">
    <![CDATA[Installed OR VersionNT >= 600]]>
</Condition>
```

You might also use the `VersionNT64` property to check if the OS is 64-bit and if so, get its version number. There's also the `ServicePackLevel` property for detecting which service pack for that OS is installed. The next example checks that the operating system is Windows XP with Service Pack 2:

```
<Condition Message=
        "This install requires Windows XP Service Pack 2.">
    <![CDATA[
        Installed OR
        VersionNT = 501 AND
        ServicePackLevel >= 2
    ]]>
</Condition>
```

Two more useful ones are `MsiNTProductType` and `Privileged`, as shown in this table:

Property name	Meaning
MsiNTProductType	Tells you if the end user's computer is a workstation (value of 1), domain controller (2), or server that isn't a domain controller (3)
Privileged	If set, installation is being performed with elevated privileges, such as by an administrator

Other Windows Installer properties can be seen at the MSDN site:

`http://msdn.microsoft.com/en-us/library/aa370905(VS.85).aspx`

You can also use environment variables in conditional statements. Prefix the variable with a percent sign (%) to reference it. The following example shows this:

```
<Condition Message=
"You need at least two processors. You have [%NUMBER_OF_PROCESSORS]">
  <![CDATA[Installed OR %NUMBER_OF_PROCESSORS >= 2]]>
</Condition>
```

This condition checks that at least two processors exist on the computer. Notice how the greater-than-or-equal-to operator is used. This may be counterintuitive since we're trying to find out if the computer has less than two, not more than. With launch conditions, though, you only want to show the error message when the condition evaluates to false. Sometimes, this means thinking backwards.

Ordinarily, you place `Condition` elements for launch conditions inside the `Product` element in your main WiX file. However, if you'd rather be more modular you can separate your launch conditions into their own WiX source file. There you can nest the `Condition` elements inside a `Fragment` element; the `LaunchConditions.wxs` file would look like so:

```
<?xml version="1.0" encoding="UTF-8"?>
<Wix xmlns="http://schemas.microsoft.com/wix/2006/wi">
  <Fragment>
    <Property Id="LaunchConditionsFile"
              Value="1" />
    <Condition Message=
                "OS must be Windows Vista, Server 2008, or higher.">
      <![CDATA[Installed OR VersionNT >= 600]]>
    </Condition>
  </Fragment>
</Wix>
```

Before these launch conditions can be included in the MSI database they have to be referenced in your main WiX file. You can add a property, as in the previous example, that can be referenced in the main file with a `PropertyRef` element. The `LaunchConditionsFile` property we have here can be referenced with a `PropertyRef` to pull in the `Condition` statement; the `Product.wxs` file would include the line:

```
<PropertyRef Id="LaunchConditionsFile" />
```

This one line will bring all of the launch conditions in the separate `Fragment` into the scope of your project. It's not a bad idea to use different source files to better organize your code, especially for large projects.

Feature conditions

A **feature condition** is where a `Condition` element is placed inside a `Feature` element. There, it can change whether or not that feature gets installed depending if the statement evaluates to true.

Recall that features contain `ComponentRef` or `ComponentGroupRef` elements and allow the end user to include entire sets of files in the install. For example, you may have a feature called "Documentation" that installs documentation files for your product. The user can choose to turn this feature off and not copy those files to their computer through the user interface or from the command line.

Feature conditions take this decision somewhat out of the end user's hands, allowing you as the developer to have the final say in whether it is appropriate to install a particular feature. In most cases, you'll evaluate properties in these statements, maybe those set from AppSearch or from a custom action.

Feature conditions work by changing the `Level` attribute of the parent `Feature` element. Every feature has a level. It's a number that tells the installer whether or not this feature should be "on". In a simple setup, having a level of 1 would include the feature in the install, a 0 would exclude it. So, if our condition sets the level to 0, the feature will *not* be installed. Here's an example:

```
<Feature Id="MainFeature"
        Title="Main Feature"
        Level="1">
  <ComponentRef Id="CMP_InstallMeTXT" />

  <Condition Level="0">
    <![CDATA[MyProperty = "some value"]]>
  </Condition>
</Feature>
```

This feature starts off with a level set to 1, meaning that by default the components that it contains will be copied to the computer. However, our condition checks that the property MyProperty equals some value. If it does, meaning the condition evaluates to true, the feature's level will be changed to 0. This is specified by the Condition element's Level attribute.

When you change a feature's level with a feature condition, it doesn't just disable that feature. It removes it completely from the list shown in the user interface. To see this in action, add the WixUI_FeatureTree dialog set from the WixUIExtension. It has a dialog with a feature tree, showing which features are available. You'll need to add a project reference to WixUIExtension.dll using the **Add Reference** option in the **Solution Explorer**.

```xml
<?xml version="1.0" encoding="UTF-8"?>
<Wix xmlns="http://schemas.microsoft.com/wix/2006/wi">
  <Product Id="B55596A8-93E3-47EB-84C4-D7FE07D0CAF4"
           Name="Awesome Software"
           Language="1033"
           Version="2.0.0.0"
           Manufacturer="Awesome Company"
           UpgradeCode="B414C827-8D81-4B4A-B3B6-338C06DE3A11">
    <Package InstallerVersion="301" Compressed="yes" />
    <Media Id="1" Cabinet="media1.cab" EmbedCab="yes" />
    <!--Directory structure-->
    <Directory Id="TARGETDIR"
               Name="SourceDir">
      <Directory Id="ProgramFilesFolder">
        <Directory Id="INSTALLLOCATION"
                   Name="Awesome Software" />
      </Directory>
    </Directory>

    <!--Components-->
    <DirectoryRef Id="INSTALLLOCATION">
      <Component Id="CMP_InstallMeTXT"
                 Guid="E8A58B7B-F031-4548-9BDD-7A6796C8460D">
        <File Id="FILE_InstallMeTXT"
              Source="InstallMe.txt"
              KeyPath="yes" />
      </Component>
    </DirectoryRef>

    <Property Id="MyProperty" Value="some value" />
    <Feature Id="MainFeature"
             Title="Main Feature"
             Level="1">
```

```
      <ComponentRef Id="CMP_InstallMeTXT" />
      <Condition Level="0">
        <![CDATA[MyProperty = "some value"]]>
      </Condition>
    </Feature>

    <!--UI-->
    <UIRef Id="WixUI_FeatureTree" />
  </Product>
</Wix>
```

Here, the condition is checking the MyProperty property for a specific value. You can change this property's value in your markup to see different results in the UI. If the condition evaluates to true the Main Feature feature will disappear from the feature tree.

The reason for this is that the installer evaluates feature conditions early in the installation process, before any dialogs are shown. Specifically, they're evaluated during the FileCost action, during which the installer checks how much disk space is going to be needed to copy your files to the system. It only makes sense for it to factor in features that won't be installed at this time. So, by the time the user sees your feature tree in a dialog, the excluded features have been removed from the list.

If you only want to show the feature as disabled but still visible, set the ADDLOCAL property to a comma-delimited list of Feature element Id attributes to enable by default, as shown:

```
  <Property Id="ADDLOCAL"
            Value="MainFeature,SecondFeature" />
```

Here, two features are enabled by default: MainFeature and SecondFeature. Any others will still be visible in the feature tree, but disabled. The user will be able to turn them back on if they want to.

Most of the time, planning ahead and authoring your features strategically so that they group related components will help you avoid using complex conditional statements in your features. Using a lot of conditional logic is sometimes a sign that features aren't mapped out well enough. For features that shouldn't be installed because some prerequisite software is missing, such as SQL Server for an SQL feature, it's often better to show the user the feature as disabled. That way, they'll know it's available if they decide to reinstall later.

At this point, let's revisit the Feature element's Level attribute because there's more to it than I've let on. You aren't forced to set it to a 1 or 0. You can, as a matter of fact, set it to any integer between 1 and 32,767.

The installer always sets a property called INSTALLLEVEL, the default value being 1. Every feature's level is compared to this number. If the level is equal to or lower, but greater than zero, it will get installed. You can change INSTALLLEVEL yourself with a Property element to give it a different default value and then change it dynamically with a custom action or from the command line.

You could use this to create a dialog with a button that says **Typical Install** and another one that says **Full Install**. "Full" might set INSTALLLEVEL to 100 when clicked and consequently install all of the features—those with a level of 100 or less. "Typical" might, on the other hand, set INSTALLLEVEL to 50 and only install some of the features.

Component conditions

Component conditions are a lot like feature conditions except that they affect whether or not a single component gets installed. In this case, you add a Condition element inside a Component element. You don't need to specify a Level attribute. In fact, these conditions don't expect any attributes. The following example only installs the CMP_InstallMeTXT component if the property MyProperty equals 1:

```
<Property Id="MyProperty"
          Value="1" />
<Component Id="CMP_InstallMeTXT"
           Guid="7AB5216B-2DB5-4A8A-9293-F6711FFAAA83">
   <File Id="FILE_InstallMeTXT"
         Source="InstallMe.txt"
         KeyPath="yes" />
   <Condition>MyProperty = 1</Condition>
</Component>
```

Again, I've hardcoded the property's value but in practice you'd set it dynamically. The benefit of component conditions is that they are much more granular than feature conditions. You're able to target a single file, folder, or registry key. For example, if the user does not have Windows PowerShell installed you could disable a component that installs a PowerShell script and instead enable one that installs a CMD shell script. Here's how it would look:

```
<PropertyRef Id="POWERSHELLVERSION" />
<DirectoryRef Id="INSTALLLOCATION">
   <Component Id="CMP_psShellScript"
              Guid="7E348141-0005-4203-A1FE-D9264EBA7E50">
     <File Id="psScript" Source="script.ps1" KeyPath="yes" />
     <Condition>POWERSHELLVERSION</Condition>
   </Component>
```

```
<Component Id="CMP_cmdShellScript"
           Guid="C1CE3886-2081-4F62-9E58-0B1E8080143D">
    <File Id="cmdScript"
          Source="script.cmd"
          KeyPath="yes" />
    <Condition>NOT POWERSHELLVERSION</Condition>
</Component>
</DirectoryRef>
```

The first thing we have to do to use this example is add a reference in our project to the WiX extension `WixPSExtension`. We're then able to pull in the `POWERSHELLVERSION` property with a `PropertyRef`. This contains the version number of PowerShell that's installed. In the `CMP_psShellScript` component, the `Condition` element checks simply if `POWERSHELLVERSION` exists. If it does then the PowerShell component is installed. Otherwise, the `CMP_cmdShellScript` is chosen. Notice that I've used the opposite condition there so there's no blurriness about which should be used. It's always either one or the other.

Ordinarily, component conditions are only evaluated during an installation and not during a reinstall. To reinstall an MSI package, which completely replaces all files, services, and environment variables (but not Registry entries), install from the command line and set the `REINSTALL` property to `ALL`.

msiexec /i myInstaller.msi REINSTALL=ALL

If you would like conditions to be re-evaluated during a reinstall, you should set the `Transitive` attribute on the parent component to `yes`. In the following example, the `Component` elements are marked as transitive, causing their conditions to be re-evaluated during a reinstall:

```
<Component Id="CMP_vistaDLL"
           Guid="7E348141-0005-4203-A1FE-D9264EBA7E50"
           Transitive="true">
    <File Id="vistaDll"
          Source="library_vista.dll"
          Name="library.dll"
          KeyPath="yes" />
    <Condition>VersionNT = 600</Condition>
</Component>

<Component Id="CMP_win7DLL"
           Guid="C1CE3886-2081-4F62-9E58-0B1E8080143D"
           Transitive="true">
    <File Id="win7Dll"
          Source="library_win7.dll"
```

```
        Name="library.dll"
        KeyPath="yes" />
    <Condition>VersionNT = 601</Condition>
</Component>
```

Here there are two components. The first has a condition to only install itself if the operating system is Windows Vista (`VersionNT = 600`) and the other only if it's Windows 7 (`VersionNT = 601`). Only one of the components will be true and be allowed to copy its file to the system. However, since we've added the `Transitive` attribute, these conditions will be checked again during a reinstall. So, if the Vista file had originally been installed and the end user has since upgraded to Windows 7, the `CMP_Win7DLL` component will replace the `CMP_VistaDLL` one.

Action state

We talked about the `Level` attribute on `Feature` elements and how it's used to enable or disable features. Behind the scenes, what you're doing is setting the action state of the feature. **Action state** is the thing that stores whether or not the end user has requested that the feature be installed. The same exists for components since we can enable and disable them too. It can have any of the following values:

- **Unknown**: The state is not known, usually because costing has not taken place. No action will be taken on the component or feature.
- **Advertised**: The feature will be installed as advertised, meaning install on demand. This doesn't exist for components.
- **Absent**: The feature or component will not be installed.
- **Local**: The feature or component will be installed to the local hard disk.
- **Source**: The feature or component will be run from source, such as from a network share.

Action state is initially unknown until **costing** has taken place. Costing is the process of finding out how much space on the hard drive will be required for your software. Action state is set during an installation step called **CostFinalize**. We'll talk about many of the install steps in detail in the next chapter.

Once it's available, you can get the action state for your features and components by using a special syntax. To get the action state of a feature, place an ampersand (`&`) in front of its name. For components, use a dollar sign (`$`). For example, the following statement checks if the feature that has an `Id` of `MainFeature` is set to be installed locally:

```
&MainFeature = 3
```

To check a component's action state, use a dollar sign:

```
$ComponentA = 3
```

You might be tempted to use this in your feature and component conditions. It won't work though. The reason is that component and feature conditions are evaluated *during* the FileCost action but action state isn't available until *after* the CostFinalize action has run. If you attempt to access it in one of these conditions, you'll always get a value of "Unknown".

So where can you use it? You can use it anywhere after CostFinalize, such as in custom actions that you schedule later in the installation process. You can also use them in conditional statements that affect UI controls, which we'll cover later in the book. You can pair these statements with "NOT Installed" to have Windows Installer evaluate them only during installation.

Before, I checked the action state against the number three. The five possible action states each correspond to a number, as listed in the following table:

Action state	Meaning
-1	Unknown
1	Advertised
2	Absent
3	Local
4	Source

Note that you don't have to use the equals sign. You can use any of the conditional operators that can be used with launch conditions. For example, you might use the "greater than" operator, as in:

```
&MainFeature > 2
```

This checks if a feature is set to be installed locally or to source. During an install, you can see action state being written to the install log. Use the l*v flag to record to a logfile, as shown:

msiexec /i myInstaller.msi /l*v install.log

Below is a snippet from the log that shows the ProductFeature with a Request:Local. That's its action state. The component, similarly, has Request:Local. The Action is what ultimately happened during the install.

```
Action ended 0:25:17: CostFinalize. Return value 1.
MSI (s) (C0:F0) [00:25:17:452]: Doing action: InstallValidate
MSI (s) (C0:F0) [00:25:17:452]: Note: 1: 2205 2:  3: ActionText
```

```
Action 0:25:17: InstallValidate. Validating install
Action start 0:25:17: InstallValidate.
MSI (s) (C0:F0) [00:25:17:452]: Feature: ProductFeature;
Installed: Absent;   Request: Local;   Action: Local
MSI (s) (C0:F0) [00:25:17:452]: Component: CMP_InstallMeTXT;
Installed: Absent;   Request: Local;   Action: Local
```

Checking the log can help out when it's unclear why a certain feature or component isn't getting installed.

Installed state

While Windows Installer uses action state to determine if a feature or component should be installed, it uses **installed state** to see if a feature or component has *already* been installed by a previous installation. In other words, does it currently exist on the computer?

Unlike action state, the value of installed state *can* be used in feature and component conditions. For features, you'll prefix the feature's Id with an exclamation mark (!), as shown:

```
!MainFeature = 3
```

For components, you'll use a question mark (?):

```
?ComponentA = 3
```

This allows you to include features and components based on whether they were installed before. You can also use them in custom actions and UI control conditions, such as to change which dialogs are displayed. Windows Installer uses this functionality itself, at least in regards to features, when you use the feature tree control. During a reinstall, it will show the features as enabled that have been selected before and disables those that haven't. This makes for a better user experience.

The same values apply for installed state as for action state. For example, 3 refers to a component or feature that was installed to the local hard disk.

Installed state	Meaning
-1	Unknown
1	Feature was installed as Advertised
2	Feature or component was Absent (not installed)
3	Feature or component was installed Local, to the hard disk
4	Feature or component was installed to Source

Summary

In this chapter, we talked about the meaning of launch conditions and how they can be used to prevent an install on a system that doesn't meet the minimum requirements you've set. When paired with AppSearch or the built-in Windows Installer properties, launch conditions are able to detect the operating system, .NET version and whether or not required software is installed.

We touched on feature and component conditions and how they allow you to exclude a specific feature or component from the install. These take the decision out of the hands of the end user and let you have the final say. Be warned that using feature conditions can completely remove a feature from a feature tree list. It may be better to use the ADDLOCAL property instead.

Towards the end, we discussed what action and installed state is. Action state can't be used in feature and component conditions like installed state can, but it can still come in handy in other types of conditions. Both come in very handy when it comes to custom actions, which we'll discuss in the next chapter, as they allow you to only run a task if a piece of the software is going to be or has already been installed.

5
Understanding the Installation Sequence

In order to coordinate the use of the WiX elements we've seen and the jobs that they do, we have two tables, **InstallUISequence** and **InstallExecuteSequence** that contain the order in which installation events should occur. For example, AppSearch always happens before launch conditions.

In this chapter, we'll talk about how these tables work. Specifically, we'll cover:

- The events that happen during the UI sequence and how to access them
- The events that happened during the execute sequence and how to access them
- How to add your own custom actions to a sequence
- The various types of custom actions
- Some tips on writing C# custom actions via the DTF library

InstallUISequence

If you use Orca to look inside your MSI package, you'll find a table called
`InstallUISequence`. This is where the actions that happen during the first half
of the installation are defined. The following image shows what it will look like:

Tables	Action	Condition	Sequence
AdminExecuteSequence	AppSearch		50
AdminUISequence	LaunchConditions		100
AdvtExecuteSequence	ValidateProductID		700
AppSearch	CostInitialize		800
Component	FileCost		900
CreateFolder	CostFinalize		1000
CustomAction	ExecuteAction		1300
Directory			
DuplicateFile			
Feature			
FeatureComponents			
File			
Font			
InstallExecuteSequence			
InstallUISequence			
LaunchCondition			

The table contains three columns: **Action**, **Condition**, and **Sequence**. For now, we're
just interested in Action and Sequence. Action is the name of the **standard action** to
run. Sequence is the order in which it happens in relation to other actions. You can
sort the Sequence column from lowest to highest by clicking on the column header.
This is the order as it happens.

You're likely to see the following standard actions in your list:

- **AppSearch**
- **LaunchConditions**
- **ValidateProductID**
- **CostInitialize**
- **FileCost**
- **CostFinalize**
- **ExecuteAction**

You've already seen some of these, but we'll go over each in the next section.

UI standard actions

We'll take a moment here to describe each of the standard actions we've listed
in the order that they'd be executed.

AppSearch

The **AppSearch** action reads the AppSearch table, which holds signatures of the searches you've authored in your WiX markup. During this phase, you could look for files and directories on the end user's system, read Registry values, or peek inside INI configuration files. The AppSearch table utilizes various other tables for this including (and in this order) CompLocator, RegLocator, IniLocator, and DrLocator.

LaunchConditions

The **LaunchConditions** action references the table called LaunchCondition, which lists conditional statements that tell the installer what's required before it can continue. If a condition is false, the installer exits.

ValidateProductID

You can collect a software registration key from the end user via the command line by having them set a property called PIDKEY. During the ValidateProductID action, this property is compared to another property you've set called PIDTemplate that defines a pattern PIDKEY must match. If everything checks out, a third property called ProductID is set for you. After ValidateProductID has run, you can check for the existence of ProductID to see if the key that was entered is in the valid format.

CostInitialize

The CostInitialize action starts the "costing" process where the disk space needed for your product is calculated. At this point, the Component and Feature tables are loaded into memory, which sets the stage for the installer to check which components and features will be installed.

FileCost

During the FileCost action, the installer starts the cost calculation. The files in the File table are examined to see how much hard drive space they require. If one of the files already exists on the end user's system, it will only be replaced if a newer version is being installed. In that case, the file will add to the disk space needed.

CostFinalize

During the CostFinalize action, the costing calculation takes into consideration the components and features that shouldn't be installed because of a component or feature-level condition. It then verifies that all target directories are writable. This phase ends the costing process.

ExecuteAction

The last standard action in the UI sequence is called ExecuteAction. It looks at a property with the same name to see which table to pass control to. As this is a normal installation that started off by reading the InstallUISequence, the property will be set to "INSTALL" and this action will pass control to the InstallExecuteSequence table.

InstallExecuteSequence

During the **InstallExecuteSequence**, changes are made to the computer such as laying down files. This part of the installation is called the "server side" and the UI portion is called the "client side", which is a way of conceptualizing that the two are run in different sessions and with different privileges. The client side runs as the user who launched the MSI while the server side is run as the *LocalSystem* user.

If you install with logging turned on you can see the split between client and server. Actions that occur during the first half start with "MSI (c)", as in the following example:

```
MSI (c) (64:80) [13:41:32:203]: Switching to server:
```

That's the last entry from the client before switching to the server. Then you'll see log entries begin with "MSI (s)".

```
MSI (s) (D0:4C) [13:41:32:218]: Grabbed execution mutex.
```

By taking ownership of the execution mutex, the server side is saying that no other MSI package can be run while the execution phase is in progress. The following actions are scheduled here.

- AppSearch
- LaunchConditions
- ValidateProductId
- CostInitialize
- FileCost

- CostFinalize
- InstallValidate
- InstallInitialize
- ProcessComponents
- UnpublishFeatures
- RemoveRegistryValues
- RemoveShortcuts
- RemoveFiles
- InstallFiles
- CreateShortcuts
- WriteRegistryValues
- RegisterUser
- RegisterProduct
- PublishFeatures
- PublishProduct
- InstallFinalize

The first six are repeats from the UI phase and will be skipped if they've already run. Note that you can skip the UI portion and go straight to Execute by setting the "quiet" flag on the command line. People sometimes do this for unattended installs.

```
msiexec /i myInstaller.msi /quiet
```

In the next section, we'll discuss the standard actions that are new.

Execute standard actions

Now, let's look at each of the standard actions that are unique to the Execute sequence.

InstallValidate

The **InstallValidate** action uses the total calculated by the costing phase to verify that there's enough disk space available and whether any running processes have a lock on files needed by the MSI.

InstallInitialize

The **InstallInitialize** action marks the beginning of the "deferred" stage of the Execute sequence, wherein actions can be rolled back if an error happens. Any actions between it and `InstallFinalize` have the opportunity to be covered by rollback.

ProcessComponents

The **ProcessComponents** action makes note of the components that are in your installer and stores their GUIDs in the Registry. It tracks which file in each component is the KeyPath file.

UnpublishFeatures

During uninstallation, **UnpublishFeatures** removes component-to-feature mappings in the Registry and discards information about which features were selected.

RemoveRegistryValues

The **RemoveRegistryValues** action looks at the MSI's `Registry` and `RemoveRegistry` tables to find Registry items to remove during an uninstall.

RemoveShortcuts

The **RemoveShortcuts** action removes any shortcuts during uninstallation that your installer created.

RemoveFiles

During uninstallation, the **RemoveFiles** action deletes files and folders that were copied to the system. You can add files and folders for it to remove by using the `RemoveFolder` and `RemoveFile` elements.

InstallFiles

The **InstallFiles** action uses information from the `Directory` and `File` tables to copy files and folder into their appropriate locations. It's smart enough that if a file already exists from a previous installation and its component GUID and version haven't changed to leave it as is.

CreateShortcuts

During installation, **CreateShortcuts** adds shortcuts as specified in the Shortcut table.

WriteRegistryValues

You can use the WiX elements RegistryKey and RegistryValue to write to the Registry. The **WriteRegistryValues** action does the work.

RegisterUser

The **RegisterUser** action records to the Registry who the user was who initiated the installation.

RegisterProduct

The **RegisterProduct** action registers your product with Add/Remove Programs and stores the MSI package locally.

PublishFeatures

During the **PublishFeatures** action, the installed state (installed, advertised, or absent) is written to the Registry and components are mapped to features.

PublishProduct

Used only by an advertised installation, the **PublishProduct** action "publishes" the product to a server, or in other words, makes it available for other computers to download.

InstallFinalize

The **InstallFinalize** action marks the end of the rollback-protected stage called the "deferred" phase. If your installation gets this far it means that it was successful.

Immediate vs. deferred

There are reasons for separating the installation into two parts. The biggest is to have an obvious time during which the end user should expect changes to be made to the system. During the UI phase, they can safely fill information into the UI's dialogs without fear that their computer will be altered. Typically, it isn't until they click a button labeled "Install" that changes begin to take effect. Therefore, the standard actions only make system changes during the second half, during the Execute sequence.

By keeping all system changes in one area, Windows Installer is able to offer something else: rollback protection if an error occurs. It works in the following way: No changes to the system are made when the Execute phase starts. At first, the installer reads what actions are in the `InstallExecuteSequence` table and prepares itself by storing a script of what's to be done. All actions *between* `InstallInitialize` and `InstallFinalize` are included. This initial phase, when the script is prepared but rollback protection hasn't started yet, is called the Execute sequence's "immediate" phase.

Once things actually start happening, it's called the "deferred" stage. If an error occurs, the installer will use the script it created to roll back the actions that had taken place up to that point. Only the deferred stage has rollback protection. The UI sequence does not have this feature and so actions that alter the system should never take place there.

In the next section, you'll learn about creating custom actions that you can add to either the UI or Execute phase. Take special care to mark those actions that make system changes as "deferred" and to schedule them to run somewhere after the `InstallInitialize` action and before `InstallFinalize` in the Execute phase. As you'll see, you'll need to create your own rollback actions to complement your deferred custom actions.

Custom actions

Knowing what the standard actions do and when prepares you for what's next: making your own actions, called **custom actions**, and scheduling them appropriately.

Any custom action that changes the system, whether it be changing files, setting up databases, or adjusting user rights, should happen during the deferred stage of the Execute sequence. Otherwise, you're free to place them where you like during either the UI or Execute sequence.

Custom actions are declared with the `CustomAction` element. Use its `Execute` attribute to define how it should run and its `Return` attribute to tell how its return status should be treated. For example, this would declare a custom action called `MyAction` that runs during the deferred stage and is checked for success upon completion.

```
<CustomAction Id="MyAction" Execute="deferred"
    Return="check" ... />
```

That's the basics, although there are seven specific types of custom actions that each add their own necessary attributes. We'll cover each of the following types of custom actions:

- Setting a Windows Installer Property
- Setting the location of a Directory
- Running embedded VBScript or JScript code
- Calling an external VBScript or JScript file
- Calling a method from a dynamic-link library
- Triggering an executable
- Sending an error that stops the installation

To add our custom action to the Execute sequence, we'd use the `InstallExecuteSequence` element and the `Custom` element.

```xml
<?xml version="1.0" encoding="UTF-8"?>
<Wix xmlns="http://schemas.microsoft.com/wix/2006/wi">
    <Product ... >
        <Package ... />
        <Media ... />

        <CustomAction Id="MyAction" Execute="deferred"
            Return="check" ... />

        <InstallExecuteSequence>
            <Custom Id="MyAction" After="InstallInitialize" />
        </InstallExecuteSequence>
    </Product>
</Wix>
```

We can use the Custom element's `After` attribute to schedule the action to run after `InstallInitialize` in the Execute sequence. You can also use the `Before` attribute to schedule it before some action or the `Sequence` attribute, which sets a specific number to use in the `InstallExecuteSequence` table's Sequence column. You can even schedule additional custom actions based upon other custom actions, as in the next example.

```xml
<InstallExecuteSequence>
    <Custom Id="MyAction" After="InstallInitialize" />
    <Custom Id="Action2" After="MyAction" />
</InstallExecuteSequence>
```

To schedule actions during the UI sequence use the `InstallUISequence` element instead. It works in the same way. The `CustomAction` element gives you more control over when it is executed through its `Execute` attribute, which you'll usually set to "immediate", "deferred", or "rollback". Note that you can run the same custom action in both sequences if need be.

These values are available for the `Return` attribute:

Return value	Meaning
asyncNoWait	The custom action will run asynchronously and execution may continue after the installer terminates.
asyncWait	The custom action will run asynchronously but the installer will wait for the return code at sequence end.
check	The custom action will run synchronously and the return code will be checked for success. This is the default.
ignore	The custom action will run synchronously and the return code will not be checked.

The `Return` attribute tells the installer whether it should wait for the custom action to complete its processing before continuing on and whether the return code should be evaluated. During the deferred stage, if a custom action returns failure and the `Return` attribute is "check" or "asyncWait", a rollback will occur, reverting any changes made up to that point. During the immediate phase, failure will end the installation prematurely.

For the rest of this section, we'll look at the different types of custom actions.

Set a Windows Installer Property

You aren't limited to setting a property with a `Property` element or from the command line. You can, through the use of a *Type 51* custom action, set one at any point during the installation. These "Type" numbers come from the *Type* column in the `CustomAction` table. To set a property, use the CustomAction element's `Property` and `Value` attributes.

```
<CustomAction
    Id="rememberInstallDir"
    Property="ARPINSTALLLOCATION"
    Value="[INSTALLLOCATION]" />
```

This is a useful example that uses the built-in `ARPINSTALLLOCATION` property to save the install directory. Any value you save to it will be stored for you in the Registry and can be recalled later during uninstallation or repair. By using square brackets around the ID of my `install` directory, I'm referencing the directory's path. That's a special case and most of the time you can set a property to a literal value. Here's our directory structure:

```
<Directory Id="TARGETDIR" Name="SourceDir">
    <Directory Id="ProgramFilesFolder">
        <Directory Id="INSTALLLOCATION" Name="MySoftware" />
    </Directory>
</Directory>
```

Then, schedule the custom action so that it happens after `InstallValidate` in the Execute sequence—that's when directories are checked for write access and truly set.

```
<InstallExecuteSequence>
    <Custom Action="rememberInstallDir"
        After="InstallValidate" />
</InstallExecuteSequence>
```

You can, during uninstallation for example, access this property using another type of custom action—one in a C# assembly, which we'll discuss later—by using the `ProductInstallation` class in you C# code.

```
ProductInstallation install =
    new ProductInstallation(session["ProductCode"]);
string installDir = install.InstallLocation;
```

When it comes to writing C# that can interact with your installer, there's a lot to cover. We'll hit some of the major points when we talk about the Deployment Tools Foundation library at the end of this chapter. It's what provides access to the underlying installer functionality.

Set the location of an Installed Directory

A *Type 35* custom action sets the value of a Directory element. Use the `CustomAction` element's `Directory` and `Value` attributes.

```
<CustomAction Id="SetAppDataDir" Directory="DataDir"
    Value="[CommonAppDataFolder]MyProduct" />
```

Assuming we've already defined a `Directory` element with an ID of "DataDir", this action will change its location to a folder called "MyProduct" in the `C:\Documents and Settings\All Users\Application Data` folder. To test this out, you'll need to add a `Directory` element with an ID of "DataDir" and place at least one component inside it.

You should schedule this to run during the Execute sequence before `InstallFiles` or, if you're installing empty folders using the `CreateFolder` element, before the `CreateFolders` action.

```
<InstallExecuteSequence>
   <Custom Action="SetAppDataDir" Before="InstallFiles" />
</InstallExecuteSequence>
```

Run embedded VBScript or JScript

A *Type 37* (JScript) or *Type 38* (VBScript) custom action executes embedded script. You'll define the script as the inner text of the `CustomAction` element and declare its type with the `Script` attribute set to either `vbscript` or `jscript`. Here's an example that displays two message boxes and returns success.

```
<CustomAction Id="testVBScript" Script="vbscript"
   Execute="immediate" >
   <![CDATA[
     msgbox "this is embedded code..."
      msgbox "MyProperty: " & Session.Property("MyProperty")
   ]]>
</CustomAction>
```

Then, we just need to schedule it to run.

```
<InstallUISequence>
   <Custom Action="testVBScript" After="LaunchConditions" />
</InstallUISequence>
```

Call an external VBScript or JScript file

A *Type 5* (JScript) or *Type 6* (VBScript) custom action calls a subroutine from an external script file. Let's say we have a file called `myScript.vbs` that contains this code:

```
Sub myFunction()
   msgbox "This comes from an external script"
End Sub
```

In our WiX markup, we must reference this file with a **Binary** element. This will store the file inside the MSI.

```
<Binary Id="myScriptVBS" SourceFile=".\myScript.vbs" />
```

Then, our `CustomAction` element uses the `BinaryKey` and `VBScriptCall`, or `JScriptCall` if this had been a JScript file, attributes to access the subroutine.

```
<CustomAction
    Id="myScript_CA"
    BinaryKey="myScriptVBS"
    VBScriptCall="myFunction"
    Execute="immediate"
    Return="check" />
```

Be sure to schedule it during one of the sequences. Remember, any code that alters the system should be marked with an Execute attribute of `deferred`.

Call a function from a dynamic-link library

A *Type 1* custom action calls a method from a dynamic-link library (`.dll`). The Votive plugin for Visual Studio provides a template you can use.

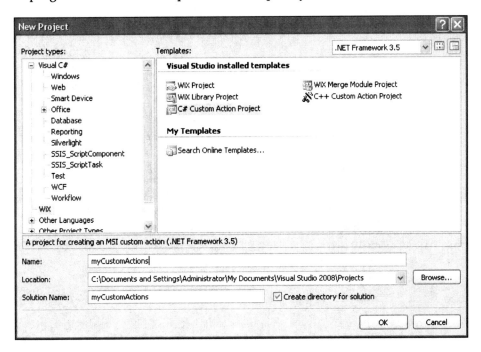

Create a new C# Custom Action Project and you'll get a source file that references the `Microsoft.Deployment.WindowsInstaller` namespace. This contains helpful classes like `Session` that allow you to access the properties, features, and components from your installer.

myCustomActions.cs

```
using System;
using Microsoft.Deployment.WindowsInstaller;

namespace myLibrary
{
    public class CustomActions
    {
        [CustomAction]
        public static ActionResult MyFunction(Session session)
        {
            string myProperty = Session["myProperty"];
            return ActionResult.Success;
        }
    }
}
```

The signature for the C# method has a return type of `ActionResult`, is decorated with the `CustomAction` attribute, and has a `Session` object as its parameter. You're free to name the function, its parent class, and namespace whatever you like. All of this comes from a framework called the **Deployment Tools Foundation** (DTF). DTF is a library that allows you to write .NET code that can interact with the lower-level Windows Installer technology.

Using this will require your end users to have .NET installed—at least .NET 2.0 for the basic functionality provided by the `Microsoft.Deployment.WindowsInstaller` namespace. If you use the additional LINQ features found in `Microsoft.Deployment.WindowsInstaller.Linq`, your end users will need .NET 3.5. So, you might consider using a launch condition to check that they have this prerequisite.

The `ActionResult` object can return any of the following values from your custom action: `Success`, `SkipRemainingActions`, `UserExit`, `Failure`, and `NotExecuted`. This will be read by the `Return` attribute of the `CustomAction` element in your WiX markup.

In the example that we just saw, our C# function returned `ActionResult.Success`. You would, in a real-world scenario, try to catch exceptions and return `ActionResult.Failure` if need be. That way, you could display a friendly error message or write to the install log before the installer rolls back. We'll cover more of what you can do with DTF at the end of this chapter.

When you compile this project you'll end up with two files: one that ends in `.dll` and one that ends `.CA.dll`. It's the second that you'll reference in your WiX project as it contains extra metadata that allows it to be packaged into the MSI. You won't use the *Add a Reference* screen to do this, but rather a WiX Binary element to point to the `.CA.dll` file. Back in our WiX markup, we'd add the following to `Product.wxs`:

```
<Binary Id="myCustomActionsDLL"
     SourceFile=".\myCustomActions.CA.dll" />
```

You'll then use the `CustomAction` element's `BinaryKey` and `DllEntry` attributes to specify the C# method to call.

```
<CustomAction
    Id="CA_myCustomAction"
    BinaryKey="myCustomActionsDLL"
    DllEntry="MyFunction"
    Execute="deferred"
    Return="check"  />
```

You can have a maximum of 16 custom action functions in a single .NET assembly. After that, you'll need to split them up into more projects. There's talk of raising this limit, but for now it holds true.

Trigger an executable

There are three ways to call an executable file (`.exe`) from a custom action. The first, a *Type 2*, uses the Binary element to store the file in the MSI and calls it from there. That way, it doesn't need to be copied to the end user's computer. Here we're referring to a file called `MyProgram.exe` in our WiX project's directory.

```
<Binary
    Id="myProgramEXE"
    SourceFile="$(sys.SOURCEFILEDIR)myProgram.exe" />

<CustomAction
    Id="myProgramEXE_CA"
    BinaryKey="myProgramEXE"
    Impersonate="yes"
    Execute="deferred"
    ExeCommand=""
    Return="check" />
```

The `CustomAction` element's `Impersonate` attribute, when set to `no`, tells the installer to run as the *LocalSystem* user (as we'll be running this during the Execute sequence and that's the user who executes actions there by default on the user's behalf). Setting it to `yes` means that the installer will impersonate the user who initiated the install. The `ExeCommand` attribute takes any command-line arguments you'd want to pass to the executable. You should always specify this, even if it's set to an empty string. It's a required attribute.

We can schedule this to run during the Execute phase.

```
<InstallExecuteSequence>
    <Custom Action="myProgramEXE_CA"
        Before="InstallFinalize" />
</InstallExecuteSequence>
```

The second way of calling an executable, called a *Type 18* custom action, is by copying it to the end user's computer first. Let's say that we're going to copy a file called `MainApp.exe` to the `INSTALLLOCATION` folder, as shown here:

```
<DirectoryRef Id="INSTALLLOCATION">
    <Component Id="CMP_MainAppEXE"
        Guid="7AB5216B-2DB5-4A8A-9293-F6711FFAAA83">

        <File Id="mainAppEXE" Source="MainApp.exe"
            KeyPath="yes" />
    </Component>
</DirectoryRef>
```

Our `CustomAction` element can then use the `FileKey` attribute to specify the ID of our File element, thereby executing it.

```
<CustomAction
    Id="RunMainApp"
    FileKey="mainAppEXE"
    ExeCommand=""
    Execute="commit"
    Return="ignore" />
```

By marking it as `commit`, it will only run if the install is successful. Also, by setting the `Return` attribute to `ignore` we're saying that we don't care if the job succeeds or fails.

The last way, called a *Type 34* custom action, is to use the `Directory` attribute, targeting the directory where the executable is on the end user's computer. The `ExeCommand` attribute should also reference this directory and the name of the `.exe` file including any command-line arguments.

```
<CustomAction
   Id="RunMainApp"
   Directory="INSTALLLOCATION"
   ExeCommand="[INSTALLLOCATION]Main_App.exe"
   Execute="commit"
   Return="ignore" />
```

Send an error that stops the installation

A *Type 19* custom action sends an error to the installer and ends it. It uses the `Error` attribute and looks like this:

```
<CustomAction Id="ErrorCA" Error="Ends the installation" />

<InstallUISequence>
   <Custom Action="ErrorCA" Before="ExecuteAction">
      <![CDATA[
         myProperty <> "1"
      ]]>
   </Custom>
</InstallUISequence>
```

I've placed a conditional statement inside the `Custom` element so that this error will only be triggered if `myProperty` is not equal to `1`. Note that these types of custom actions can only be run during the immediate phase.

Rollback custom actions

Custom actions that are scheduled as "deferred" execute during the Execute sequence's rollback-protected phase. To give those actions rollback capabilities, you'll need to author separate custom actions that undo the work. These are scheduled as "rollback". Rollback custom actions are scheduled before the action they're meant to revert in case of an error. Here's an example:

```
<CustomAction Id="systemChangingCA" Execute="deferred"
Script="vbscript">
      msgbox "Imagine this changes the system in some way"
</CustomAction>

<CustomAction Id="myRollbackCA" Execute="rollback"
Script="vbscript">
      msgbox "Imagine this undoes the changes"
</CustomAction>
```

```
<CustomAction Id="causeError" Execute="deferred"
    Script="vbscript">
        return failure
</CustomAction>
```

We'll schedule these during the Execute sequence.

```
<InstallExecuteSequence>
    <Custom Action="myRollbackCA" Before="systemChangingCA" />
    <Custom Action="systemChangingCA"
        After="InstallInitialize" />
    <Custom Action="causeError" After="systemChangingCA" />
</InstallExecuteSequence>
```

Now, the deferred custom action, called `SystemChangingCA`, is written down in the script during the Execute sequence's immediate phase. The rollback action, called `myRollbackCA`, is recorded as coming before. It won't run unless there's an error. The `CauseError` action happens during the deferred stage and causes a rollback after `SystemChangingCA` has run. Both deferred and rollback actions are always scheduled between `InstallInitalize` and `InstallFinalize`.

The WiX toolset provides a custom action for stimulating rollback called `WixFailWhenDeferred`. It's available as part of the `WixUtilExtension` and you can find more information at `http://wix.sourceforge.net/manual-wix3/wixfailwhendeferred.htm`. You could use it to test your rollback methods.

Having a rollback action for every deferred one is a good idea as it covers you, reverting your changes if need be. Of course, you'll need to author the code of your rollback action so that it really does revert what you've done.

Accessing properties in a deferred action

If you try to access a property from a custom action during the Execute sequence's deferred stage, you'll find that you get an error. This is because only a finite number of properties are available here. As a workaround, you can store the value of your properties in another property called `CustomActionData` and pass that to the custom action.

There are two ways to do this: from your WiX code or from inside another C# custom action. In your WiX markup, you can set a property with a custom action that has a `Property` attribute that matches the custom action you want to pass the property to.

In the next example, we want to pass the MYPROPERTY property to a custom action called myDeferredCA. So, we create another action called SetProperty that sets a property, also called myDeferredCA, to the value of MYPROPERTY.

```
<Property Id="MYPROPERTY" Value="my value" />

<CustomAction Id="SetProperty" Property="myDeferredCA"
Value="[MYPROPERTY]"  />

 <InstallExecuteSequence>
<Custom Action="SetProperty" Before="myDeferredCA" />
    <Custom Action="myDeferredCA" After="InstallInitialize" />
</InstallExecuteSequence>
```

Now, myDeferredCA will have access to our property, indirectly, through the Session object's CustomActionData property.

```
[CustomAction]
public static ActionResult myDeferredCA(Session session)
{
    string myProperty = session.CustomActionData;
    return ActionResult.Success;
}
```

You can also store several properties in CustomActionData by separating them with commas.

```
<CustomAction Id="SetProperty" Property="myDeferredCA"
    Value="[MYPROP],[PROP2],[PROP3]"  />
```

You can then split CustomActionData to get all of the properties.

```
[CustomAction]
public static ActionResult myDeferredCA(Session session)
{
    string[] properties =
    session.CustomActionData.ToString().Split(new string[] {
        "," }, StringSplitOptions.None);

    foreach (string prop in properties)
    {
        MessageBox.Show(prop);
    }

    return ActionResult.Success;
}
```

It's also possible to set the data directly in an immediate custom action. So, instead of using a WiX CustomAction element, you could set the value from code:

```
[CustomAction]
public static ActionResult myImmediateCA(Session session)
{
    CustomActionData data = new CustomActionData();
    data["property1"] = "abc";
    data["property2"] = "def";
    data["property3"] = "ghi";

    session["myDeferredCA"] = data.ToString();

    return ActionResult.Success;
}
```

You can then access the data from within your deferred custom action like this:

```
[CustomAction]
public static ActionResult myDeferredCA(Session session)
{
    CustomActionData data = session.CustomActionData;
    string property1 = data["property1"];

    return ActionResult.Success;
}
```

Adding conditions to custom actions

After you've defined your custom actions and scheduled them into either the InstallUISequence or the InstallExecuteSequence, you have the option of adding conditions to them. These are added as the inner text of the Custom element and prevent the action from running if the condition is false. A common use for this is to only run the action during installation by using the "NOT Installed" condition.

```
<InstallExecuteSequence>
  <Custom Action="myCustomAction" After="InstallInitialize">
    NOT Installed
  </Custom>
</InstallExecuteSequence>
```

Other common conditions are "Installed", which is true if the software is already installed, and "REMOVE", which contains a list of features that are being uninstalled.

You can also use the action state and installed state of features and components or check the values of properties. Look back to *Chapter 4* to review the discussion about these types of conditional statements. It's a good idea to try out an installation and uninstallation of your product just to make sure your custom actions are running only when you expect them to. You can see this in the install log by looking for the words "Doing action".

Deployment Tools Foundation

Writing custom actions with .NET code means making use of the Deployment Tools Foundation (DTF). Here, we'll touch on some of the more common parts of the DTF library. However, you should also take a look at the DTF documentation that comes with WiX if you'd like to explore some of its other features. For example, although we won't cover it here, DTF has support for LINQ and CAB file compression. The examples in this section draw from DTF's `Microsoft.Deployment.WindowsInstaller` namespace.

Session object

When the `InstallUISequence` and `InstallExecuteSequence` tables run through their lists of actions, they're doing so in their own memory space—called a *session*. You've seen how this requires you to mark WiX properties as public (uppercase) to get them from one session to the other. In DTF, the **Session** object is your pipeline into each sequence's running state. Every .NET custom action method receives Session in its parameter list. If you remember, the generic signature of one of these custom actions is this:

```
[CustomAction]
public static ActionResult TestCustomAction(Session session)
```

You'll use Session as the starting place for almost everything you do when working with the `WindowsInstaller` namespace. Its methods and properties return the various other objects that DTF provides. The following sections each use this object in some way to accomplish a task.

Getting and setting properties

To access a WiX property, such as those set with the `Property` element, use the Session object's indexer. Here is an example:

```
[CustomAction]
public static ActionResult CustomAction1(Session session)
{
    string myProperty = session["MY_PROPERTY"];
    return ActionResult.Success;
}
```

Setting properties is just as easy. You'll set the value by referencing the key with the name of your property. Here's an example:

```
[CustomAction]
public static ActionResult CustomAction1(Session session)
{
    session["MY_PROPERTY"] = "abc";
    return ActionResult.Success;
}
```

If the property doesn't exist when you set it, it will be created. Similarly, you can clear a property by settings its value to null. Creating or changing property values from a custom action doesn't stop the installer from displaying those properties in the install log. So, if a property holds information that ought to be hidden, you're better off declaring it in your WiX markup first and setting its `Hidden` attribute to `yes`.

```
<Property Id="MY_PROPERTY" Hidden="yes" />
```

Logging

You can add your own messages to the install log by using the Session object's **Log** method. The simplest way is to just pass it as string.

```
session.Log("This will show up in the log.");
```

You can also pass it a formatted string, as in the next example.

```
string currentTime =
    System.DateTime.Now.ToString("HH:mm:ss",
        CultureInfo.CurrentCulture);
string functionName = "CustomAction1";
string message = "This will show up in the log.";

session.Log("{0} : Method = {1}: {2}", currentTime,
    functionName, message);
```

This will produce the following message in the log:

```
18:05:19 : Method = CustomAction1: This will show up in
the log.
```

You can also use the `Message` method for the same effect. You'll need to create a `Record` object that contains your text and pass it along with `InstallMessage.Info` to the method. Here's an example:

```
Record record = new Record(0);
record[0] = "This will show up in the log";
session.Message(InstallMessage.Info, record);
```

Be aware that the Log and Message methods don't work when the custom action is called from a UI control such as a button click. You'll learn about calling custom actions from UI controls using the `DoAction` event in *Chapter 8*.

Showing a MessageBox

The `Message` method can also be used to display a MessageBox to the user. All you need to do is change the first parameter to `InstallMessage.Warning` or `InstallMessage.Error`. Either will show a MessageBox although the icon shown will differ.

The following example displays a warning message to the user.

```
[CustomAction]
public static ActionResult CustomAction1(Session session)
{
    Record record = new Record(0);
    record[0] = "This is a warning!";
    session.Message(InstallMessage.Warning, record);

    return ActionResult.Success;
}
```

Here's the result:

To show an error MessageBox, use `InstallMessage.Error` instead.

```
[CustomAction]
public static ActionResult CustomAction1(Session session)
{
    Record record = new Record(0);
    record[0] = "This is an error!";
    session.Message(InstallMessage.Error, record);

    return ActionResult.Success;
}
```

Here's the result. Notice that the icon has changed.

Note that these only provide an **OK** button. If you need more than that, you'll need to use something like a Windows Forms dialog, which you can do by adding the appropriate assembly. Something else to consider is that, as we did when logging, we're using the Message method here. So, it will not work if called from a UI control.

Accessing feature and component states

To access a feature's action or installed state, use the `Features` collection. You can look up a feature by name.

```
FeatureInfo productFeature =
    session.Features["ProductFeature"];

//will return "Absent" during an installation
InstallState installedState = productFeature.CurrentState;

//will return "Local" during an installation
InstallState actionState = productFeature.RequestState;
```

Here, we're using the `FeatureInfo` object's `CurrentState`, for installed state, and `RequestState`, for action state, properties to get the info we want. You can do the same thing for components by using the `Components` collection.

```
ComponentInfo cmpInfo = session.Components["cmp_myFile"];
InstallState cmpCurrentState = cmpInfo.CurrentState;
InstallState cmpRequestState = cmpInfo.RequestState;
```

Querying the MSI database

You can read any of the data that's in the MSI database. First, get a reference to the MSI database with the `Session` object's `Database` property.

```
Database db = session.Database;
```

Next, if you just want to get one value from a table, use the `ExecuteScalar` method. This will return the value from the column in your SQL query. Here's an example:

```
string property = "ProductName";

string value = (string)db.ExecuteScalar(
    "SELECT `Value` FROM `Property` WHERE `Property` = '{0}'",
property);

db.Close();
```

Notice that I cast the result to a string. This works in this example because the `Value` column on the `Property` table contains strings. If, on the other hand, the column had contained integers I would have had to cast the result to an integer.

If you'd like to get multiple rows back from your query, use the `ExecuteQuery` method. It returns a collection of type `System.Collections.IList`.

```
string query =
    "SELECT `Property` FROM `Property` ORDER BY `Property`";
System.Collections.IList result = db.ExecuteQuery(query);
db.Close();
```

Inserting rows into the MSI database

You can't insert new data into the MSI database while it's installing and unfortunately, that's often exactly when you want to! To get around this, you can make *temporary* inserts using the `View` object's `InsertTemporary` method. You can get a View by calling the `OpenView` method on the Database object, passing in a `SELECT` statement of the data you want to work with. Here's an example that adds a new property, called NEW_PROPERTY, to the `Property` table:

```
Database db = session.Database;
View view = db.OpenView("SELECT * FROM `Property`");
Record rec = new Record("NEW_PROPERTY", "new_value");
view.InsertTemporary(rec);
```

The first thing we did here was use the Database object's OpenView method to get a View. We selected all of the existing rows from the Property table and then inserted a new row with InsertTemporary. It's perfectly acceptable to get a smaller view by adding a WHERE clause to the SQL query.

You'll need to know the order of the columns in the Property table before you start inserting new rows. When you create your Record object, you have to place the values in the same order as the columns. You can omit columns you don't use as long as they come at the end.

A practical use for this technique is to add a new control to a dialog during the course of the install. Just be sure to add it *before* CostInitialize in the UI phase or your change will go unnoticed. In the following example, we'll add a Text control to the ProgressDlg dialog. This is assuming you're using one of WiX's built-in dialog sets and that ProgressDlg exists.

```
[CustomAction]
public static ActionResult AddControl(Session session)
{
    Database db = null;

    try
    {
        db = session.Database;

        //create control on ProgressDlg:
        View view = db.OpenView("SELECT * FROM `Control`");

        Record record = new Record(
            "ProgressDlg",
            "MyText",
            "Text",
            "20",
            "150",
            "150",
            "15",
            "1");

        view.InsertTemporary(record);

        //subscribe that control to the ActionData event:
        View view2 =
            db.OpenView("SELECT * FROM `EventMapping`");

        Record record2 = new Record("ProgressDlg",
```

```
                "MyText", "ActionData", "Text");

        view2.InsertTemporary(record2);
    }
    catch (Exception err)
    {
        session.Log(err.Message + ": " + err.StackTrace);
        return ActionResult.Failure;
    }

    return ActionResult.Success;
}
```

First, we get a handle to the MSI database by using `session.Database`. Next, we insert a new temporary record into the `Control` table. That will be our Text control. To make things interesting, we've also added a record to the `EventMapping` table, subscribing our Text control to the `ActionData` event. We'll discuss control events in more detail later. For now, know that this will cause the Text control to automatically update itself with any status messages of actions that occur during the installation.

It's a good idea to catch any exceptions that might happen and return `ActionResult.Failure`. This is better than allowing uncaught exceptions to bubble up and kill the installation. This also allows us to log exactly what went wrong.

Summary

In this chapter, we discussed standard actions, which are actions that are built into Windows Installer, and custom actions, which are actions that you add yourself. We saw that there are two sequences: `InstallUISequence` and `InstallExecuteSequence` and how we can access them from our WiX markup. We covered the various types of custom actions and investigated the Deployment Tools Foundation. Knowing how the installer executes its tasks will help you in the next chapter where we cover adding dialogs to your installer.

6

Adding a User Interface

The WiX toolset ships with several User Interface wizards that are ready to use out of the box. You can drop one into your installer by first adding a reference to WixUIExtension.dll and then adding a UIRef element with the name of the wizard. We'll briefly discuss each of the available sets and then move on to learning how to create your own from scratch. In this chapter, you'll learn about:

- Adding dialogs into the InstallUISequence
- Linking one dialog to another to form a complete wizard
- Getting basic text and window styling working
- Including necessary dialogs like those needed to display errors

WiX standard dialog sets

The wizards that come prebuilt with WiX won't fit every need, but they're a good place to get your feet wet. To add any one of them, you first have to add a project reference to WixUIExtension.dll, which can be found in the bin directory of your WiX program files.

Adding this reference is sort of like adding a new source file. This one contains dialogs. To use one, you'll need to use a UIRef element to pull the dialog into the scope of your project. For example, this line, anywhere inside the Product element, will add the "Minimal" wizard to your installer:

```
<UIRef Id="WixUI_Minimal" />
```

It's definitely minimal, containing just one screen.

It gives you a license agreement, which you can change by adding a `WixVariable` element with an `Id` of `WixUILicenseRtf` and a `Value` attribute that points to a Rich Text Format (`.rtf`) file containing your new license agreement:

```
<WixVariable Id="WixUILicenseRtf"
             Value="newLicense.rtf" />
```

You can also override the background image (red wheel on the left, white box on the right) by setting another `WixVariable` called `WixUIDialogBmp` to a new image. The dimensions used are 493x312. The other available wizards offer more and we'll cover them in the following sections.

WixUI_Advanced

The "Advanced" dialog set offers more: It has a screen where the end user can change the folder that files are installed to, another with a feature tree where features can be turned on or off, and a screen that lets the user choose to install for just the current user or for all users, as in the following screenshot:

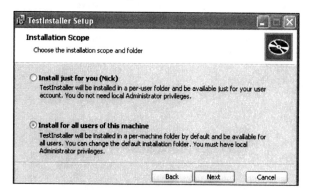

You'll need to change your `UIRef` element to use `WixUI_Advanced`. This can be done by adding the following line:

```
<UIRef Id="WixUI_Advanced" />
```

You'll also have to make sure that your install directory has an `Id` of `APPLICATIONFOLDER`, as in this example:

```
<Directory Id="TARGETDIR"
           Name="SourceDir">
  <Directory Id="ProgramFilesFolder">
    <Directory Id="APPLICATIONFOLDER"
               Name="My Program" />
  </Directory>
</Directory>
```

Next, set two properties: `ApplicationFolderName` and `WixAppFolder`. The first sets the name of the install directory as it will be displayed in the UI. The second sets whether this install should default to being per user or per machine. It can be either `WixPerMachineFolder` or `WixPerUserFolder`.

```
<Property Id="ApplicationFolderName"
          Value="My Program" />
<Property Id="WixAppFolder"
          Value="WixPerMachineFolder" />
```

This dialog uses a bitmap that the Minimal installer doesn't: the white banner at the top. You can replace it with your own image by setting the `WixUIBannerBmp` variable. Its dimensions are 493x58. It would look something like this:

```
<WixVariable Id="WixUIBannerBmp"
             Value="myBanner.bmp" />
```

WixUI_FeatureTree

The `WixUI_FeatureTree` wizard shows a feature tree like the Advanced wizard, but it doesn't have a dialog that lets the user change the install path. To use it, you only need to set the `UIRef` to `WixUI_FeatureTree`, like so:

```
<UIRef Id="WixUI_FeatureTree" />
```

This would produce a window that would allow you to choose features as shown in the following screenshot:

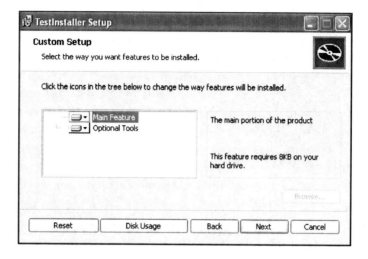

Notice that in the image, the **Browse** button is disabled. If any of your `Feature` elements have the `ConfigurableDirectory` attribute set to the `Id` of a `Directory` element, then this button will allow you to change where that feature is installed to. The `Directory` element's `Id` must be all uppercase.

WixUI_InstallDir

`WixUI_InstallDir` shows a dialog where the user can change the installation path. Change the `UIRef` to `WixUI_InstallDir`, like so:

```
<UIRef Id="WixUI_InstallDir" />
```

Here, the user can chose the installation path. This is seen in the following screenshot:

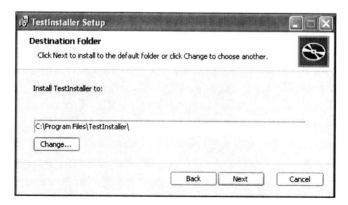

You'll have to set a property called `WIXUI_INSTALLDIR` to the `Id` you gave your install directory. So, if your directory structure used `INSTALLLDIR` for the `Id` of the main install folder, use that as the value of the property.

```
<Directory Id="TARGETDIR"
           Name="SourceDir">
  <Directory Id="ProgramFilesFolder">
    <Directory Id="INSTALLDIR"
               Name="My Program" />
  </Directory>
</Directory>

<Property Id="WIXUI_INSTALLDIR"
          Value="INSTALLDIR" />
```

WixUI_Mondo

The `WixUI_Mondo` wizard gives the user the option of installing a "Typical", "Complete" or "Custom" install. **Typical** sets the `INSTALLLEVEL` property to 3 while **Complete** sets it to 1000. You can set the `Level` attribute of your `Feature` elements accordingly to include them in one group or the other. Selecting a **Custom** install will display a feature tree dialog where the user can choose exactly what they want. To use this wizard, change your `UIRef` element to `WixUI_Mondo`.

```
<UIRef Id="WixUI_Mondo" />
```

This would result in a window like the following:

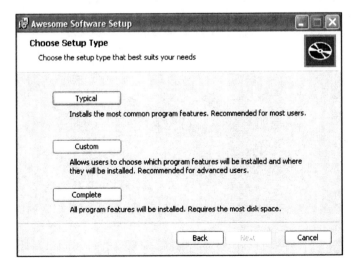

Customizing a standard dialog set

Each of the dialog sets shown can be customized by adding screens, removing some, or changing the look and text. Usually, this means downloading the WiX source code and changing the markup in the dialogs. You can find them under the `src\ext\UIExtension\wixlib` folder of the source code.

The general procedure is to copy the `.wxs` file that has the name of the wizard, such as `WixUI_Minimal.wxs`, to your project with a different name. Then, using the other `.wxs` files in that folder as a reference, add or remove `DialogRef` elements to add or remove dialogs. `DialogRefs` are the references to the dialogs in the other files. Files such as `WixUI_Minimal.wxs` just tie them all together into a wizard. For example, here's part of what you'd find in the Minimal wizard's main source file:

```
<DialogRef Id="ErrorDlg" />
<DialogRef Id="FatalError" />
<DialogRef Id="FilesInUse" />
<DialogRef Id="MsiRMFilesInUse" />
<DialogRef Id="PrepareDlg" />
<DialogRef Id="ProgressDlg" />
<DialogRef Id="ResumeDlg" />
<DialogRef Id="UserExit" />
<DialogRef Id="WelcomeEulaDlg" />
```

Here, you could remove the welcome dialog from the wizard by removing the `WelcomeEulaDlg` line. The Minimal wizard is pretty small to begin with so you're probably better off customizing a set like Mondo.

Scanning through the rest of the file, you'll find that it uses `Publish` elements to define where the **Next** button on each dialog takes you to. You can, in your custom file, change that. Here's what you'd find in `WixUI_Mondo.wxs`:

```
<Publish Dialog="WelcomeDlg"
         Control="Next"
         Event="NewDialog"
         Value="LicenseAgreementDlg">1</Publish>

<Publish Dialog="LicenseAgreementDlg"
         Control="Back"
         Event="NewDialog"
         Value="WelcomeDlg">1</Publish>

<Publish Dialog="LicenseAgreementDlg"
         Control="Next"
         Event="NewDialog"
         Value="SetupTypeDlg"
         Order="2">LicenseAccepted = "1"</Publish>
```

This is all unfamiliar still and we'll go over the Publish element in more detail when we talk about creating our own dialogs. For now, notice that we pair `Dialog` and `Control` attributes to find a particular UI control, such as a button, on a specific dialog. The first Publish element, for example, finds the **Next** button on the `WelcomeDlg` dialog. Use the `Event` attribute to add an event such as `NewDialog` to the button.

Here, we're saying we want the **Next** button to fire the `NewDialog` event with a `Value` of `LicenseAgreementDlg`. This means that when the button is clicked, `WelcomeDlg` will be replaced with `LicenseAgreementDlg`. You can customize any control on any dialog from here, usually to change where the **Next** and **Back** buttons take you. This allows you to insert new dialogs or skip one you don't want.

Here's an example that inserts a custom dialog between the `WelcomeDlg` and the `LicenseAgreementDlg`. Add this to the `CustomWixUI_Mondo.wxs` file:

```
<Publish Dialog="WelcomeDlg"
        Control="Next"
        Event="NewDialog"
        Value="MyDialog">1</Publish>

<Publish Dialog="MyDialog"
        Control="Back"
        Event="NewDialog"
        Value="WelcomeDlg">1</Publish>

<Publish Dialog="MyDialog"
        Control="Next"
        Event="NewDialog"
        Value="LicenseAgreementDlg">1</Publish>

<Publish Dialog="LicenseAgreementDlg"
        Control="Back"
        Event="NewDialog"
        Value="MyDialog">1</Publish>
```

Remember, you'd need to get the original `WixUI_Mondo.wxs` file from the WiX source and rename it to something like `CustomWixUI_Mondo.wxs` before adding it to your project. You'll then reference the custom file with a `UIRef`. We'll explain more about referencing dialog sets when we discuss creating dialogs from scratch.

Creating your own dialogs

In this section, we'll discard the premade dialogs and create our own. This should give you a much deeper understanding of how things work.

ICE20 errors

For these first exercises, you'll have to ignore some of WiX's warnings. Go to the **Properties** page for the project, select **Tools Settings** and add a rule to ignore the validation test **ICE20**. This test checks that you've added `FilesInUse`, `Error`, `FatalError`, `UserExit`, and `Exit` dialogs. That's a lot to start out with, so for now just ignore those rules.

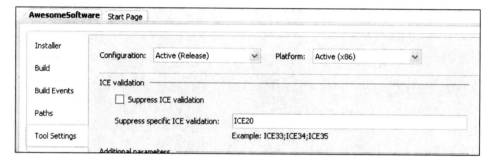

What are these dialogs? They are all windows that serve the purpose of showing an error or a message explaining that the installation has completed successfully. They show up automatically when they're needed. Later in the chapter, I'll show how you can create these dialogs to meet the requirements of ICE20.

Adding dialog files

Let's remove the reference to the `WixUIExtension.dll` and the `UIRef` that points to a standard dialog. We'll be creating everything ourselves now to get the best working knowledge. Each dialog window that you create should be placed into its own WiX source file (`.wxs`). In Visual Studio, you can right-click on your project and select **Add | New Item | WiX File**.

This will create an XML file containing a `Wix` root element and a `Fragment` element. Fragments can be used to split your code into separate files and as such can be used for many different purposes. To create a dialog out of one, you'll need to add two more elements: `UI` and `Dialog`. In this example, I've added a `UI` element and given it an `Id` of `InstallDlg_UI`. Inside that, I've nested a `Dialog` element, which I've called `InstallDlg`. The `InstallDlg.wxs` file should look like this:

```
<Wix xmlns="http://schemas.microsoft.com/wix/2006/wi">
  <Fragment>
    <UI Id="InstallDlg_UI">
      <Dialog Id="InstallDlg">
        <!--Controls like buttons and text go here-->
      </Dialog>
    </UI>
  </Fragment>
</Wix>
```

This is the basic structure that you'll use for each new dialog. The first dialog that you create can serve as the entry point for the others. If, for example, we created a second dialog called SecondDlg, we could set it up in the same way. On additional dialogs, you can omit the UI element's Id attribute, but be sure to change the Dialog element's Id to something new. Use the following snippet to build your SecondDlg. wxs file:

```
<Wix xmlns="http://schemas.microsoft.com/wix/2006/wi">
  <Fragment>
    <UI>
      <Dialog Id="SecondDlg">
        <!--Controls like buttons and text go here-->
      </Dialog>
    </UI>
  </Fragment>
</Wix>
```

Then, to reference SecondDlg in our first dialog, add a DialogRef element to out InstallDlg.wxs file:

```
<Wix xmlns="http://schemas.microsoft.com/wix/2006/wi">
  <Fragment>
    <UI Id="InstallDlg_UI">
      <DialogRef Id="SecondDlg"/>

      <Dialog Id="InstallDlg">
      </Dialog>
    </UI>
  </Fragment>
</Wix>
```

To add both dialogs to our project, use a `UIRef` in your main source file. Its `Id` should match the `Id` you gave to your `UI` element in `InstallDlg`. Add this line to `Product.wxs`:

```
<UIRef Id="InstallDlg_UI"/>
```

Scheduling dialogs

For now, we only need to schedule one of our dialogs in the UI sequence. To do that, place a `Show` element inside an `InstallUISequence` element with a `Dialog` attribute set to the `Id` of `InstallDlg` file's `Dialog` element. Then add a `Before` attribute and schedule it before `ExecuteAction`. The following snippet shows this:

```
<InstallUISequence>
  <Show Dialog="InstallDlg"
        Before="ExecuteAction" />
</InstallUISequence>
```

Now, when the installer is launched our first dialog will be shown. To get from our first dialog to our second one, we'll add a **Next** button that takes us there. We'll cover buttons in detail in the next chapter, but basically, you'll add a `Control` element of `Type = "PushButton"` inside the `InstallDlg` file's `Dialog` element. It will, in turn, contain another element called `Publish` that closes the current dialog and opens the second. The InstallDlg.wxs file will contain this code:

```
<Dialog ...>
  <Control Id="Next"
           Type="PushButton"
           X="245"
           Y="243"
           Width="100"
           Height="17">
    <Publish Event="NewDialog"
             Value="SecondDlg" />
  </Control>
</Dialog>
```

This technique can be used to navigate from one dialog to another, or even to go back via **Back** buttons. You only need to change the value of the `Publish` element's `Value` attribute to the `Id` of a different `Dialog`. We could add a **Back** button on our `SecondDlg` file that takes us back to `InstallDlg`:

```
<Dialog ...>
  <Control Id="Back"
           Type="PushButton"
```

```
            X="180"
            Y="243"
            Width="100"
            Height="17">
    <Publish Event="NewDialog"
            Value="InstallDlg" />
    </Control>
    </Dialog>
```

Of course, you'd also need to change the Id of the Control and change its X and Y attributes, otherwise all of your buttons would sit on top of one another and have the same key in the MSI's *Control* table. Here's an image of a dialog that has a **Back** and **Next** button:

Dialog element

Our InstallDlg won't work properly yet. We still need to add more attributes to the Dialog element to set its size, title, and whether or not it can be minimized:

```
<Dialog Id="InstallDlg"
        Width="370"
        Height="270"
        Title="Amazing Software"
        NoMinimize="no">
```

You can set the Width and Height larger or smaller, but these are the dimensions used by the WiX dialog sets. Together, these define the size of the window. The Title attribute sets the text that will be displayed at the top of the window. Setting NoMinimize to no means that the user will be able to minimize the dialog. This is the default so specifying it isn't strictly necessary. There's one other attribute that you're likely to use early on and that's Modeless, which can be set to yes. This will make the dialog not wait for user input and is often used for progress bar dialogs. We'll cover it later on in the chapter.

Adding TextStyle elements

Our dialog isn't useable yet. It needs at least one `TextStyle` element to set the default font for the text on the window. You'll only need to do this for the first dialog you create. The other dialogs can reuse the styles you set there. A `TextStyle` element uses the `FaceName`, `Size`, `Bold`, `Italic`, and `Underline` attributes to set a font. The following example creates a vanilla 8pt Tahoma font to be used as our default:

```
<TextStyle Id="Tahoma_Regular"
           FaceName="Tahoma"
           Size="8" />
<Property Id="DefaultUIFont"
          Value="Tahoma_Regular" />
```

Since this will be our default font, we have to add a `Property` with an `Id` set to `DefaultUIFont` and a `Value` set to the `Id` of our `TextStyle` element. These will go inside our `UI` element as siblings to our `Dialog` element. You can add more `TextStyle` elements for titles, fine print, and so on.

```
<Wix xmlns="http://schemas.microsoft.com/wix/2006/wi">
  <Fragment>
    <UI Id="InstallDlg_UI">
      <TextStyle Id="Tahoma_Regular"
                 FaceName="Tahoma"
                 Size="8" />
      <Property Id="DefaultUIFont"
                Value="Tahoma_Regular" />

      <TextStyle Id="Tahoma_Bold"
                 FaceName="Tahoma"
                 Size="8"
                 Bold="yes" />
      <TextStyle Id="Tahoma_Italic"
                 FaceName="Tahoma"
                 Size="8"
                 Italic="yes" />
      <TextStyle Id="Tahoma_Title"
                 FaceName="Tahoma"
                 Size="12"
                 Underline="yes" />

      <Dialog Id="InstallDlg"
              Width="370"
              Height="270"
              Title="Amazing Software"
```

```
                   NoMinimize="no">
       </Dialog>
     </UI>
   </Fragment>
 </Wix>
```

You can use these styles on, for example, a `Control` of `Type = "Text"`, which displays a label, by adding the `TextStyle` element's `Id` in curly brackets to the `Control` element's `Text` attribute. Prefix the `Id` with a backslash as shown:

```
<Control Id="myText"
          Type="Text"
          X="10" Y="10"
          Width="200"
          Height="17"
          Text="{\Tahoma_Bold}Here is some text" />
```

The following table lists the possible attributes for your `TextStyle` elements:

Attribute	Meaning
Blue	Set to a number between 0 and 255 of how blue the text should be.
Green	Set to a number between 0 and 255 of how green the text should be.
Red	Set to a number between 0 and 255 of how red the text should be.
Italic	If yes, the text will be italic.
Bold	If yes, the text will be bold.
Size	Sets the numeric size of the text.
Strike	If yes, the text will have line through it.
Underline	If yes, the text will be underlined.
FaceName	The font face of the text.

Here is an example that uses several `TextStyle` elements in `Text` controls:

Adding a tabbable control

Our `InstallDlg` still isn't ready. We need to add at least one control that can be tabbed to inside our `Dialog` element. For this, we can add a button like the **Next** button you saw before. It used the `Publish` element to take us to a dialog called `SecondDlg`:

```
<Control  Id="Next"
          Type="PushButton"
          X="50"
          Y="50"
          Width="100"
          Height="17">
   <Publish  Event="NewDialog"
             Value="SecondDlg" />
</Control>
```

Suppose we don't have a `SecondDlg` though, and we just want a button that, when clicked, will continue the installation. It could say **Install** on it. For that, we'll create a button that publishes the `EndDialog` event with a `Value` of `Return`. This is illustrated in the following:

```
<Control  Id="InstallButton"
          Type="PushButton"
          Text="Install"
          Height="17"
          Width="56"
          X="245"
          Y="243">
   <Publish  Event="EndDialog"
             Value="Return" />
</Control>
```

We can also add a button that says **Cancel**. It will also publish the `EndDialog` event, but with a `Value` of `Exit`. If we add the `Cancel` attribute to it, this button will be triggered if the user clicks the **X** button on the window or presses *Escape*.

```
<Control  Id="CancelButton"
          Type="PushButton"
          Text="Cancel"
          Height="17"
          Width="56"
          X="180"
          Y="243"
          Cancel="yes">
   <Publish  Event="EndDialog"
             Value="Exit" />
</Control>
```

Here's our `InstallDlg` now, ready for use:

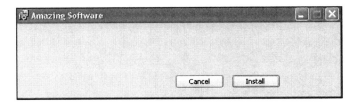

Here's the entire markup:

```
<?xml version="1.0" encoding="UTF-8"?>
<Wix xmlns="http://schemas.microsoft.com/wix/2006/wi">
  <Fragment>
    <UI Id="InstallDlg_UI">
      <TextStyle Id="Tahoma_Regular"
                 FaceName="Tahoma"
                 Size="8" />
      <Property Id="DefaultUIFont"
                Value="Tahoma_Regular" />

      <Dialog Id="InstallDlg"
              Width="370"
              Height="270"
              Title="Amazing Software"
              NoMinimize="no">

        <Control Id="InstallButton"
                 Type="PushButton"
                 Text="Install"
                 Height="17"
                 Width="56"
                 X="245"
                 Y="243">
          <Publish Event="EndDialog"
                   Value="Return" />
        </Control>

        <Control Id="CancelButton"
                 Type="PushButton"
                 Text="Cancel"
                 Height="17"
                 Width="56"
                 X="180"
```

```
                    Y="243"
                    Cancel="yes">
            <Publish Event="EndDialog"
                    Value="Exit" />
        </Control>
      </Dialog>

      <InstallUISequence>
        <Show Dialog="InstallDlg"
              Before="ExecuteAction" />
      </InstallUISequence>
    </UI>
  </Fragment>
</Wix>
```

When adding controls it's important to know that the order in which they appear in your XML markup (from top to bottom) will be their tab order on the window. So, you should place the button you'd want to receive the focus first at the top of your markup, followed by the control that you'd want to receive the focus on next, down the line. In our example, the **Install** button would be focused when the window first loads and pressing **Tab** would take you to the **Cancel** button.

You can prevent a control from being the default focused control by setting its TabSkip attribute to yes.

 Note that TabSkip only prevents a control from having the focus when the dialog is first shown. The user will still be able to tab to that control once the dialog is loaded.

Adding a progress dialog

So what happens when we click the **Install** button? It installs but there's no indication that anything has happened. We need a dialog that shows a progress bar to inform the user that the install is happening. Add a new WiX source file to your project and call it ProgressDlg.wxs. Add a UI element, like before, and then a Dialog element with the Id = "ProgressDlg" to differentiate it in the MSI database. The ProgressDlg.wxs file will look like the following:

```
<Wix xmlns="http://schemas.microsoft.com/wix/2006/wi">
  <Fragment>
    <UI>
      <Dialog Id="ProgressDlg"></Dialog>
    </UI>
  </Fragment>
</Wix>
```

Back in `InstallDlg.wxs`, add a `DialogRef` element inside the `UI` element to reference this new file:

```
<Fragment>
  <UI ...>
    <DialogRef Id="ProgressDlg" />
```

The `Dialog` element in `ProgressDlg.wxs` will use the `Modeless` attribute to signify that it shouldn't wait for user interaction. The installation process will continue, but it will allow this dialog to remain up for the remainder of the installation. This allows the dialog to respond to events that fire during the Execute sequence, which will enable the dialog's progress bar to increment itself.

```
<Dialog Id="ProgressDlg"
        Width="370"
        Height="270"
        Title="Amazing Software"
        Modeless="yes">
```

If you like, you can add a **Cancel** button to this dialog, just in case the user decides to cancel at this point. Refer back to `InstallDlg` for the markup. We'll also add a `Control` of type `ProgressBar` that uses the `Subscribe` element to receive progress updates:

```
<Control Id="MyProgressBar"
         Type="ProgressBar"
         X="70"
         Y="150"
         Width="200"
         Height="20"
         ProgressBlocks="yes">

  <Subscribe Event="SetProgress"
             Attribute="Progress" />
</Control>
```

By subscribing to the SetProgress event, the progress bar is able to increment itself as actions occur. Here's what it will look like:

Before, when we talked about adding a **Next** button to take us to a second dialog, there would have been no need to explicitly add that dialog to the UI sequence. The button takes us to it. It would have been up to that second dialog to then have an **Install** button that ended the dialog wizard and allowed the rest of the install to continue. In other words, we must always end with a button that publishes the EndDialog event with a Value of Return. Usually, that button is marked **Install**.

Our ProgressDlg, however, will remain up as the rest of the install continues. It's "Modeless". Therefore, we should schedule it to run after InstallDlg and before ExecuteAction. This is shown in the following code:

```
<InstallUISequence>
   <Show Dialog="ProgressDlg"
         After="InstallDlg" />
</InstallUISequence>
```

If you look at the InstallUISequence table in Orca, you can see how things look:

Action	Condi...	Seque...
ValidateProductID		700
CostInitialize		800
FileCost		900
CostFinalize		1000
InstallDlg		1298
ProgressDlg		1299
ExecuteAction		1300

Even if we'd had a second, third, and fourth dialog, each arrived at by clicking a **Next** button on the dialog before, we wouldn't see any of them in this table. The InstallDlg is our entry point. When it closes, via the EndDialog event, ProgressDlg pops up. Since ProgressDlg is Modeless, ExecuteAction fires immediately and takes us into the Execute sequence. Here's a complete sample for the progress dialog:

```xml
<?xml version="1.0" encoding="UTF-8"?>
<Wix xmlns="http://schemas.microsoft.com/wix/2006/wi">
  <Fragment>
    <UI>
      <Dialog Id="ProgressDlg"
              Width="370"
              Height="270"
              Title="Amazing Software"
              Modeless="yes">

        <Control Id="CancelButton"
                 Type="PushButton"
                 TabSkip="no"
                 Text="Cancel"
                 Height="17"
                 Width="56"
                 X="180"
                 Y="243"
                 Cancel="yes">
          <Publish Event="EndDialog"
                   Value="Exit" />
        </Control>

        <Control Id="MyProgressBar"
                 Type="ProgressBar"
                 X="70"
                 Y="150"
                 Width="200"
                 Height="20"
                 ProgressBlocks="yes">
          <Subscribe Event="SetProgress"
                     Attribute="Progress" />
        </Control>
      </Dialog>

      <InstallUISequence>
        <Show Dialog="ProgressDlg"
              After="InstallDlg" />
      </InstallUISequence>
    </UI>
  </Fragment>
</Wix>
```

Modal windows

Up to this point, closing one dialog opened another in its place. You can also create "modal" windows that pop up on top of the current window. Instead of publishing the NewDialog event inside a button, such as with our **Next** button, we can publish the SpawnDialog event.

Modal windows are usually a little bit smaller in size than normal windows so that the parent window can be seen in the background. Suppose we had a dialog called PopupDlg; we could use the SpawnDialog event to open it modally. Typically, modal windows have an **OK** button that publishes the EndDialog event with a Value of Return. This allows them to be closed and have focus return to the parent window.

Here's what a button on InstallDlg would look like if it were set to open PopupDlg modally:

```
<Control  Id="PopupButton"
          Type="PushButton"
          Text="Show Popup"
          Height="17"
          Width="56"
          X="245"
          Y="243"
          Default="yes">
    <Publish Event="SpawnDialog"
          Value="PopupDlg" />
</Control>
```

Here's what the result looks like:

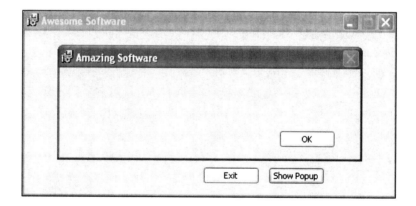

ICE20 revisited

ICE20 is the validation check that makes sure you have the necessary dialogs defined to handle things like showing a friendly message when the user cancels the install. We initially suppressed this check in the project's properties. Now, let's remove that suppression and add these dialogs. Note that all are defined in the WiX source files and you may find it easier to simply copy them to your project.

We need to define five dialogs: `FilesInUse`, `Error`, `FatalError`, `UserExit`, and `Exit`.

FilesInUse

The `FilesInUse` dialog allows the user to shut down applications that are accessing files the installer needs to update or delete. The MSI finds this dialog by looking in the MSI `Dialog` table for a dialog with an `Id` of `FilesInUse`. So, in our new WiX source file, the `Dialog` element's `Id` must match this name. The `FilesInUseDlg.wxs` file will look like like the following:

```
<?xml version="1.0" encoding="UTF-8"?>
<Wix xmlns="http://schemas.microsoft.com/wix/2006/wi">
  <Fragment>
    <UI>
      <Dialog Id="FilesInUse"
              Width="370"
              Height="270"
              Title="Amazing Software">
      </Dialog>
    </UI>
  </Fragment>
</Wix>
```

To show which applications are using the files, we need to add a `ListBox` control that sets a property called `FilesInUseProcess`.

```
<Control Id="InUseFiles"
         Type="ListBox"
         Width="300"
         Height="150"
         X="30"
         Y="60"
         Property="FileInUseProcess"
         Sorted="yes" />
```

We also need to add three buttons, **Ignore**, **Retry**, and **Exit**. Set the EndDialog event
to these values:

```
<Control Id="Retry"
        Type="PushButton"
        X="304"
        Y="243"
        Width="56"
        Height="17"
        Default="yes"
        Cancel="yes"
        Text="Retry">
  <Publish Event="EndDialog"
        Value="Retry">1</Publish>
</Control>

<Control Id="Ignore"
        Type="PushButton"
        X="235"
        Y="243"
        Width="56"
        Height="17"
        Text="Ignore">
  <Publish Event="EndDialog"
        Value="Ignore">1</Publish>
</Control>

<Control Id="Exit"
        Type="PushButton"
        X="166"
        Y="243"
        Width="56"
        Height="17"
        Text="Cancel">
  <Publish Event="EndDialog"
        Value="Exit">1</Publish>
</Control>
```

Remember to add a DialogRef to this dialog in your InstallDlg.wxs file:

```
<DialogRef Id="FilesInUseDlg" />
```

Error

An installer uses the `Error` dialog to display error messages. Create a new source file and call it `ErrorDlg.wxs`. This file should set a property called `ErrorDialog` to the value you've set the `Dialog` element's `Id`. In addition, the `Dialog` element should set the `ErrorDialog` attribute to `yes`. The file should contain this snippet:

```
<?xml version="1.0" encoding="UTF-8"?>
<Wix xmlns="http://schemas.microsoft.com/wix/2006/wi">
  <Fragment>
    <UI>
      <Property Id="ErrorDialog"
                Value="ErrorDlg" />

      <Dialog Id="ErrorDlg"
              Width="370"
              Height="270"
              Title="Amazing Software"
              ErrorDialog="yes">
      </Dialog>
    </UI>
  </Fragment>
</Wix>
```

You'll also need to add a `Text` control inside the `Dialog` element and set its `Id` to `ErrorText`. This will be used to display the error message.

```
<Control Id="ErrorText"
         Type="Text"
         X="50"
         Y="15"
         Width="200"
         Height="60" />
```

Next, add seven new buttons. Each will publish the `EndDialog` event with one of the following `Values`:

- `ErrorAbort`
- `ErrorCancel`
- `ErrorIgnore`
- `ErrorNo`
- `ErrorOk`
- `ErrorRetry`
- `ErrorYes`

For example, here's the first that sets the `ErrorAbort` button:

```
<Control Id="A"
         Type="PushButton"
         X="100"
         Y="80"
         Width="56"
         Height="17"
         TabSkip="yes"
         Text="Cancel">
   <Publish Event="EndDialog"
         Value="ErrorAbort">1</Publish>
</Control>
```

You can change the `Text` attribute of each button so that it matches the type, such as `Yes` for `ErrorYes` and `No` for `ErrorNo`. The `X` and `Y` attributes can remain the same. Remember to reference this new dialog with a `DialogRef` in your `InstallDlg` file.

FatalError

The `FatalError` dialog is shown when an unrecoverable error is encountered during the install, causing a premature end. Add a new WiX source file and call it `FatalErrorDlg.wxs`. The message will always be the same so you can add a `Text` control that displays a static message, as in the following example:

```
<?xml version="1.0" encoding="UTF-8"?>
<Wix xmlns="http://schemas.microsoft.com/wix/2006/wi">
  <Fragment>
    <UI>
      <Dialog Id="FatalErrorDlg"
              Width="370"
              Height="270"
              Title="Amazing Software">

        <Control Id="Description"
                 Type="Text"
                 X="50"
                 Y="70"
                 Width="220"
                 Height="80"
                 Text="[ProductName] Setup Wizard ended
                     prematurely because of an error. Your system
                     has not been modified. To install this
                     program at a later time, run Setup Wizard
                     again." />
```

```
        <Control Id="Finish"
                 Type="PushButton"
                 X="180"
                 Y="243"
                 Width="56"
                 Height="17"
                 Default="yes"
                 Cancel="yes"
                 Text="Finish">
          <Publish Event="EndDialog"
                   Value="Exit" />
        </Control>
      </Dialog>
    </UI>

    <InstallUISequence>
      <Show Dialog="FatalErrorDlg"
            OnExit="error" />
    </InstallUISequence>

    <AdminUISequence>
      <Show Dialog="FatalErrorDlg"
            OnExit="error" />
    </AdminUISequence>
  </Fragment>
</Wix>
```

The Text control uses the Text attribute to set the message to display. You should also add a button that publishes the EndDialog event with a Value of Exit to allow the user to quit the install.

Notice that we add this dialog into two sequences: InstallUISequence and AdminUISequence. This is required even if you aren't supporting administrative installs. In both cases, set the Show element's OnExit attribute to error. This will schedule the dialog in the appropriate place in those sequences.

UserExit

The UserExit dialog appears when the user cancels the install. Typically, it contains some text and a Finish button that publishes the EndDialog event with a Value of Exit. Like the FatalError dialog, it must appear in both the InstallUISequence and the AdminUISequence. This time, we'll set the Show element's OnExit attribute to cancel.

Here's an example:

```xml
<?xml version="1.0" encoding="UTF-8"?>
<Wix xmlns="http://schemas.microsoft.com/wix/2006/wi">
  <Fragment>
    <UI>
      <Dialog Id="UserExitDlg"
              Width="370"
              Height="270"
              Title="Amazing Software">

        <Control Id="Description"
                 Type="Text"
                 X="50"
                 Y="70"
                 Width="220"
                 Height="80"
                 Text="[ProductName] setup was interrupted. Your
                       system has not been modified. To install
                       this program at a later time, please run the
                       installation again." />

        <Control Id="Finish"
                 Type="PushButton"
                 X="180"
                 Y="243"
                 Width="56"
                 Height="17"
                 Default="yes"
                 Cancel="yes"
                 Text="Finish">
          <Publish Event="EndDialog"
                   Value="Exit" />
        </Control>
      </Dialog>
    </UI>

    <InstallUISequence>
      <Show Dialog="UserExitDlg"
            OnExit="cancel" />
    </InstallUISequence>

    <AdminUISequence>
      <Show Dialog="UserExitDlg"
```

```
                OnExit="cancel" />
        </AdminUISequence>
    </Fragment>
</Wix>
```

Exit

The Exit dialog is shown at the end of a successful installation. Typically, it contains some text and a **Finish** button. It must also be added to both the InstallUISequence and AdminUISequence. Here, set the Show element's OnExit attribute to success. Here's an example:

```
<?xml version="1.0" encoding="UTF-8"?>
<Wix xmlns="http://schemas.microsoft.com/wix/2006/wi">
  <Fragment>
    <UI>
      <Dialog Id="ExitDlg"
              Width="370"
              Height="270"
              Title="Amazing Software">

        <Control Id="Description"
                Type="Text"
                X="50"
                Y="70"
                Width="220"
                Height="80"
                Text="[ProductName] setup has completed
                      successfully. Click 'Finish' to exit the
                      Setup Wizard." />

        <Control Id="Finish"
                Type="PushButton"
                X="180"
                Y="243"
                Width="56"
                Height="17"
                Default="yes"
                Cancel="yes"
                Text="Finish">
          <Publish Event="EndDialog"
                  Value="Exit" />
        </Control>
      </Dialog>
```

```
      </UI>

      <InstallUISequence>
        <Show Dialog="ExitDlg"
             OnExit="success" />
      </InstallUISequence>

      <AdminUISequence>
        <Show Dialog="ExitDlg" OnExit="success" />
      </AdminUISequence>
    </Fragment>
  </Wix>
```

Remember to add a `DialogRef` to reference this file in your `InstallDlg` file.

Summary

In this chapter, we covered the basics of making simple dialogs. There are a few required dialogs, as required by the ICE20 validation check, but for the most part you're free to create as many of your own customized dialogs as you want. In the next chapter, we'll explore UI controls such as buttons, text, and lists. This should give you plenty of options when designing your install wizard.

7
Using UI Controls

Now that you've seen how to create windows for your user interface, it's time to explore the controls you can use on them. Controls are the buttons, text boxes, lists, and images that we've all interacted with before and that make up any graphical UI. In this chapter, we'll discuss the following topics:

- The Control element and its basic attributes
- The various types of controls and their unique features

Controls

Placing a **Control** element inside a Dialog adds a new control to that window. You'll use its Type attribute to specify which kind of control it is: PushButton, Text, and so on. Beware that these names are case sensitive. "Pushbutton" isn't the same as "PushButton" and will give you an install time error.

Positioning and sizing are always the same: Use the **X** and **Y** attributes to place your control at a specific coordinate on the window and the Width and Height attributes to size it. You must also always give it an **ID** attribute that uniquely identifies it on that dialog. So, you can have two buttons with the same ID if they're on two different dialogs, but not if they're on the same dialog.

In the following sections, we will explore each type of control.

PushButton

A button is one of the most basic types of controls and the one you'll probably use the most. In WiX, it's created by setting the Control element's `Type` attribute to "PushButton". Use its `Text` attribute to set its label.

```
<Control
    Id="MyButton"
    Type="PushButton"
    Text="Click Me!"
    X="50"
    Y="50"
    Height="17"
    Width="75">

    <Publish Event="EndDialog" Value="Return" />
</Control>
```

Here's what it looks like:

You always need to add a `Publish` element inside it or else the button won't do anything. The `Publish` element executes an action when the button is clicked. In the last example, I'm calling the `EndDialog` event to continue the install. There are many control events available. Another good example is `DoAction`, which will execute the custom action you specify with `Value`.

```
<Control
    Id="MyButton"
    Type="PushButton"
    ... >

    <Publish Event="DoAction" Value="MyCustomAction" />
</Control>
```

You can also set a property by using the `Property` attribute. The next example sets the `INSTALLLEVEL` property to set certain features as "on".

```
<Control
    Id="MyButton"
    Type="PushButton"
    ... >

    <Publish Property="INSTALLLEVEL" Value="2" />
</Control>
```

To execute more than one action, add more `Publish` elements and use the `Order` attribute to order them.

```
<Control
    Id="MyButton"
    Type="PushButton"
    ... >

    <Publish Event="DoAction" Value="MyCustomAction"
        Order="1">1</Publish>
    <Publish Property="MY_PROPERTY" Value="my value"
        Order="2">CA_RESULT = 1</Publish>
    <Publish Event="EndDialog" Value="Return"
        Order="3">1</Publish>
</Control>
```

Whenever you use more than one, you should also add inner text to each with a conditional statement that determines if that action should run. You can use just a "1" to always execute the action or, as in this example, check some property. This is just to give you a feeling for what **control events** are. We'll explore them in more detail in the next chapter.

As far as styling your buttons, you can add `TextStyle` references to the `Text` attribute to use a particular font.

```
<Control
    Id="MyButton"
    Type="PushButton"
    Text="{\Tahoma_Bold}Click me!"
    ... >
```

You can also use an icon instead of text. In that case, set the `Text` attribute to the ID of a Binary element that uses its `SourceFile` attribute to point to an `.ico` file. Also, set the `Control` element's `Icon` attribute to `yes` and its `IconSize` attribute to the size of your icon: 16, 32, or 48.

```
<Binary Id="myIcon" SourceFile="iconFile.ico" />

<Dialog ...>
    <Control
        Id="myButton"
        Type="PushButton"
        Text="myIcon"
        Icon="yes"
        IconSize="48"
        Height="50"
```

```
        Width="50"
        X="50"
        Y="50">

        <Publish Event="EndDialog" Value="Return" />
    </Control>
</Dialog>
```

Here's the result:

Something else to consider is whether to add a keyboard shortcut for your button. To do so, add an ampersand (&) in front of one of the letters in the Text attribute. Then, pressing *Alt* and that letter will trigger the button. You'll want to use the **Text** element inside your control instead of the Text attribute so that you can surround the text with CDATA tags.

```
<Control
    Id="InstallButton"
    Type="PushButton"
    ... >

    <Text><![CDATA[&Install]]></Text>
    <Publish Event="EndDialog" Value="Return" />
</Control>
```

One last thing to look at is placing a **Condition** element inside your PushButton control. This uses an Action attribute to enable/disable or hide/show your button, depending upon the state of some property.

```
<Control
    Id="myButton"
    Type="PushButton"
    ... >

    <Condition Action="disable">
        <![CDATA[myProperty <> "abc"]]>
    </Condition>

    <Condition Action="enable">
        myProperty = "abc"
    </Condition>
</Control>
```

Here, we're enabling the button only if the property called `myProperty` is set to `abc`. Instead of using an `Action` of `enable` and `disable`, I could also use `hide` and `show` to toggle the button's visibility. This sort of thing is used in the WiX dialog sets to enable the **Next** button when the user license agreement is accepted.

Text

A Text control places a block of text on the dialog. Here's an example:

```
<Control
    Id="SampleText"
    Type="Text"
    Text="This text comes from a Text control"
    Height="17"
    Width="200"
    X="50"
    Y="50" />
```

This is what it will look like:

Be sure to make it wide enough so that the text isn't clipped. Another option is to make the `Height` bigger and then set the `NoWrap` attribute to `no` so that the text wraps to a new line when it runs out of width space. If the text runs out of height space it gets clipped and will be replaced with an ellipsis (...).

Two other useful attributes are Transparent and RightAlligned. `Transparent` allows any background behind the control, such as a bitmap image, to show through. `RightAlligned` right justifies the text.

ScrollableText

The `ScrollableText` control is used to display large amounts of text that wouldn't fit on the dialog window otherwise. It creates a read-only text box with a scrollbar and is often used to show a license agreement. To set the text, either use a Text element that points to a Rich Text Format (`.rtf`) file:

```
<Control
    Id="myScrollableText"
    Type="ScrollableText"
    Height="150"
    Width="300"
```

```
        X="50"
        Y="50"
        Sunken="yes">

    <Text SourceFile="Document.rtf" />
</Control>
```

Or you can add the RTF text directly inside the `Text` element:

```
<Control
    Id="myScrollableText"
    Type="ScrollableText"
    Height="150"
    Width="300"
    X="50"
    Y="50"
    Sunken="yes">

    <Text>                        <![CDATA[{\rtf1\ansi\ansicpg1252\
deff0\deflang1033{\fonttbl{\f0\fswiss\fcharset0 Arial;}}
{\*\generator Msftedit 5.41.21.2500;}\viewkind4\uc1\pard\f0\fs20 This
is a bunch of text...\par
}]]>
    </Text>
</Control>
```

The RTF text created by Microsoft's WordPad tends to work better than that created by Microsoft Word. Here's what it might look like:

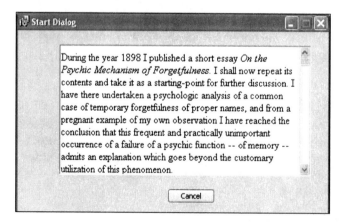

If you'd rather see the scrollbar on the left, set the `LeftScroll` attribute to `yes`.

Line

A Line control is definitely the simplest of all. It creates a visible horizontal line starting at the point specified by X and Y and stretching the length specified by Width. You can set Height to 0, as the attribute is ignored.

```
<Control Id="sampleLine" Type="Line" Height="0" Width="370"
    X="2" Y="50" />
```

It looks like this:

You might use this to separate bold title text on your dialogs from other content like text fields and buttons.

GroupBox

A close relative to the Line control is the GroupBox. It creates a rectangle that you can use to visually group other controls. You have the option of displaying a caption at the top by setting the Text attribute. Here's an example:

```
<Control
    Id="myGroupBox"
    Type="GroupBox"
    Text="My GroupBox"
    X="10"
    Y="10"
    Height="100"
    Width="200" />
```

To have controls appear inside the box, you'll have to position them there manually using the X and Y attributes of each one. The GroupBox doesn't offer any functionality. You can, however, stylize its caption by referencing a TextStyle in its Text attribute. Here's what a basic GroupBox looks like:

Bitmap

Bitmap controls show images on your dialog. You could use this to show a picture on only a portion of the window or to skin the entire area. First, you must use a Binary element to point to an image file. Then, reference that element's ID in your Control's `Text` attribute.

```
<UI>
    <Binary Id="myPic" SourceFile="gradientBackground.jpg" />

    <Dialog ... >
        <Control
            Id="myBitmap"
            Type="Bitmap"
            Text="myPic"
            Height="270"
            Width="370"
            X="0"
            Y="0"
            TabSkip="no" />
```

Here, we're using an image that will cover the entire window. So, we set `X` and `Y` to `0` so that it will line up with the top-left corner.

If you add Text controls, set their `Transparent` attributes to `yes` so that the background image can be seen behind them. Things also tend to work out better when you place the Bitmap control first in the markup and set its `TabSkip` attribute to `no`. Here's what it might look like, with several other elements on top:

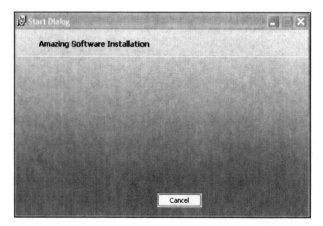

Icon

The Icon control is used to display an `.ico` image on your dialog. Like the Bitmap control, you'll need to first reference the `.ico` file with a Binary element.

```
<Binary Id="myIcon" SourceFile="myIcon.ico" />
```

Then, add a Control element of Type "Icon" and reference the Binary element's ID in the `Text` attribute. Use the `IconSize` attribute to specify the size of the icon: `16`, `32`, or `48`.

```
<Control
    Id="myIcon"
    Type="Icon"
    Text="myIcon"
    X="50"
    Y="50"
    Height="48"
    Width="48"
    IconSize="48" />
```

Here's what it might look like:

Edit

An Edit control creates a text box that the user can type into. You'll use its `Property` attribute to set the value of a property to what the user types. It isn't necessary to declare this property beforehand, as it will be created on the fly. Here's an example that sets a property called USER_NAME.

```
<Control
    Id="myEdit"
    Type="Edit"
    Property="USER_NAME"
    Height="17"
    Width="100"
    X="50"
    Y="50" />
```

It looks like this:

You can see this property being created by keeping a log of the install and then searching it for the name of the property. Here's the entry:

```
MSI (c) (54:98) [13:33:25:734]: PROPERTY CHANGE: Adding USER_NAME
property. Its value is 'Nick'.
```

If you're collecting a password or other sensitive data, you can hide the user's input by setting the Control's `Password` attribute to `yes`. This will only show asterisks (*) as the user types. To be even more secure, you can declare the property before and set its `Hidden` attribute to `yes`. That way, the value won't be visible in the install log either.

```
<Control
    Id="myPassword"
    Type="Edit"
    Property="USER_PASSWORD"
    Password="yes"
    Height="17"
    Width="100"
    X="50"
    Y="50" />
```

You can also limit the number of characters that the user can enter by adding the maximum number in curly brackets to the `Text` attribute. This can even be combined with a `TextStyle`, as in the next example:

```
<Control
    Id="myEdit"
    Type="Edit"
    Text="{\Tahoma_Bold}{50}"
    Height="17"
    Width="100"
    X="50"
    Y="50"
    Property="MY_PROPERTY" />
```

MaskedEdit

The `MaskedEdit` control is used with the `ValidateProductID` standard action to validate a product serial number. To use it you'll first need to define a **mask**, which is the pattern that the user's input must match. You'll define this with a `Property` element called `PIDTemplate`. Be sure to mark it as `Hidden` so that the user can't see the mask in the install log.

Here's a mask that says the user must enter three numbers, a dash, three numbers, another dash, and then four numbers. The pound signs (#) stand for numbers and the dashes are literal characters.

```
<Property Id="PIDTemplate" Hidden="yes">
   <![CDATA[<###-###-####>]]>
</Property>
```

The following table explains the characters that have special meaning in a mask.

Symbol	Meaning
#	Can be any number.
&	Can be any letter.
?	Can be a number or letter.
^	Can be any letter, but it will always be converted to uppercase.
@	Creates a random number. This is only used in the "hidden" part of the mask.
<	Marks the beginning of the visible text box (visible part of the mask).
>	Marks the end of the visible text box.

In the previous example, our mask began with the less than symbol (<) and ended with the greater than symbol (>). These mark the beginning and end of the part of the mask that the user must match. You can also add characters before and after this part and these extra characters will be added to what the user enters. For example, the next mask prepends "12345" to the beginning of user's input and five random numbers to the end.

```
12345<###-###-####>@@@@@
```

To use this in a `MaskedEdit` control, set the Control's `Text` attribute to the ID of the property. Surround it with square brackets.

```
<Control
    Id="myMaskedEdit"
    Type="MaskedEdit"
    Text="[PIDTemplate]"
    Property="PIDKEY"
```

```
Height="17"
Width="150"
X="50"
Y="50" />
```

Here's what it looks like:

As we're using a property called PIDKEY and a mask called PIDTemplate, the ValidateProductID action will run and check the value. If it's a match, a new property called ProductID will be set that combines the user's input with the hidden characters in the mask. If not, that property won't be set. Either way, you'll know if the user's input was valid. You would expect to see this in the log:

```
Property(C): PIDKEY = 123-456-7890
Property(C): ProductID = 12345-123-456-7890-64010
```

From here, you could execute a custom action that truly checks the serial number. For example, you could write a C# method that calls a Web Service, passing it the serial number, to evaluate its validity. You'd likely add a conditional statement to this custom action so that it only runs if ProductID has been set. Be aware that because you're collecting the number during the UI, ValidateProductID won't have a chance to validate it until it runs in the Execute sequence. So, your custom action should run after that.

PathEdit

A PathEdit control is used to change the path that one of your Directory elements points to. To use it, the Directory must have an ID that's a public property, meaning it must be uppercase. Suppose that this was our directory structure:

```
<Directory Id="TARGETDIR" Name="SourceDir">
   <Directory Id="ProgramFilesFolder">
      <Directory Id="INSTALLLOCATION"
         Name="Amazing Software" />
   </Directory>
</Directory>
```

Here, our main install directory has an ID of INSTALLLOCATION. Now, we can reference this directory in the Property attribute of our control.

```
<Control
    Id="myPathEdit"
    Type="PathEdit"
    Property="INSTALLLOCATION"
    Height="17"
    Width="150"
    X="50"
    Y="50" />
```

Here's what it looks like:

C:\Program Files (x86)\Awesome Software\

The user can edit this and when they do the installation path will be changed. There's just one thing: The installer won't know that it's changed. To alert it, we need to fire the SetTargetPath event and pass it our new path. This is best called by a PushButton so let's add one.

```
<Control Id="OKButton" Type="PushButton" Height="17"
    Width="56" X="50" Y="70" Text="OK">

    <Publish Event="SetTargetPath" Value="INSTALLLOCATION">
        1
    </Publish>
</Control>
```

The PushButton publishes the SetTargetPath event with a Value set to the ID of our directory. When the user clicks it, the new path will be set.

CheckBox

A CheckBox control is a checkbox that the user can click to set a property. You'll specify which property to set with the Property attribute and what to set it *to* with the CheckBoxValue attribute. If you want to stress that this value is meant to be a number, set the Integer attribute to yes. Here's an example:

```
<Control
    Id="myCheckbox"
    Type="CheckBox"
    Property="myCheckboxResult"
```

```
CheckBoxValue="my value"
Text="Check the box please."
X="50"
Y="50"
Height="10"
Width="150" />
```

The Text attribute is the text that appears to the right of the checkbox and explains what the box is for. Be sure to make the control wide enough to fit all of this text in. Here's what it looks like:

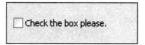

When the user checks the box, the property myCheckboxResult will be set to my value. Deselecting the box will delete the property. If you declare the property beforehand with a Property element, the box will be checked by default.

```
<Property Id="myCheckboxResult" Value="my value" />
```

RadioButtonGroup

A RadioButtonGroup control creates a list of radio buttons, only one of which can be selected at a time. As one of the buttons has to be selected by default, you must create a Property element first and reference it on the control. Below, a Property element is created with a value of 1. The radio button with that value will be selected as the default.

```
<Property Id="buttonGroup" Value="1" />
```

To reference this property, set the Control element's Property attribute to its ID.

```
<Control
    Id="myRadioGroup"
    Type="RadioButtonGroup"
    Property="buttonGroup"
    Height="100"
    Width="100"
    X="50"
    Y="50">
</Control>
```

Now to add our radio buttons. Although you can define them outside of the Control element—by instead adding them inside the UI element--it's more common to add them as children to the Control. Each button is created with a RadioButton element that sets the text to display next to it with the `Text` attribute and the value the property will be set to with the `Value` attribute. They're all held inside a `RadioButtonGroup` element that also references our property. Here's our control has three radio buttons nested inside:

```
<Control
    Id="myRadioGroup"
    Type="RadioButtonGroup"
    Property="buttonGroup"
    Width="100"
    Height="100"
    X="50"
    Y="50">

    <RadioButtonGroup Property="buttonGroup">
        <RadioButton Value="1" Text="One" Height="17" Width="50"
            X="0" Y="0" />
        <RadioButton Value="2" Text="Two" Height="17" Width="50"
            X="0" Y="20" />
        <RadioButton Value="3" Text="Three" Height="17"
            Width="50" X="0" Y="40" />
    </RadioButtonGroup>
</Control>
```

Here's what it looks like:

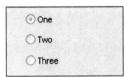

Selecting a different radio button will set the `buttonGroup` property to that button's value.

You can change the look of the buttons with the Control element's `HasBorder`, `Sunken`, and `RightAligned` attributes. **HasBorder** will put a `GroupBox` around the buttons, although you should then change the `X` and `Y` attributes of the `RadioButton` elements so that they have some padding. **Sunken** will place a sunken border edge around the buttons. **RightAligned** will place the text (`One`, `Two`, `Three`) on the left side of the buttons.

You also have the option of displaying icons next to your radio buttons instead of text. For that, replace the `Text` attribute on the `RadioButton` with an `Icon` attribute set to the ID of a Binary element that points to an `.ico` file.

ComboBox

A `ComboBox` control creates a drop-down list of selectable items. First, create a
Control element of Type "ComboBox" and set its `Property` attribute to the name
of a property that will store the item the user selects from the list. If you want your
items to be sorted alphabetically, set the `Sorted` attribute to `yes`. Also, be sure to
always set the `ComboList` property to `yes`. Here's an example where the option the
user selects will be stored in a property called `selectedItem`:

```
<Control
    Id="myComboBox"
    Type="ComboBox"
    Width="100"
    Height="50"
    X="50"
    Y="50"
    Property="selectedItem"
    ComboList="yes"
    Sorted="yes">

</Control>
```

The items in your list are defined with `ListItem` elements nested inside a `ComboBox`
element. Although you can place this outside of the Control element, it's clearer to
place it directly inside. The `ComboBox` element uses its `Property` attribute to tie it to
the control. Each `ListItem` sets a `Text` attribute, which is what gets displayed, and
a `Value` attribute that sets the value of the item. Let's add three items to our list:

```
<Control ... >

    <ComboBox Property="selectedItem">
        <ListItem Text="One" Value="1" />
        <ListItem Text="Two" Value="2" />
        <ListItem Text="Three" Value="3" />
    </ComboBox>

</Control>
```

If you want to set one of the items as the default, set a `Property` element with an ID
that matches the property name we're using in our control and a `Value` attribute that
matches the value of the `ListItem`. This, for example, would set the default item
selected to the `ListItem` that has a `Value` attribute to `2`:

```
<Property Id="selectedItem" Value="2" />
```

This is what it will look like:

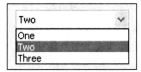

ListBox

A `ListBox` control is similar to a `ComboBox` except that the options are all displayed at once. Create a Control element and set its `Type` attribute to `ListBox`. This control also uses the `Property` and `Sorted` attributes like a `ComboBox`. You can add list items in the same way as before, using `ListItem` elements, except that this time they'll be contained inside a `ListBox` element.

```
<Control
    Id="myListBox"
    Type="ListBox"
    Width="100"
    Height="45"
    X="50"
    Y="50"
    Property="selectedItem"
    Sorted="yes">

    <ListBox Property="selectedItem">
        <ListItem Text="One" Value="1" />
        <ListItem Text="Two" Value="2" />
        <ListItem Text="Three" Value="3" />
    </ListBox>
</Control>
```

If you want to set a default selected item, create a `Property` element with an ID that matches your ListBox's property and a `Value` that's the same as the value of one of the `listItems`.

```
<Property Id="SelectedItem" Value="2" />
```

It looks like this:

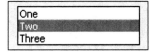

You can also add the `Sunken` attribute, set to yes, to give your `ListBox` a sunken border.

ListView

A `ListView` is like a `ListBox` except that it displays an icon *and* text for each
selectable option. For each item, you'll need to define a Binary element that
points to an icon file.

```
<Fragment>
  <UI>
    <Binary Id="face1" SourceFile="icons/alien1.ico" />
    <Binary Id="face2" SourceFile="icons/alien2.ico" />
    <Binary Id="face3" SourceFile="icons/alien3.ico" />
```

The next step is to create a Control element of Type "ListView" and set the `IconSize`
attribute to the size of your icons: `16`, `32`, or `48`. Also, set its `Property` attribute to
store the option the user selects.

```
<Control
    Id="myComboBox"
    Type="ListView"
    Width="200"
    Height="150"
    X="10"
    Y="10"
    Property="selectedItem"
    IconSize="32">

    <ListView Property="selectedItem">
        <ListItem Text="Alien 1" Icon="face1" Value="1" />
        <ListItem Text="Alien 2" Icon="face2" Value="2" />
        <ListItem Text="Alien 3" Icon="face3" Value="3" />
    </ListView>
</Control>
```

Here, we've added a `ListView` element inside the control with a `ListItem` for each
option. Each one gets a `Text` attribute for the displayed text, an `Icon` attribute that
references one of the Binary elements, and a `Value` attribute to hold the value of the
item. Here's what it looks like:

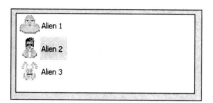

To set a default selected item, set a `Property` element with an ID that matches your control's `Property` attribute to the value of one of your `ListItems`. As you can see from this example, the image quality is usually poor, even if your `.ico` files are good.

DirectoryList

A `DirectoryList` control displays a directory and the folders that are in it. It can be used to set the path of one of your Directory elements. Here's one that sets a Directory with an ID of `INSTALLLOCATION`:

```
<Control
    Id="myDirectoryList"
    Type="DirectoryList"
    Property="INSTALLLOCATION"
    Height="150"
    Width="320"
    X="10"
    Y="30" />
```

If you add this to one of your dialogs, you won't be very impressed with the result. All you'll see is a blank box. That's because you're looking inside the `INSTALLLOCATION` directory—a directory that hasn't been installed yet and no folders exist inside it.

To get some benefit from this, we need to add some more controls around it to alert the user to where they are in the folder hierarchy. At the very least, you should add a `PathEdit` control that displays the current directory. Something like this:

```
<Control
    Id="myPath"
    Type="PathEdit"
    Height="17"
    Width="320"
    X="10"
    Y="10"
    Property="INSTALLLOCATION" />
```

The following image shows a dialog with even more bells and whistles:

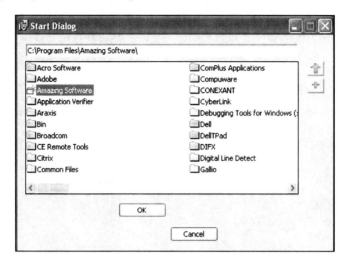

Here, the giant `DirectoryList` in the middle of the dialog is showing the **Program Files** folder after we navigated out of `INSTALLLOCATION` (whose friendly name is **Amazing Software**). Creating a button that navigates up one directory is done by adding a `PushButton` control to the same dialog as your `DirectoryList` and having it publish the `DirectoryListUp` event with a value of 0. In this example, it uses an icon that looks like an arrow pointing up.

```
<Control
    Id="DirUpButton"
    Type="PushButton"
    Height="17"
    Width="20"
    X="340"
    Y="30"
    Icon="yes"
    Text="upIcon"
    IconSize="16">

    <Publish Event="DirectoryListUp" Value="0" />
</Control>
```

There's also a button for creating new directories (labeled with a plus sign icon). It publishes the `DirectoryListNew` event.

```
<Control
    Id="NewDirButton"
    Type="PushButton"
    Height="17"
    Width="20"
    X="340"
    Y="50"
    Icon="yes"
    Text="addIcon"
    IconSize="16">

    <Publish Event="DirectoryListNew" Value="0" />
</Control>
```

Once the user has highlighted the directory that they want to set the path to, you'll need to save it. To do that, add a button that publishes the `SetTargetPath` event with a value set to the ID of the Directory element. Here, I add such a button and also have it close the current dialog (assuming this is a modal window). This is the **OK** button from the screenshot that we just saw.

```
<Control
    Id="OK_Button"
    Type="PushButton"
    Height="17"
    Width="56"
    X="120"
    Y="190"
    Text="OK">

    <Publish
        Event="SetTargetPath"
        Value="INSTALLLOCATION"
        Order="1">1</Publish>

    <Publish
        Event="EndDialog"
        Value="Return"
        Order="2">1</Publish>
</Control>
```

The WiX "Mondo" dialog set comes with a window just like this, called BrowseDlg. It looks like this:

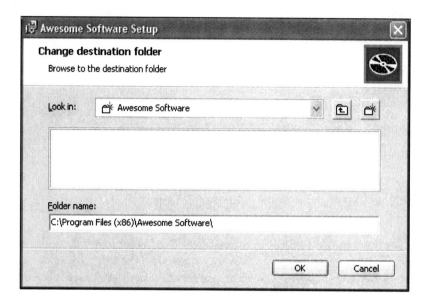

It also uses a DirectoryCombo control, which we'll cover next.

DirectoryCombo

A DirectoryCombo displays a drop-down list of directories and drives. You can use it to show the install directory and other drives it can be changed to. The next example shows the INSTALLLOCATION directory and any remote and fixed drives that are accessible.

```
<Control
    Id="myDirectoryCombo"
    Type="DirectoryCombo"
    Property="INSTALLLOCATION"
    Fixed="yes"
    Remote="yes"
    X="10"
    Y="10"
    Width="200"
    Height="100" />
```

Here's the result:

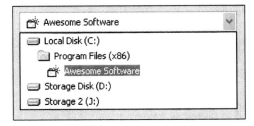

This example displays the available fixed (otherwise known as internal) and remote drives. The following table explains all of your options:

Attribute	Description
Fixed	List fixed internal hard drives.
Remote	List remote volumes.
Removable	List removable drives.
CDROM	List CD-ROM volumes.
Floppy	List floppy drives.
RAMDisk	List RAM disks.

A DirectoryCombo by itself cannot drill down into drives and their directories. Therefore, it works best when paired with another control that can, such as a DirectoryList.

SelectionTree

A SelectionTree displays a tree of the features defined in your installer. The user can use this to include or exclude certain features at install time. Be sure to add the Property attribute to the Control element, specifying your main install directory.

```
<Control
    Id="MySelectionTree"
    Type="SelectionTree"
    Property="INSTALLLOCATION"
    X="10"
    Y="30"
    Width="200"
    Height="120" />
```

Here is what it looks like:

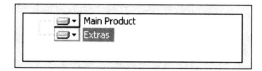

When you click on one of the features you're given the option to install it locally, install it as an advertised feature, or to not install it. The text for these options has to be defined by UIText elements inside the UI element. Define the following elements: MenuLocal, MenuAllLocal, MenuAdvertise, and MenuAbsent.

```
<UIText Id="MenuLocal">The feature will be installed    locally.
</UIText>

<UIText Id="MenuAllLocal">The feature and all of its    subfeatures
will be installed locally.</UIText>

<UIText Id="MenuAdvertise">The feature will be installed when
needed.</UIText>

<UIText Id="MenuAbsent">The feature will not be    installed.</UIText>
```

Your Feature elements, defined in your main .wxs file, can use the Description attribute to show information about what they contain, as in this example:

```
<Feature Id="ProductFeature" Title="Main Product" Level="1"
    Description="The main feature for the product">

    <ComponentRef Id="cmp_myFile" />
</Feature>
```

To show this on the dialog that has your SelectionTree, add a Text control that subscribes to the SelectionDescription event. The Subscribe element's Attribute must be set to Text. You can also show the size of the feature by subscribing another Text control to the SelectionSize event.

```
<Control Id="MySelectionDescription" Type="Text" X="220"
    Y="30" Width="100" Height="30">
    <Subscribe Event="SelectionDescription" Attribute="Text" />
</Control>

<Control Id="MySelectionSize" Type="Text" X="220" Y="70"
    Width="100" Height="50">
    <Subscribe Event="SelectionSize" Attribute="Text" />
</Control>
```

When you use `SelectionSize`, you have to define a few more `UIText` elements:

```
<UIText Id="Bytes">Bytes</UIText>
<UIText Id="KB">KB</UIText>
<UIText Id="MB">MB</UIText>
<UIText Id="GB">GB</UIText>

<UIText Id="SelChildCostPos">Feature will use [1] on your hard
drive.</UIText>
<UIText Id="SelChildCostNeg">Feature will free [1] on your     hard
drive.</UIText>
<UIText Id="SelChildCostPending">Figuring space needed for     this
feature...</UIText>
```

Here's the final result:

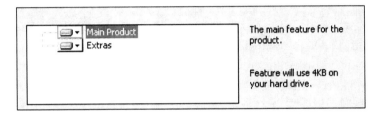

VolumeCostList

A `VolumeCostList` control displays available hard drives and the amount of disk space your installation will require on them.

```
<Control
    Id="myVolumeCostList"
    Type="VolumeCostList"
    Fixed="yes"
    Text="{50}{50}{70}{50}{50}"
    X="10"
    Y="10"
    Width="300"
    Height="100" />
```

In this example, we're only showing the space required on the fixed drives. Any of the attributes available to the `DirectoryCombo` control are available here. The `Text` attribute sets the widths of each column in the `VolumeCostList`. Here's what it looks like:

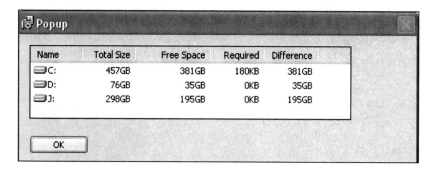

You'll need to define the following `UIText` elements inside the UI element, some of which are repeats from the `SelectionTree` control.

```
<UIText Id="Bytes">Bytes</UIText>
<UIText Id="KB">KB</UIText>
<UIText Id="MB">MB</UIText>
<UIText Id="GB">GB</UIText>

<UIText Id="VolumeCostAvailable">Free Space</UIText>
<UIText Id="VolumeCostDifference">Difference</UIText>
<UIText Id="VolumeCostRequired">Required</UIText>
<UIText Id="VolumeCostSize">Total Size</UIText>
<UIText Id="VolumeCostVolume">Name</UIText>
```

Typically, this control is shown on a pop up, or "modal", window during the installation. The user may click a button that says something like "Disk Cost" on the main window and the modal window will be displayed over top. There's a practical reason for doing this. If you try to show a `VolumeCostList` too soon, such as on the very first dialog, the numbers won't be calculated yet. You'd likely see a column of zeroes in the "Required" column. This is because these numbers aren't available until several properties, including `CostingComplete`, have been set. This happens during the costing phase at the beginning of the install.

VolumeSelectCombo

A `VolumeSelectCombo` control is a drop-down list that shows available drives. Using the `TARGETDIR` property, you might use this to change the drive that your files are installed to. In the next example, I display all fixed drives in the list:

You might pair it with a `PathEdit` control that shows the user what the install path is currently set to. If you don't want to let the user edit the `PathEdit` control, set its `Disabled` attribute to `yes`.

When the user selects a new option, the install path will be changed to use that drive.

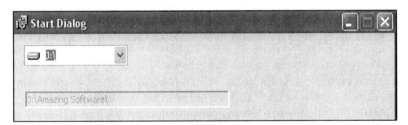

Notice that if they select the **D:** or **J:** drive in this example, we don't target the `Program Files` folder as that only exists on the `C:\` drive. Instead, we just install to the root folder of that drive. Here's the control's markup:

```
<Control
    Id="myVolumeSelectCombo"
    Type="VolumeSelectCombo"
    Property="TARGETDIR"
    Fixed="yes"
    Remote="yes"
    X="10"
    Y="10"
    Width="100"
    Height="17">
```

```
<Publish
    Property="INSTALLLOCATION"
    Value="[ProgramFilesFolder]Amazing Software\"
    Order="1">
        <![CDATA[TARGETDIR = "C:\"]]>
</Publish>

<Publish
    Property="INSTALLLOCATION"
    Value="[TARGETDIR]Amazing Software\"
    Order="2">
        <![CDATA[TARGETDIR <> "C:\"]]>
</Publish>

<Publish
    Event="SetTargetPath"
    Value="INSTALLLOCATION"
    Order="3">
        <![CDATA[1]]>
</Publish>
</Control>
```

In the Control element, we've set the `Type` to `VolumeSelectCombo` and the `Property` to `TARGETDIR`. By using the `Fixed` and `Remote` attributes, we're saying we only want to see those types of drives in the list.

The first `Publish` element sets the property `INSTALLLOCATION` to the path `[ProgramFilesFolder]Amazing Software\`, but only if the user has selected the `C:\` drive. In essence, what we're saying here is that we want to use the built-in `ProgramFilesFolder` property, which always maps back to the `C:\` drive anyway. The conditional statement inside the `Publish` element checks `TARGETDIR`.

The second Publish element is only used if the user has *not* chosen the `C:\` drive. In that case, we set `INSTALLLOCATION` to `[TARGETDIR]Amazing Software\`, which would be `J:\Amazing Software` for example.

The last `Publish` element calls the `SetTargetPath` event to save the new install path to the install session. Without that, the change wouldn't really be noticed by the installer.

Billboard

A `Billboard` control displays a slideshow to entertain the user while the installation is in progress. Unlike the other controls we've seen, which are shown during the UI sequence, a `Billboard` can only be used during the deferred stage of the Execute sequence. Therefore, you'll need to place it on a "Modeless" dialog shown at the end of your wizard, just like the progress dialog we saw in the last chapter.

Remember, to create this type of dialog, set the Dialog element's `Modeless` attribute to `yes`.

```
<Wix xmlns="http://schemas.microsoft.com/wix/2006/wi">
    <Fragment>
        <UI>
            <Dialog Id="BillboardDlg" Width="370" Height="270"
                Title="Amazing Software" NoMinimize="no"
                Modeless="yes">

                <!--Our Billboard will go here-->

            </Dialog>

            <InstallUISequence>
                <Show Dialog="BillboardDlg" After="InstallDlg" />
            </InstallUISequence>
        </UI>
    </Fragment>
</Wix>
```

Here, we've set up a new dialog called `BillboardDlg` and set it to be shown after `InstallDlg`. This will allow it to stay up as the installer enters the Execute phase. Remember to add a `DialogRef` to this dialog in `InstallDlg`:

```
<DialogRef Id="BillboardDlg" />
```

Now to add our `Billboard` control: Add a Control element of `Type Billboard` inside your new dialog and have it subscribe to the `SetProgress` event. This allows it to change its picture as the install progresses. Make sure that the Control's `Width` and `Height` attributes are big enough for your images to fit into.

```
<Dialog Id="BillboardDlg" ...>
    <Control Id="MyBillboard" Type="Billboard" X="10" Y="10"
        Height="200" Width="300">
        <Subscribe Event="SetProgress" Attribute="Progress" />
    </Control>
```

To set the images to display, add Binary elements that point to your image files.

```
<Binary Id="Image1" SourceFile="Image1.jpg" />
<Binary Id="Image2" SourceFile="Image2.jpg" />
<Binary Id="Image3" SourceFile="Image3.jpg" />
```

Next, add a `BillboardAction` element inside the UI element of `BillboardDlg.wxs`. Its `Id` will determine which Execute sequence action this image will be shown during. For example, this `BillboardAction` will be displayed during the `InstallFiles` action:

```
<BillboardAction Id="InstallFiles">
    <Billboard Id="BB1" Feature="ProductFeature">
        <Control
            Id="AgreeBitmap"
            Type="Bitmap"
            X="0"
            Y="0"
            Height="200"
            Width="300"
            Text="Image2" />
    </Billboard>
</BillboardAction>
```

The `Billboard` element inside the `BillboardAction` contains the Bitmap control to display. You can think of this as being one slide in the slideshow. By adding more Billboard elements, we get more slides—but only during the `InstallFiles` action. To cover other actions, you'll need to add more `BillboardAction` elements.

The `Billboard` element's `Feature` attribute tells the installer to only show this set of slides if that feature is being installed. The `Bitmap` control inside sets it `X` and `Y` attribute to `0` to line it up with the top left corner of the `Billboard` control. It's possible to have one `Billboard` element contain multiple controls, such as `Text` controls positioned over `Bitmap` controls. This would give you a layered effect of text and images.

Often, it takes a moment for anything in your billboard to be displayed because the Execute sequence first runs through its `immediate` phase, gathering information before proceeding to the `deferred` stage. During this immediate phase, your billboard won't be displayed. For that reason, you may decide to add a Bitmap or some text that is displayed from the very start. This will be replaced by the billboard when it's ready. The Bitmap control can be positioned in the same spot as where your Billboard will go.

```
<Dialog Id="BillboardDlg" ...>

    <Control
        Id="Image1"
        Type="Bitmap"
        X="10"
        Y="10"
        Height="200"
        Width="300"
        Text="Image1" />
```

ProgressBar

A `ProgressBar` control is a bar that incrementally fills with tick marks to illustrate the installation's progress. Like the Billboard control, a ProgressBar should appear on a Modeless dialog that's sequenced as the last dialog during the UI phase. That way, it can remain up during the Execute sequence and show the progress of the `deferred` stage. The markup looks like this:

```
<Control Id="MyProgressBar" Type="ProgressBar" X="50" Y="50"
    Width="250" Height="20">
    <Subscribe Event="SetProgress" Attribute="Progress" />
</Control>
```

This control should subscribe to the `SetProgress` event so that it can update itself as the install continues. It looks like this:

If you add the `ProgressBlocks` attribute to the Control element, set to `yes`, the look changes:

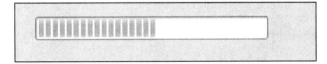

It's possible to reset and increment a `ProgressBar` from a C# custom action. This is done by using the Session object's `Message` method. This method can accept a variety of message types, including a Progress message. We'll use a `Record` object, which is a type of collection, to set our message. You can find documentation about setting Record objects at http://msdn.microsoft.com/en-us/library/aa370354%28VS.85%29.aspx. The following code, where the first value in the record is 0, resets the ProgressBar:

```
private static void ResetProgress(Session session)
{
    Record record = new Record(4);
    record[1] = "0"; // "Reset" message
    record[2] = "1000"; // total ticks
    record[3] = "0"; // forward motion
    record[4] = "0"; // execution is in progress
    session.Message(InstallMessage.Progress, record);
}
```

The `Message` method sets its type through the `InstallMessage` enumeration, which we've set to `Progress`. To increment the bar a certain number of ticks, set the record's first value to 2 and its second to the number of ticks to add:

```
private static void IncrementProgress(Session session, int ticks)
{
    Record record = new Record(2);
    record[1] = "2"; // "Increment" message
    record[2] = ticks.ToString(); // ticks to increment
    session.Message(InstallMessage.Progress, record);
}
```

You could then call these methods in your custom action:

```
[CustomAction]
public static ActionResult MyCustomAction(Session session)
{
    //reset bar
    ResetProgress(session);

    //do some stuff for the custom action...

    //add 100 tick marks
    IncrementProgress(session, 100);

    return ActionResult.Success;
}
```

If you'd rather have things happen more or less on their own without you having to specify each time how many tick marks to add, then we'll need to do things differently. This other way goes hand-in-hand with displaying info about what's happening in a Text control above the ProgressBar. First, add a Text control to your dialog that subscribes to the `ActionData` event:

```
<Control Id="InfoText" Type="Text" X="50" Y="130" Width="250"
Height="17">
    <Subscribe Event="ActionData" Attribute="Text" />
</Control>
<Control Id="MyProgressBar" Type="ProgressBar" X="50" Y="50"
    Width="250" Height="20">
    <Subscribe Event="SetProgress" Attribute="Progress" />
</Control>
```

This new control will display messages about what's going on at any point during the install. To get a message about your custom actions to show up, add a `ProgressText` element to you dialog, inside the UI element.

```
<ProgressText Action="MyCustomAction"
    Template="Doing Stuff: [1]" />
```

Its `Action` attribute tells the installer when to show this message (during which action) and `Template` is what to display. The [1] in the template is where your messages will fill in as your custom action executes.

Now, at the beginning of your custom action, set up how many tick marks to add for each update you send. Here's a method that does that:

```
private static void NumberOfTicksPerActionData(Session session, int
ticks)
{
    Record record = new Record(3);
    record[1] = "1"; // Bind progress bar to progress messages
    record[2] = ticks.ToString(); // number of ticks to move
                                   // for each message
    record[3] = "1"; // enable
    session.Message(InstallMessage.Progress, record);
}
```

The next method we create will do two things: display a message in the Text control and increment the ProgressBar:

```
private static void DisplayActionData(Session session, string message)
{
    Record record = new Record(1);
    record[1] = message;
    session.Message(InstallMessage.ActionData, record);
}
```

Here's a custom action that illustrates how they're used. So that you have time to see the messages get displayed, we'll have the code sleep for two seconds between each update.

```
[CustomAction]
public static ActionResult MyCustomAction(Session session)
{
    ResetProgress(session);
    NumberOfTicksPerActionData(session, 100);

    DisplayActionData(session, "Sleeping for two seconds...");
    System.Threading.Thread.Sleep(2000);

    DisplayActionData(session, "Sleeping for another two
seconds...");
    System.Threading.Thread.Sleep(2000);

    DisplayActionData(session, "This is my third message");
    System.Threading.Thread.Sleep(2000);
    return ActionResult.Success;
}
```

Here's the result:

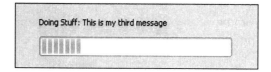

Summary

In this chapter, we discussed all of the available controls that you can use on your WiX dialogs. They range from simple lines and buttons to progress bars and billboards. With this knowledge, you can either create your own dialogs from scratch or add new controls to the dialogs that come with the WiX toolset's UIExtension library.

In the next chapter, we'll dig into the meaning of control events. These are used to subscribe a control to a particular Windows Installer event or to have a control publish one itself.

8
Tapping into Control Events

Windows Installer defines a limited number of events that your UI controls can listen out for or trigger. For example, a progress bar can listen for actions that say progress has taken place and then react by showing more ticks. Or, a button can trigger an action that closes the current window. Listening for an event is known as "subscribing" and triggering one is known as "publishing".

Because these events happen within `Control` elements they're known as **Control Events**. We've covered several examples of control events already, but we'll cover others that you haven't seen and show how the whole process works. In this chapter, you will:

- Use the `Publish` and `Subscribe` elements to connect to events
- Get some hands on experience with both types

Publish element

To trigger an event, nest a `Publish` element inside a `Control` element. For example, to cause a `PushButton` control to open a new modal window, add a `Publish` element inside it that specifies the `SpawnDialog` event with its `Event` attribute, as in the following snippet:

```
<Control Id="ShowPopupButton"
         Type="PushButton"
         Text="Show Popup"
         Height="17"
         Width="56"
         X="245"
         Y="243"
         Default="yes">
    <Publish Event="SpawnDialog"
         Value="PopupDlg">1</Publish>
</Control>
```

You'll find that different events require different arguments in the `Value` attribute. Here, `Value` takes the `Id` of the `Dialog` element you want to open. Also, notice that we've used a conditional statement as the inner text of the `Publish` element. Setting it to 1 means that it will always be true and always trigger the event. However, you can also test that a property, perhaps set by another control event or a custom action, evaluates to some expected value. If the condition is false, the event won't be published. Here's an example:

```
<Control ... >
  <Publish Event="SpawnDialog"
           Value="PopupDlg">
    MY_PROPERTY = 1
  </Publish>
</Control>
```

This event will be published only if `MY_PROPERTY` is equal to 1. The following table lists the events that can be published and which controls can use them:

Event	Used by	What it does
AddLocal	PushButton CheckBox SelectionTree	Sets which features to install locally
AddSource	PushButton CheckBox SelectionTree	Sets which features to install and run from source
CheckExistingTargetPath	PushButton SelectionTree	Checks if an existing path, given in Value, can be written to
CheckTargetPath	PushButton SelectionTree	Given a file path via the Value attribute, checks if it's a valid path
DirectoryListNew	PushButton	Create a new folder in a DirectoryList control. Value set to 0
DirectoryListOpen	PushButton	Selects a folder in a DirectoryList control. Value set to 0
DirectoryListUp	PushButton	Moves up one directory in a DirectoryList control. Value set to 0

Event	Used by	What it does
DoAction	PushButton	Executes the custom action specified by Value.
	CheckBox	
	SelectionTree	
EnableRollback	PushButton	Turn rollback on or off, depending on if Value is True or False.
	SelectionTree	
EndDialog	PushButton	Closes the current dialog window. Value can be exit, retry, ignore or return.
	SelectionTree	
NewDialog	PushButton	Closes current dialog and shows dialog specified by Value.
	SelectionTree	
Reinstall	PushButton	Sets which features to reinstall.
	SelectionTree	
ReinstallMode	PushButton	Specifies a string defining the type of reinstall to do.
	SelectionTree	
Remove	PushButton	Sets which features to remove.
	CheckBox	
	SelectionTree	
Reset	PushButton	Undoes any changes on controls on the current window. Value set to 0.
	SelectionTree	
SelectionBrowse	PushButton	Spawns a Browse dialog
SetInstallLevel	PushButton	Sets an integer that defines the install level for features.
	SelectionTree	
SetTargetPath	PushButton	Sets the selected path. Value set to the Directory element's Id.
	SelectionTree	
SpawnDialog	PushButton	Displays the modal dialog window specified by Value.
	SelectionTree	
SpawnWaitDialog	PushButton	Displays a dialog while a condition is false.
	SelectionTree	
ValidateProductID	PushButton	Validates the ProductID property.
	SelectionTree	

It's possible to stack several `Publish` elements inside a single control. For example, the following `PushButton` first calls the `DoAction` event and then the `SpawnDialog` event. Use the `Order` attribute to set which event occurs first:

```
<Control  Id="ShowPopupButton"
          Type="PushButton"
          Text="Show Popup"
          Height="17"
          Width="56"
          X="245"
          Y="243"
          Default="yes">

   <Publish Event="DoAction"
            Value="MyCustomAction"
            Order="1">1</Publish>

   <Publish Event="SpawnDialog"
            Value="PopupDlg"
            Order="2">1</Publish>
</Control>
```

If the `MyCustomAction` custom action had set a property, you could have evaluated it in the inner text of the `SpawnDialog` event. If the statement then evaluated to false, the `SpawnDialog` event wouldn't be called. Notice that both `Publish` elements in this example use an `Order` attribute, causing the `DoAction` event to be called first.

Subscribe element

Some events can't be published, only listened for. In that case, you'll use a `Subscribe` element inside a `Control` element. Use its `Event` attribute to specify the event to listen for and `Attribute` to set the required argument. The next example shows a `ProgressBar` control that subscribes to the `SetProgress` event. Whenever a standard or custom action notifies the installer that progress has been made, the `ProgressBar` will know about it and add more ticks.

```
<Control  Id="MyProgressBar"
          Type="ProgressBar"
          X="50"
          Y="50"
          Width="200"
          Height="20"
          ProgressBlocks="yes">
   <Subscribe Event="SetProgress"
              Attribute="Progress" />
</Control>
```

Unlike the `Publish` element, the `Subscribe` element can't have a conditional statement as its inner text. A single control can, however, subscribe to more than one event. One example is to subscribe a `Text` control to both the `ScriptInProgress` and `TimeRemaining` events. The first will display a message while the Execute sequence is being loaded and the second will show the time left until completion.

The following table lists the events that can be subscribed to and their required arguments.

Event	Used by	Attribute argument
`ActionData`	Text control to show info about latest action.	`Text`
`ActionText`	Text control to show name of latest action.	`Text`
`IgnoreChange`	`DirectoryCombo` to not update itself if folder is highlighted but not opened in neighboring `DirectoryList`.	`IgnoreChange`
`ScriptInProgress`	Text control to show a message while the Execute sequence loads up.	`Visible`
`SelectionAction`	Text control to describe the highlighted item in a neighboring `SelectionTree`.	`Text`
`SelectionDescription`	Text control to display the description of a highlighted feature in a neighboring `SelectionTree`.	`Text`
`SelectionNoItems`	`PushButton` to disable itself if no items are present in a neighboring `SelectionTree`. (Personally, I've found that this event has no effect.).	`Enabled`
`SelectionPath`	Text control to display the path of the highlighted item in a neighboring `SelectionTree`. Works if item is set to be run from source.	`Text`
`SelectionPathOn`	Text control to display whether or not there's a path for the highlighted item in a neighboring `SelectionTree`.	`Visible`
`SelectionSize`	Text control to display the size of the highlighted item in a neighboring `SelectionTree`.	`Text`
`SetProgress`	`ProgressBar` to increment ticks.	`Progress`
`TimeRemaining`	Text control to display time remaining in installation.	`TimeRemaining`

Publish events

In the following sections, we'll take a look at several events that you can publish. This should give you a good idea about how the `Publish` element works.

AddLocal

The `SelectionTree` control can be used to show the available features in your install package and gives the user the ability to select which ones they want. Windows Installer keeps track of which features to install through the `ADDLOCAL` property, which is a comma-delimited list of features to install locally. When it comes to the `SelectionTree`, all of the logic of setting the `ADDLOCAL` property is handled for you behind the scenes. However, if you wanted to, you could do away with the `SelectionTree` and create your own device for including features. For that, you'd publish the `AddLocal` control event.

`AddLocal`, like the property by the same name, can be used to set which features get installed. You'll set the `Publish` element's `Value` attribute to either the `Id` of a single `Feature` element or the string `ALL`, which will include all features. You can publish the event more than once to include additional features.

The next example puts this into action. Two `CheckBox` controls set properties indicating a certain feature to be installed. Later, we'll evaluate whether or not these checkboxes were checked via these properties and set the value of the `AddLocal` event accordingly:

```
<Control Id="Feat1Box"
        Type="CheckBox"
        X="10"
        Y="120"
        Width="75"
        Height="10"
        Text="Main Product"
        Property="MainProductFeatureChecked"
        CheckBoxValue="on" />

<Control Id="Feat2Box"
        Type="CheckBox"
        X="10"
        Y="140"
        Width="75"
        Height="10"
        Text="Extra Stuff"
        Property="ExtraStuffFeatureChecked"
        CheckBoxValue="on" />
```

Now, use a PushButton control to trigger the AddLocal event to include only the features in the install for which a box was checked. We use conditional statements inside the Publish elements for this:

```
<Control Id="OKButton"
         Type="PushButton"
         Text="OK"
         Height="17"
         Width="56"
         X="220"
         Y="173">

    <Publish Event="Remove"
             Value="ALL"
             Order="1">1</Publish>

    <Publish Event="AddLocal"
             Value="ProductFeature"
             Order="2">
      <![CDATA[MainProductFeatureChecked]]>
    </Publish>

    <Publish Event="AddLocal"
             Value="ExtraStuff"
             Order="3">
      <![CDATA[ExtraStuffFeatureChecked]]>
    </Publish>

    <Publish Event="EndDialog"
             Value="Return"
             Order="4">1</Publish>
</Control>
```

If we add these controls to a modal dialog window, with a SelectionTree so that we can see the changes, it would look like this:

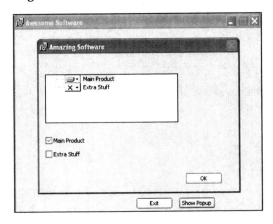

When you click the **OK** button, the checkboxes will be evaluated, the AddLocal event called, features set, and the window will close. You must reopen the modal window to see the changes in the SelectionTree since dialog windows aren't smart enough to redraw themselves dynamically.

So, what happened? Here's the process in detail:

- The first Publish element triggers an event called Remove to remove all features from the install. This gets us to a clean state.

```
<Publish Event="Remove"
         Value="ALL"
         Order="1">1</Publish>
```

- The second Publish element checks if the MainProductFeatureChecked property has been set and if it has, calls the AddLocal event for the ProductFeature feature. This adds that feature to the list to install.

```
<Publish Event="AddLocal"
         Value="ProductFeature"
         Order="2">
  <![CDATA[MainProductFeatureChecked]]>
</Publish>
```

- The third Publish element does the same for the ExtraStuff feature.

```
<Publish Event="AddLocal"
         Value="ExtraStuff"
         Order="3">
  <![CDATA[ExtraStuffFeatureChecked]]>
</Publish>
```

- The last Publish element calls the EndDialog event with a value of Return, which closes the modal window.

```
<Publish Event="EndDialog"
         Value="Return"
         Order="4">1</Publish>
```

DoAction

The DoAction event calls a custom action that you've declared elsewhere in your markup. For example, suppose we'd defined a custom action called CA_ShowMessage that simply displays a message box with the text **You clicked?**:

```
<CustomAction Id="CA_ShowMessage"
              Script="vbscript"
              Execute="immediate">
  <![CDATA[msgbox "You clicked?"]]>
</CustomAction>
```

We could then trigger this action with a `PushButton` by publishing the `DoAction` event with a value of `CA_ShowMessage`.

```
<Control Id="DoActionButton"
         Type="PushButton"
         X="120"
         Y="100"
         Width="56"
         Height="17"
         Text="Click Me!">
  <Publish Event="DoAction"
           Value="CA_ShowMessage">1</Publish>
</Control>
```

Clicking the button will show the message:

Often, you'll use this technique to validate a property or set one before other events are triggered.

EndDialog

The `EndDialog` event, which is used on a `PushButton` control, is used to close the current dialog window and can accept one of four values: `Exit`, `Retry`, `Ignore` or `Return`.

In practice, you'll only ever use `Exit` or `Return`. The other two are used by the `FilesInUse` dialog and don't have much application elsewhere. `Exit` closes the current dialog and ends the installation. It's usually used on a **Cancel** button, as in this example:

```
<Control Id="CancelButton"
         Type="PushButton"
         Text="Exit"
         Height="17"
         Width="56"
         X="180"
         Y="243"
         Cancel="yes">
  <Publish Event="EndDialog"
           Value="Exit">1</Publish>
</Control>
```

A `Value` of `Return` closes the current window, but continues the installation. It's usually used on an **Install** button on the last dialog in your UI. You'll also use it to close modal dialog windows and return control to the parent window. Here's an example **Install** button:

```
<Control Id="InstallButton"
        Type="PushButton"
        Text="Install"
        Height="17"
        Width="56"
        X="245"
        Y="243"
        Default="yes">
  <Publish Event="EndDialog"
        Value="Return">1</Publish>
</Control>
```

NewDialog

The `NewDialog` event closes the current window and opens the one specified by the `Value` attribute. Typically, you'll use this for **Next** and **Back** buttons that move you from one dialog to another. For example, the following `PushButton` control opens a dialog called `NextDlg`:

```
<Control Id="NextButton"
        Type="PushButton"
        Text="Next"
        Height="17"
        Width="56"
        X="180"
        Y="243">
  <Publish Event="NewDialog"
        Value="NextDlg">1</Publish>
</Control>
```

This is the perfect place to add a conditional statement so that the user may see one dialog instead of another, depending on the state of some property. In the next example, if the property USE_SQLSERVER is set, then the dialog `SetSqlCredentialsDlg` is shown; otherwise, we show the `NoSqlDlg` dialog:

```
<Control Id="NextButton"
        Type="PushButton"
        Text="Next"
        Height="17"
        Width="56"
```

```
            X="180"
            Y="243">

    <Publish Event="NewDialog"
             Value="SetSqlCredentialsDlg">USE_SQLSERVER</Publish>

    <Publish Event="NewDialog"
             Value="NoSqlDlg">NOT USE_SQLSERVER</Publish>
</Control>
```

Here, I use a different conditional statement for each `Publish` element. The first evaluates to true only if the `USE_SQLSERVER` property has been set and the second only if it hasn't.

Publishing a property

There's another event that you can publish, called `SetProperty`, that's used to assign a property's value. However, in WiX you won't set it in the normal way, but rather use the `Publish` element's `Property` and `Value` attributes. For example, here's a button that sets the value of a property called `MYPROPERTY` to `123`:

```
<Control Id="MyButton"
         Type="PushButton"
         Text="Click me!"
         Height="17"
         Width="56"
         X="50"
         Y="50">
    <Publish Property="MYPROPERTY"
             Value="123">1</Publish>
</Control>
```

Subscribe events

In the following sections, we'll look at the `Subscribe` element.

ScriptInProgress

You can subscribe a `Text` control to the `ScriptInProgress` event so that its text is only shown during the "immediate" phase of the `InstallExecuteSequence`. This is when that sequence prepares itself for its "deferred" stage by creating a rollback script containing all of the actions it will need to perform.

You'd use this technique on a progress bar dialog. As you can see in the next example, all it does is show some text telling the user that things are gearing up.

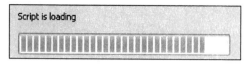

Here, we have a dialog called `ProgressDlg` that is shown during the `InstallExecuteSequence`. It contains the following markup:

```xml
<?xml version="1.0" encoding="UTF-8"?>
<Wix xmlns="http://schemas.microsoft.com/wix/2006/wi">
  <Fragment>
    <UI>
      <Dialog Id="ProgressDlg"
              Width="370"
              Height="270"
              Title="Awesome Software"
              Modeless="yes">

        <Control Id="CancelButton"
                 Type="PushButton"
                 TabSkip="no"
                 Text="Cancel"
                 Height="17"
                 Width="56"
                 X="180"
                 Y="243"
                 Cancel="yes">
          <Publish Event="EndDialog" Value="Exit" />
        </Control>

        <Control Id="MyProgressBar"
                 Type="ProgressBar"
                 X="70"
                 Y="150"
                 Width="200"
                 Height="20"
                 ProgressBlocks="yes">
          <Subscribe Event="SetProgress"
                     Attribute="Progress" />
        </Control>

        <Control Id="InfoText"
```

```
                Type="Text"
                X="70"
                Y="130"
                Width="200"
                Height="17"
                Text="Script is loading">
        <Subscribe Event="ScriptInProgress"
                Attribute="Visible" />
      </Control>
    </Dialog>

    <InstallUISequence>
      <Show Dialog="ProgressDlg"
            Before="ExecuteAction" />
    </InstallUISequence>
  </UI>
  </Fragment>
</Wix>
```

The control named `InfoText` on `ProgressDlg` subscribes to the `ScriptInProgress` event. `Attribute` is set to `Visible`. Even though we're using a `Text` control to subscribe to this event, it only works if there's a `ProgressBar` nearby. This is often the case with the `Subscribe` element, there must be a neighboring control that gives the event meaning.

SelectionAction

The `SelectionAction` event is used by a `Text` control to display the current action state of the highlighted feature in a neighboring `SelectionTree`. In the following example, a feature called **Main Product** has been set to be installed locally. A `Text` control to the right displays the message **Feature will be installed locally**. It subscribes to `SelectionAction`.

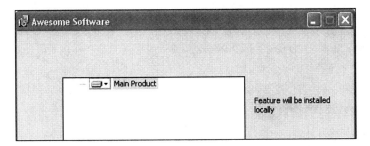

The first thing to do is add three new `UIText` elements inside the `UI` element on your dialog. These should have the following `Id` values:

- `SelAbsentLocal`
- `SelAbsentAdvertise`
- `SelAbsentAbsent`

These will contain the generic text to display as the user changes the action state of a feature. We can set them as follows:

```
<UIText Id="SelAbsentLocal">
  Feature will be installed locally
</UIText>

<UIText Id="SelAbsentAdvertise">
  Feature will be installed as advertised
</UIText>

<UIText Id="SelAbsentAbsent">
  Feature will not be installed
</UIText>
```

Our `Text` control, which must be on the same dialog as the `SelectionTree`, subscribes to `SelectionAction` and sets the `Subscribe` element's `Attribute` to `Text`, as in the following:

```
<Control Id="SelectionAction"
         Type="Text"
         X="260"
         Y="70"
         Height="50"
         Width="100">
   <Subscribe Event="SelectionAction"
              Attribute="Text" />
</Control>
```

As the user changes a feature's inclusion in the `SelectionTree`, the text will change to reflect the new status.

TimeRemaining

The `TimeRemaining` event allows you to display the time left before the installation is complete. It looks like the following:

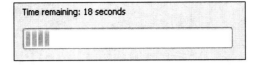

You'll need to add a `UIText` element with an `Id` of `TimeRemaining` and inner text defining the text to show. It should follow this format:

```
<UIText Id="TimeRemaining">
  <![CDATA[Time remaining: {{[1] minutes }{[2] seconds}]]>
</UIText>
```

The inner text defines a template in which the minutes and seconds of remaining time are shown. Next, add a `Text` control that subscribes to the `TimeRemaining` event. Its `Publish` element should set `Attribute` to `TimeRemaining` too.

```
<Control Id="TimeRemaining"
        Type="Text"
        X="70"
        Y="130"
        Width="200"
        Height="17">
  <Subscribe Event="TimeRemaining"
          Attribute="TimeRemaining" />
</Control>
```

The standard actions in the `InstallExecuteSequence` don't publish any `TimeRemaining` data. So, to see the effect, you'll have to publish it yourself from a custom action. Add a new C# custom action project to your solution and add the following code to it:

```
namespace CustomAction1
{
    using Microsoft.Deployment.WindowsInstaller;
    public class CustomActions
    {
        [CustomAction]
        public static ActionResult ShowTime(Session session)
        {
            ResetProgress(session);
            NumberOfTicksPerActionData(session, 100);
            DisplayActionData(session, "Message 1");
            System.Threading.Thread.Sleep(2000);

            DisplayActionData(session, "Message 2");
            System.Threading.Thread.Sleep(2000);
```

```
                DisplayActionData(session, "Message 3");
                System.Threading.Thread.Sleep(2000);

                return ActionResult.Success;
            }

            private static void ResetProgress(Session session)
            {
                Record record = new Record(4);
                record[1] = "0";
                record[2] = "1000";
                record[3] = "0";
                record[4] = "0";
                session.Message(InstallMessage.Progress, record);
            }

            private static void NumberOfTicksPerActionData(
                                        Session session, int ticks)
            {
                Record record = new Record(3);
                record[1] = "1";
                record[2] = ticks.ToString();
                record[3] = "1";
                session.Message(InstallMessage.Progress, record);
            }

            private static void DisplayActionData(Session session,
                                                string message)
            {
                Record record = new Record(1);
                record[1] = message;
                session.Message(InstallMessage.ActionData, record);
            }
        }
    }
```

This sets up a custom action called ShowTime and three methods to support it. The first, ResetProgressBar, resets the ticks in the ProgressBar control to zero and sets up how many tick marks there should be in total. The second, NumberOfTicksPerActionData, sets up how many ticks to add for each action performed. The third, DisplayActionData, shows a message that any controls subscribing to the ActionData event will pick up. The TimeRemaining event uses all of this information to gauge how much time it should allot for this custom action.

When you add this custom action to the deferred stage of the InstallExecuteSequence, you'll see that our Text control that's monitoring the TimeRemaining event will update itself with the approximate time left. Here's the markup to add to your main .wxs file to include this new custom action:

```
<Binary Id="CA_DLL"
        SourceFile="CustomAction1.CA.dll" />

<CustomAction Id="CA_ShowTime"
              BinaryKey="CA_DLL"
              DllEntry="ShowTime"
              Execute="deferred"
              Return="check" />

<InstallExecuteSequence>
  <Custom Action="CA_ShowTime"
          After="InstallInitialize">NOT Installed</Custom>
</InstallExecuteSequence>
```

Here, the name of the assembly file is CustomAction1.CA.dll, but you should change this if yours is different.

Summary

In this chapter, we looked at the Publish and Subscribe elements that are used to trigger and listen for Control Events. Knowing the exact arguments to use for each event can be tricky, so be sure to consult the Windows Installer SDK to get specifics. Probably one of the most powerful events is DoAction, which lets you publish your own custom action. Pairing this with the ability to stack several events inside one control and to set the order in which they're called gives you quite a bit of latitude.

In the next chapter, we will explore the WiX command line. This will give you the knowledge to compile and link your project even without Visual Studio.

9
Working from the Command Line

Creating an MSI file with WiX takes two steps: compiling your source files and then linking them together into a single package. A tool called Candle handles the compiling, transforming your `.wxs` files into `.wixobj` files. The linking phase is handled by a tool called Light.

In this chapter, we'll discuss the following topics:

- The arguments to use when calling Candle and Light from the command line
- Compile-time and link-time variables
- How to build an MSI without using Visual Studio

Candle.exe

Candle, the WiX compiler, can be run from the command line to build your WiX source files. Behind the scenes, Visual Studio is really just calling this tool for you. When you use it yourself you can give it any of a number of arguments, which we'll discuss in the next section.

To make things easy, you should consider adding the WiX `bin` directory (under `Program Files/Windows Installer XML v3/bin`) to your computer's PATH environment variable. This is where Candle and all the rest of the WiX tools are. Right-click on **My Computer** in your **Start** menu, select **Properties**, then the **Advanced** tab, and click **Environment Variables**. From there, you can find the PATH variable and append the path of the `bin` directory. Note that WiX adds an environment variable during its installation called `%WIX%` that points to its main folder, but not its `bin` folder.

Command-line arguments (compiling)

In this section, we'll look at the basic syntax for using Candle on the command line. This is helpful in Visual Studio, too, as you can add extra arguments via your project's `Properties` page. You can see information about Candle by opening a command prompt and typing `candle -?`. The general usage is:

```
candle.exe [-?] [-nologo] [-out outputFile] sourceFile [sourceFile ...]
[@responseFile]
```

As you can see, you should specify an output file, via the `-out` flag, to give a name to the `.wixobj` file that's created. The `SourceFile` argument refers to the name of the `.wxs` file you want to compile. You should also give the `-arch` flag, set to `x64` or `x86`, to set the target processor architecture of your software. If you've used any WiX extensions, such as the `WixUIExtension`, you should specify its path with the `-ext` flag. Here's a simple example that compiles one file:

```
candle.exe -arch x86 -out ".\wixobj\Product.wixobj" -ext "WixUIExtension.
dll" Product.wxs
```

You can also use a wildcard (*) to compile all `.wxs` files in a directory and then output the `.wixobj` files to another directory. In that case, the `.wixobj` files will have the same name as the `.wxs` files. Here's an example:

```
candle.exe -arch x86 -out ".\wixobj\" ".\*.wxs"
```

There are a number of optional flags available. We'll discuss them briefly.

-arch

The `-arch` flag sets the architecture for the build. This is important because certain elements in the MSI package, such as components, need to marked as 64-bit if they are to be installed in a computer's 64-bit directories. This flag, if set to `x64`, also causes the compiler to check that you've specified an installer version of 2.0.0 or higher, as this is the minimum version needed for a 64-bit package.

-d

This `-d` flag, for "define", allows you to set compile-time variables. These are translated into their literal values when Candle creates the `.wixobj` file. We'll discuss this in more detail later in the chapter.

-ext

This flag is used to include a WiX extensions, such as `WixUIExtension` or `WixUtilExtension`. Include it when your source file depends on a WiX extension.

-fips

Enabling FIPS compliant algorithms with the `-fips` flag causes the installer to switch its hashing algorithm from MD5 to SHA1. FIPS, which stands for Federal Information Processing Standards Publications, is a governmental standard for ensuring security and interoperability when hashing data.

-I

A **WiX include file**, with a `.wxi` extension, can be created to hold preprocessor variables and conditional statements. There's a Visual Studio template for it. Although you can add this file to your project with the **Add a Reference** window, a more dynamic way is to add the `-I` flag on the command line, set to the path of the directory that contains the `.wxi` file. Candle will search that directory for the file.

Reference the file in your markup with `<?include ?>` tags. For example, suppose you wanted to include a `.wxi` file in the `C:\` directory. You'd add `-I"C:\"` and then add the following line to one of your WiX source files:

```
<?include myIncludeFile.wxi ?>
```

-nologo

Candle prints its version number and copyright at the top its output. However, if you supply the `-nologo` flag this will be suppressed.

-o

The `-o` or `-out` argument tells Candle where to place the new `.wixobj` file after compiling the WiX source code and what the name of that file will be.

-p

An intermediate step performed by Candle is to process your `.wxs` file into a well-formed XML document. You can see this intermediate XML document by adding the `-p` flag.

-pedantic

Turning on "pedantic" messages with the `-pedantic` flag tells the compiler to show messages that you wouldn't normally see. Examples include having GUIDs with lowercase letters and not explicitly setting a KeyPath for a component.

-sfdvital

Ordinarily, all File elements in WiX are marked as "Vital". This means that if, during an installation, a file cannot be copied to the end-user's system, the installer won't be able to proceed. Setting the `-sfdvital` flag switches this default behavior off.

-ss

As Candle compiles your project, it validates it against the WiX schema found in `wix.xsd`. You can turn this validation off by adding the `-ss` flag.

-sw

If you don't care much about compiler warnings (maybe you only care about errors), you can suppress them with the `-sw` flag. Without any argument, all warnings will be suppressed. To exclude only a specific warning, reference its ID, such as, -sw1009. You can find a full list of errors and their message IDs by downloading the WiX source files, by opening the *Wix* solution and looking at `messages.xml`.

-trace

If you get a compile-time error, such as when an include file cannot be found, you may consider turning on trace logging.

-v

The `-v` flag, for "verbose", tells the compiler to display *Information* level messages during processing. As of WiX 3.0, these messages are mostly absent from Candle.

-wx

To treat all compile-time warnings as errors, add the `-wx` flag. You can also supply a specific message ID (from `messages.xml` in the WiX source files) to elevate only that particular warning to error status.

Response files

Sometimes, your calls to Candle will be simple and it won't be much trouble entering them on the command line. However, when you start adding optional arguments you could easily start to see them span several rows of the console window. In that case, you may find it easier to store your arguments in a **response file**, which can be a simple text file. Following is an example called `MyCommands.txt` that contains several compiler arguments.

```
-out "C:\MyProjects\Installer\obj"
-dConfig=Release
-trace
-arch x86
-ext "C:\Program Files\Windows Installer XML v3\bin\WixUtilExtension.
dll"
-ext "C:\Program Files\Windows Installer XML v3\bin\WixUIExtension.
dll"
```

You reference a response file by prefixing its name with the @ symbol. Here's an example:

```
candle.exe "C:\MyProjects\Installer\Product.wxs" @"C:\MyProjects\
Installer\MyCommands.txt"
```

.wixobj files

The compilation process ultimately produces a .wixobj file for every .wxs file. The linking phase will later combine all of the .wixobj files into a single MSI package. A .wixobj file consists of XML code with mainly table, row, and field elements. Together, these elements describe the rows in each table of the MSI database. The top-level element of a .wixobj file is wixObject.

```
<?xml version="1.0" encoding="utf-8"?>
<wixObject version="3.0.2002.0"
    xmlns="http://schemas.microsoft.com/wix/2006/objects">
```

Nested inside of the wixObject element are references to various MSI tables. Following is a section describing the File table with a single row for a text file called ReadMe.txt. The sourceLineNumber attribute of the row element has been truncated for space.

```
<table name="File">
    <row sourceLineNumber="C:\InstallPractice\Product.wxs*21">
        <field>file_readmeTXT</field>
        <field>cmp_readmeTXT</field>
        <field>ReadMe.txt</field>
        <field>0</field>
        <field />
        <field />
        <field>512</field>
        <field />
    </row>
</table>
```

You should never need to alter these files directly, but knowing how they work should help you to understand what the compiling stage does.

Compile-time variables

WiX lets you specify variables that are evaluated at compile time. You might use this to get environmental variables from the build machine, get the directory where your source files are, or access custom variables you've set up in a separate WiX include file (`.wxi`).

WiX has three classifications for preprocessor variables: *Environment*, *System*, and *Custom*. We'll discuss each in the following sections.

Environment variables

Environment variables are set in the environment where the build process is running, usually from the command prompt. The following command sets an environment variable called `myVar` to the value `myvalue`:

```
set myVar=myvalue
```

To pass this to your project, build your `.wxs` files from the same command window using Candle. Now access the environment variable in your WiX markup by using a dollar sign and parentheses, prefixing the variable name with `env`. Here's an example:

```
<Property Id="property1" Value="$(env.myVar)" />
```

System variables

System variables are a lot like environment variables. They have a similar syntax (in this case you'll prefix the variable name with `sys`), but there are a finite number of them and they're defined for you. The following system variables, which are always uppercase, are available:

- CURRENTDIR: The current directory where the build process is running
- SOURCEFILEDIR: The directory containing the file being processed
- SOURCEFILEPATH: The full path to the file being processed
- BUILDARCH: The platform (Intel, x64, Intel64) this package is compiled for (set by the Package element's Platform attribute)

The first two, which contain directory paths, always end in a backslash. So, you can use them like this:

```
$(sys.SOURCEFILEDIR)myFile.wxs
```

Custom variables

To set your own custom preprocessor variables, use the **define** keyword in your WiX markup:

```
<?define myVar = "myvalue" ?>
```

Although you can do this in any of your .wxs files, it's common to do it in a separate .wxi file, for which there is a Visual Studio template. To include this file in your project, add an **include** directive to one of your .wxs files, such as your main Product.wxs file:

```
<?include Include1.wxi?>
```

Then to use the variable, use the dollar sign and parentheses syntax, but prefix the variable name with var. Here's an example that includes a component in the final MSI only if myVar is equal to myvalue. Otherwise, the markup is skipped.

```
<DirectoryRef Id="INSTALLLOCATION">
    <?if $(var.myVar) = "myvalue" ?>
       <Component ...>
           <File ... />
       </Component>
    <?endif?>
</DirectoryRef>
```

We'll talk more about preprocessor conditional statements a little later on. You can also define variables from the command line by using the -d flag.

```
candle.exe -dmyVar=myValue ...
```

Preprocessor extensions

You can create your own variable prefixes and even call methods at compile time by writing a **preprocessor extension**. You'll need to make a new C# class library. We'll walk through each step and then look at the complete code afterwards.

First, in your new class library, add a reference to Wix.dll from the WiX bin directory and add a using statement for Microsoft.Tools.WindowsInstallerXml. Next, add a class that extends the WixExtension class. Here, we've called it MyWixExtension:

```
using Microsoft.Tools.WindowsInstallerXml;

namespace MyPreprocessorExtension
{
    public class MyWixExtension : WixExtension
```

```
        {
            //our extension code will go here
        }
    }
```

The purpose of this class is to override the `PreprocessorExtension` property from the `WixExtension` class so that instead of returning null, it returns an instance of the next class we'll create—which we'll call `MyPreprocessorExtension`. We'll define that class in a moment. Add this property to the `MyWixExtension` class:

```
public override PreprocessorExtension
    PreprocessorExtension
    {
        get
    {
        if (this.preprocessorExtension == null)
        {
            this.preprocessorExtension = new
                MyPreprocessorExtension();
        }

        return this.preprocessorExtension;
    }
    }
```

The next step is to define the `MyPreprocessorExtension` class. It must extend the `PreprocessorExtension` base class and set up the prefixes you want to use for your new compile-time variables. Here's where we do that:

```
public class MyPreprocessorExtension :
    PreprocessorExtension
    {
        private static string[] prefixes = { "company" };

        public override string[] Prefixes { get { return
            prefixes; } }
```

This sets our prefix to be `company`, although you'll likely use the actual name of your company or something else more inspired. As you can see, the *prefixes* variable is an array of strings so if you wanted to, you could create multiple new prefixes here.

The next step is to override the `GetVariableValue` method, which sets up a switch statement that returns a value for the variable you'll have passed in from your WiX markup. In other words, we can't set these variables dynamically, they are all hardcoded here.

```
public override string GetVariableValue(
string prefix, string name)
    {
        string result = null;
        switch (prefix)
        {
          case "company":
            switch (name)
            {
                // define all the variables under
                // this prefix here...
                case "myvar":
                    result = "myvalue";
                    break;
            }
            break;
        }

        return result;
    }
```

For this example, there's only one variable defined under the company prefix: myVar, which has a value of myvalue. In your WiX markup, you could access this using the dollar sign and parentheses syntax:

```
<Property Id="myVar" Value="$(company.myvar)" />
```

If you want to get fancy, you can add code that calls a pre-processor method. For this, you must override EvaluateFunction.

```
public override string EvaluateFunction(
string prefix, string function, string[] args)
{
    string result = null;
        switch (prefix)
        {
          case "company":
            switch (function)
            {
                // add any functions that you can
                // call with your prefix...
                case "sayHelloWorld":
                    result = "Hello, World!";
                    break;
            }
            break;
        }
        return result;
}
```

In this example, we've added a function called `sayHelloWorld` to our `company` prefix. When called in WiX, it will return the string `Hello, World!`. In real-world scenarios, it might return a version number of some other string that you'd like to perform some calculation to get.

In WiX, we can now call this function as follows:

```
<Property Id="checkVar" Value="$(company.sayHelloWorld())" />
```

If you'd like to pass arguments to this method, alter `EvaluateFunction` so that it uses its `args` parameter: Here's a simple example that turns the first parameter that was passed in to uppercase and then returns it:

```
case "sayHelloWorld":
    if(args.Length > 0)
    {
        result = args[0].ToUpper();
    }
    else
    {
        result = String.Empty;
    }
    break;
}
return result;
```

Before your new extension will work, you'll need to do one more thing: Add the following `using` statement and attribute to the `AssemblyInfo.cs` file of the class library:

```
using Microsoft.Tools.WindowsInstallerXml;
[assembly: AssemblyDefaultWixExtension(typeof(
MyPreprocessorExtension.MyWixExtension))]
```

Of course, you'll want to replace `MyPreprocessorExtension.MyWixExtension` with whatever names you gave to your class and its namespace. Then, compile the project to create a new `.dll`. The final step is to add a reference to it in your WiX project. Be careful not to include the project, if it's in the same solution as your WiX project. You must reference the built `.dll` file.

This is the complete code for the pre-processor extension:

```
using Microsoft.Tools.WindowsInstallerXml;

namespace MyPreprocessorExtension
{
    public class MyWixExtension : WixExtension
```

```
{
    private MyPreprocessorExtension preprocessorExtension;

    public override PreprocessorExtension
        PreprocessorExtension
        {
            get
            {
             if (this.preprocessorExtension == null)
               {
                 this.preprocessorExtension =
                             new MyPreprocessorExtension();
               }

             return this.preprocessorExtension;
           }
         }
}

public class MyPreprocessorExtension :
    PreprocessorExtension
    {
        private static string[] prefixes = { "company" };

        public override string[] Prefixes { get {
                                    return prefixes; } }

        public override string GetVariableValue(
                              string prefix, string name)
          {
             string result = null;
           switch (prefix)
             {
               case "company":
                   switch (name)
                   {
                     // define all the variables under
                     // this prefix here...
                       case "myvar":
                       result = "myvalue";
                        break;
                   }
                   break;
           }
```

```
            return result;
        }

    public override string EvaluateFunction(
            string prefix, string function, string[] args)
        {
        string result = null;
        switch (prefix)
        {
            case "company":
                switch (function)
                {
                    // add any functions that you can
                    // call with your prefix...
                    case "sayHelloWorld":
                        result = "Hello, World!";
                        break;
                }
                break;
        }
        return result;
        }
    }
}
```

Conditional statements and iterations

In this section, we'll take a look at the conditional and looping statements that are available at compile time.

if...elseif...else

The **if** statement checks that a preprocessor variable is set to a certain value. If it does, the code between it and the closing **endif** statement will be compiled. Optionally, it can be followed by an **elseif** or **else** statement, allowing you to compile other code if the initial condition is false. The entire block must end with an **endif**. Here's an example that only compiles a Property element if the preprocessor variable myVar is equal to 10.

```
<?if $(var.myVar) = 10 ?>
    <Property Id="newProperty" Value="5" />
<?endif?>
```

Here's a more complex example that utilizes the elseif and else statements:

```
<?if $(var.myVar) = 10 ?>
    <Property Id="newProperty" Value="5" />
<?elseif $(var.myVar) > 10?>
    <Property Id="newProperty" Value="6" />
<?else?>
    <Property Id="newProperty" Value="7" />
<?endif?>
```

Other conditional operators are available including not equal to (!=), greater than (>), greater than or equal to (>=), less than (<) and less than or equal to (<=). In addition, you can use the **Or** and **And** keywords to combine conditions. Use the **Not** keyword to negate a conditional statement:

```
<?if Not $(var.myVar) = 10 And Not $(var.myVar) = 11 ?>
    <Property Id="newProperty" Value="5" />
<?endif?>
```

ifdef

The **ifdef** statement is used to evaluate whether a preprocessor variable is defined. If it is, the WiX markup that follows will be compiled. The variable should be the name only, not the $(var.myVariable) syntax. Here is an example that checks if myVar is defined:

```
<?ifdef myVar ?>
    <Property Id="newProperty" Value="1" />
<?endif?>
```

ifndef

The **ifndef** statement is similar to the ifdef statement, except that it checks if a variable is *not* defined. Here's an example:

```
<?ifndef myVar ?>
        <Property Id="newProperty" Value="1" />
<?endif?>
```

Iterations

WiX has a preprocessor statement, **foreach,** which you can use to repeat a block of code a number of times. For example, you might loop through a list of directory names and create a new Directory element for each one; maybe to create a directory for each language your software supports.

First, you'll need to define a list to iterate through in the form of a string containing several values, each separated by a semicolon. To keep things clear, you could define a preprocessor variable to hold it, as in this example:

```
<?define myLanguages=en_us;de_de;it_it?>
```

Next, define a top-level folder to hold all of your new directories. Here, we'll call it `languages` and place it inside our `install` directory:

```
<DirectoryRef Id="INSTALLLOCATION">
    <Directory Id="languagesFolder" Name="languages" />
</DirectoryRef>
```

Now you can use a foreach statement to loop through each value in the `myLanguages` string. For each iteration, the current value is stored in a temporary variable called `tempVar`.

```
<?foreach tempVar in $(var.myLanguages)?>
    <DirectoryRef Id="languagesFolder">
        <Directory Id="$(var.tempVar)" Name="$(var.tempVar)">
            <Component Id="MyComponent.$(var.tempVar)" Guid="*">
                <File
                    Id="$(var.tempVar)File"
                    Source="..\$(var.tempVar).xml"
                    KeyPath="yes" />
            </Component>
        </Directory>
    </DirectoryRef>
<?endforeach?>
```

For each language, a new Directory element is created under the `languagesFolder` directory. We set the directory's `Id` and `Name` to tempVar's value. We also use it to set the ID of the Component element. By using an asterisk (*) as the Guid, WiX will autogenerate a new one for each Component. Then, we use the temporary variable again for the `Id` and `path` of the language-specific XML file. Be sure that the files `en_us.xml`, `de_de.xml`, and `it_it.xml` really exist! The entire structure ends with an **endforeach** statement.

The last thing to do is to add all of our new components to a feature. Here, we can use another foreach. Notice that we don't include this part in the first loop because that would compile multiple instances of the same Feature element, causing an error.

```
<Feature Id="MainFeature" Title="Main Feature" Level="1">
    <?foreach tempVar in $(var.myLanguages)?>
        <ComponentRef Id="MyComponent.$(var.tempVar)"/>
    <?endforeach?>
</Feature>
```

Errors and warnings

Another thing that WiX gives you is the ability to trigger compile-time errors and warnings. For this, use the `<?error error-message ?>` and `<?warning warning-message?>` syntax. An error stops the compilation and shows the error in the build log. A warning will also show up in the log, but won't stop the build.

Here's an example that triggers an error if the preprocessor variable `myVariable` isn't defined:

```
<?ifndef myVariable ?>
   <?error myVariable must be defined ?>
<?endif?>
```

Adding warnings and errors like this allows you to keep a closer eye on things, making sure that critical variables are defined like they should be. The example that we just saw used an error, which stops the build if hit. A warning works the same way, but won't stop the build. Here's an example:

```
<?ifndef myVariable ?>
   <?warning myVariable should be defined ?>
<?endif?>
```

Light.exe

Light is the WiX linker and binder. It's job is to first resolve all of the references to files, directories and so on stored in the `.wixobj` files (the `linking` phase) and then to stream all of that data into the MSI file, compressing it along the way (the `binding` phase). To see information about its usage type `light -?` at the command prompt. Here's what you should see:

```
light.exe [-?] [-b basePath] [-nologo]
[-out outputFile] objectFile [objectFile ...] [@responseFile]
```

You'll use the `-out` flag to give a name to the resulting MSI package. You must then reference all of the `.wixobj` files, either individually or with an asterisk (*). For example, this creates an MSI out of three `.wixobj` files that are in the current directory:

```
light.exe -out "myInstaller.msi" Product.wixobj Fragment1.wixobj
Fragment2.wixobj
```

We can also use an asterisk:

```
light.exe -out "myInstaller.msi" *.wixobj
```

If you've created any `.wixlib` files, you can reference them in the same way:

```
light.exe -out "myInstaller.msi" *.wixobj LibraryOne.wixlib LibraryTwo.
wixlib
```

In the following sections, we'll cover the other arguments that you can pass to Light. Although some affect linking and others binding, you'll specify both during the same call to Light.

Command-line arguments (linking)

In this section, we will explore the arguments that you can pass to Light that affect linking.

-ai

The `.wixobj` files that Candle creates are made up of sections and rows that will eventually make up the structure of the MSI database. Usually, if Light finds two rows that are the same, it throws an error about duplicate entries. By using the `-ai` flag, Light will only log this as a warning.

-b

The `-b` flag, which can be set to a directory path, tells Light where to look for the `.wixobj` files. You can add more than one directory by adding more `-b` flags.

-bf

The `-bf` flag is always used with the -xo flag, which tells Light to output a `.wixout` file instead of an MSI file. The `.wixout` format is XML as opposed to binary. However, by adding the `-bf` flag, the binary data that would be stored in the MSI are included with the XML.

-binder

You can define a custom binder in a WiX extension DLL. Use the `-binder` flag to identify the class that represents your custom binder that will be used to replace the default `Microsoft.Tools.WindowsInstallerXml.Binder` class. This is an advanced topic and won't be covered in this book.

-cultures

The `-cultures` flag tells WiX which `.wxl` files to load for localization. It accepts a culture string, such as en_us. Only one culture, and in turn one language, can be specified here. This is because an MSI can only be localized for a single language.

-d

Use the `-d` flag to define a linker variable. Linker variables can be referenced with the `!(wix.VariableName)` syntax. Unlike compile time preprocessor variables, linker variables are evaluated and resolved at link time. They're often used to reference files late in the build process. We'll discuss these in detail later in the chapter.

-dut

The WiX compiler and linker use extra tables, peculiar to WiX, to store metadata about how elements get grouped together. These extra tables don't exist in the MSI specification, and they're not used in the final MSI file. So, they're called "unreal" tables. You can drop these tables from the `.wixout` or `.wixpdb` files by adding the `-dut` flag.

-ext

Use the `-ext` flag to link in WiX extensions, such as the `WixUIExtension.dll`. This loads all of the C# code and `.wxs` files found in that extension.

```
-ext "C:\Program Files\Windows Installer XML v3.5\bin\WixUIExtension.dll"
```

-loc

When you've created `.wxl` files that contain localized strings for your MSI, you'll link them in (specify their paths and file names) with `-loc` flags. Those with a culture that matches the `-cultures` flag will be used.

-nologo

Light prints a message at the top of the console window when you use it showing its version and copyright information. You stop this by adding the `-nologo` flag.

-notidy

Light produces some temporary files during the course of its processing. It ordinarily cleans up after itself, deleting these files once it's finished. However, by adding the -notidy flag, these files will not be deleted. You'll need to add the -v flag to see where the temporary files are being stored. Look for an entry in the verbose log that says something like "temporary directory located at".

-o[ut]

Use the -o or -out flag to tell Light the name of the resulting MSI or .wixout file.

-pedantic

To see extra linking information, usually of low importance, add the -pedantic flag.

-sadmin

Often at times, you won't use the AdminExecuteSequence or the AdminUISequence tables during your install. To prevent those tables from being created in the MSI database, add the -sadmin flag.

-sadv

The AdvtExecuteSequence table is used for advertised installations. If you don't need it, you can suppress its creation by adding the -sadv flag.

-sloc

To prevent Light from processing localized variables in your .wxs files, add the -sloc flag. Then, output a file with the .wixout extension via the -o flag. It will contain the variable, such as !(loc.myVariable) instead of the literal value that it would have been expanded to. However, if you specify the -loc or -cultures flag, -sloc will be ignored. You must also specify the -xo flag when you want the output with the .wixout format.

-sma

In WiX, you can tell your installer to load a file into the Global Assembly Cache by setting the Assembly attribute on that file's File element. This will add two new tables to your MSI: MsiAssembly and MsiAssemblyName. It will also add a new action to the InstallExecuteSequence called MsiPublishAssemblies.
To suppress this action and these tables from being processed, add the -sma flag.

-ss

Light performs schema validation, using the XML schema found in `outputs.xsd`, to check that the syntax of the `.wixout` or `.wxipdb` file is correct. You can suppress this validation by adding the `-ss` flag.

-sts

Light uses GUIDs to identify row elements in `.wixout` and `.wixpdb` files. You can stop Light from showing these GUIDS in these files by adding the `-sts` flag.

-sui

You can choose to suppress the UI phase of the install by adding the `-sui` flag. This will remove the `InstallUISequence` and `AdminUISequence` tables from the MSI. You might do this to simplify an MSI that has no user interface.

-sv

The output from Light can be represented in XML format in either a `.wixout` or `.wixpdb` file. These files represent an intermediate state of the data before it's turned into an MSI by Light's binding process. They always contain an element called `wixOutput` that has a `version` attribute. When Light reads these intermediate XML files and transforms them into a finished MSI, it checks that the `version` attribute in the file matches the version of Light that's installed. That way, it can be sure that the data can be processed correctly. After all, it's possible to build an MSI from `.wixout` or `.wixpdb` files at a later time and your version of Light may have changed. You can suppress this validation by adding the `-sv` flag.

-sw[N]

Light produces several warnings and errors if files can't be found or things can't be linked properly. To turn off all warnings, add the `-sw` flag. You can also specify a particular warning to suppress by setting `-sw` to that warning's number. These numbers can be found in `messages.xml` in the WiX source code.

-usf <output.xml>

Use the `-usf` flag with the name of an XML file, such as `-usf unrefSymbols.xml` to log the symbols from Light's output that were not referenced. For example, adding the `WixUIExtension` but not using any of its dialogs will cause some symbols to be orphaned.

-v

In order to see what's going on behind the scenes with Light, you'll need to add the -v flag. This displays Light's logging messages such as ICE validation, file copying and CAB file creation.

-wx[N]

Ordinarily, warnings from Light don't stop the linking process. However, by adding the -wx flag, warnings will be treated as errors, which do stop the process. You can also specify a specific warning message to treat as an error by adding its message number.

-xo

When you add the -xo flag to Light, it outputs XML in the .wixout format. So, you'll need to also specify a .wixout file name with the -out flag. You may also want to add the -bf flag to append binary data for the installer to the .wixout file.

Command-line arguments (binding)

In this section, we will explore the arguments that affect Light's binding phase.

-bcgg

When creating a Component element in WiX, you'll usually specify a GUID to uniquely identify it. However, you can specify an asterisk (*) instead, in which case Light will choose the GUID for you. The default algorithm Light uses to create a GUID involves the SHA1 hash. However, by adding the -bcgg flag, you're telling it to use the older MD5 hash. This is a more backwards compatible algorithm, but is rarely needed.

-cc <path>

The binding process creates a .cab file, which is a type of file that holds compressed data, to store the files that the MSI will install. If you plan on calling Light several times, you can save some time by caching the .cab file and reusing it. To cache it, specify the -cc flag and the path to cache it to. Later on, you can add the -reusecab flag to tell Light to look for the .cab file in the path you've specified. For example, you could specify that the .cab file be cached to a directory called cabcache like this:
-cc ".\cabcache".

-ct <N>

You can change the number of threads Light uses when creating `.cab` files. The default is to use the number stored in the `%NUMBER_OF_PROCESSORS%` environment variable. You can change it by setting the `-ct` flag to a number.

-cub <file.cub>

Windows Installer uses files with the .cub extension to store ICE validation checks. There are two files it uses routinely: `darice.cub` (for MSIs) and `mergemod.cub` (for MSMs). To add your own `.cub` file with new ICE tests, specify the path to it with the `-cub` flag. We won't cover how to create custom ICE checks in this book.

-dcl:level

By default, Light uses MSZIP to compress `.cab` files. You can change the compression by adding the `-dcl` flag and setting it to one of the following: `low`, `medium`, `high`, `none`, or `mszip`.

-eav

Light uses a workaround to prevent Windows Installer from complaining if the version stored in the `MsiAssemblyName` table doesn't fit the `fileVersion` column created by the `-fv` flag. By specifying `-eav`, you're telling Light to not use this workaround.

-fv

If you add the `-fv` flag, Light will add a column called `fileVersion` to the `MsiAssemblyName` table. This is a table used to install assemblies to the GAC. The recommended way to update an assembly in the GAC is to install the new version with a new strong name. You'd use `-fv` when you want to ignore this recommendation and update an assembly in the GAC without changing its strong name.

-ice<ICE>

If you've created your own ICE checks and referenced their containing file with the `-cub` flag, you'll need to specify which to use with the `-ice` flag. For example, to add a test called `ICE9999`, add the following: `-ice:ICE9999`. Specify the number of the test after a semicolon. Refer to the MSDN documentation for more information about creating your own ICE checks:

`http://msdn.microsoft.com/en-us/library/aa372423%28VS.85%29.aspx.`

-pdbout <output.wixpdb>

Light ordinarily creates a `.wixpdb` file that has the same name as the MSI that you're creating. However, you can change the name of the `.wixpdb` by specifying it with the `-pdbout` flag.

-reusecab

If you've used the `-cc` flag to cache the `.cab` files that Light creates, you can tell Light to reuse those cabinets by adding the `-reusecab` flag. You'll need to specify the `-cc` flag again, which tells Light where the `.cab` files have been cached. If Light can't find the `.cab` files there, it will resort to creating them again.

-sa

When storing an assembly in the GAC, Light finds the file information on the `.dll` for you (culture, name, architecture, public key token, and version) and stores it in a table called `MsiAssemblyName`. You can suppress this by adding the `-sa` flag.

Light can't use reflection on .NET assemblies that use a newer version of the Common Language Runtime (CLR) then was available when Light was built. You can see the supported runtimes by opening `light.exe.config`, found in the WiX `bin` folder, in a text editor and searching for the `supportedRuntime` element.

In such a situation, you may be better off using `-sa` and adding the assembly information to the *MsiAssemblyName* table yourself. That is, unless there's a newer version of Light available for download.

-sacl

During Light's binding phase, it copies the finished MSI file to your output folder. If the file can't be copied because its permissions (its ACLs) are too restrictive (adopted from the permissions of the source directory), then Light changes the file's permissions to be Full Control for the current user.

Once it has copied the file to the output folder, it sets things right again by giving the MSI file the permissions of the output folder. If you add the `-sacl` flag, Light will skip this step and the MSI will be left with the unrestricted permissions. You might do this if the permissions of the output folder are also too restrictive. For example, you're sending the output to a network share, but you don't want the MSI to adopt the permissions of that share.

-sf

The `-sf` flag has the same behavior as the `-sa` and `-sh` flags added together.

-sh

If you add the `-sh` flag, Light will not add the `MsiFileHash` table to the final MSI. This table is used to eliminate unnecessary copying of file if the end user's computer already has a file that's scheduled to be installed.

-sice:<ICE>

You can suppress a specific ICE validation check by adding its number after the `-sice` flag. You should specify a new `-sice` flag for each check that you want to suppress. For example, to suppress ICE20, add the following: `-sice:ICE20`.

-sl

By adding the `-sl` flag, you're telling Light to not embed the CAB file in the MSI package. Once the MSI is built, you can check the `Media` table and see that the `Cabinet` column's value does *not* start with a pound sign (#), showing that the CAB is not embedded.

-spdb

The `-spdb` flag tells WiX to not create a `.wixpdb` file.

-sval

To prevent Light from running any of the ICE validation checks, add the `-sval` flag.

Link-time variables

Like Candle, Light allows you to specify variables that will be interpreted when your project is built. Here, however, the variables are processed at link time. There are three types of link time variables: *localization*, *binder*, and *custom*. We will take a look at each in the following sections.

Localization variables

WiX gives you something unique in the MSI-building world—a way to reuse one set of .wxs files for many different languages. The way to do it is to use a variable anywhere that you'd normally place text such as on dialog controls, feature labels, directory names, and so on. At link time, these **localization variables** will be swapped with the text specific to the language you're building.

Use the !(loc.VariableName) syntax in your WiX markup, such as:

```
<Directory Id="TARGETDIR" Name="SourceDir">
   <Directory Id="ProgramFilesFolder">
      <Directory Id="INSTALLLOCATION"
         Name="!(loc.InstallDirName)" />
   </Directory>
</Directory>
```

Here, we're not setting the name of our install directory in stone. We're using a variable instead and will swap it out with real text at link time. You can then create a .wxl file to store the meaning of your variable. One .wxl file for each language.

We'll talk more about this later in the book when we discuss localization. For now, it's enough to know that these variables are expanded at link time.

Binder variables

There are a number of **binder variables** that are predefined for you and that become available just before Light creates the final output. You'll use the !(bind. VariableName) syntax to access them.

The following list shows the variables that are available. You'll replace FileID with the ID of the File element you're trying to get information about. The first two are available to all of the files that you add with the File element. The remainder are only available to those that specified the Assembly attribute and set it to either .net or win32.

Variable name	Example
bind.fileLanguage.FileID	!(bind.fileLanguage.MyFile)
bind.fileVersion.FileID	!(bind.fileVersion.MyFile)
bind.assemblyCulture.FileID	!(bind.assemblyCulture.MyAssembly)
bind.assemblyFileVersion.FileID	!(bind.assemblyFileVersion. MyAssembly)
bind.assemblyFullName.FileID	!(bind.assemblyFullName. MyAssembly)

Variable name	Example
`bind.assemblyName.FileID`	`!(bind.assemblyName.MyAssembly)`
`bind.assemblyProcessorArchitecture.FileID`	`!(bind.assemblyProcessorArchitecture.MyAssembly)`
`bind.assemblyPublicKeyToken.FileID`	`!(bind.assemblyPublicKeyToken.MyAssembly)`
`bind.assemblyType.FileID`	`!(bind.assemblyType.MyAssembly)`
`bind.assemblyVersion.FileID`	`!(bind.assemblyVersion.MyAssembly)`

Custom variables

There are two ways to define a custom variable: via the command line with the `-d` flag or in your WiX markup with the `WixVariable` element. When using the `-d` flag, you can specify the variable name and its value, separated by an equal sign.

```
-dmyVariable="some value"
```

When using the WixVariable element, you'll use its `Id` attribute to define its name and its `Value` attribute to define its value.

```
<WixVariable Id="myVariable" Value="my value" />
```

Either way, the variable can be referenced elsewhere in your markup by using the `!(wix.VariableName)` syntax. The following example inserts the value of the variable as the name of a file that's scheduled to be installed.

```
<Component Id="cmp_myFile" Guid="8E74ECD6-782F-45e7-9432-
6F4FB4E08CED">
   <File Id="file_myFile" Source="!(wix.myVariable)" KeyPath="yes" />
</Component>
```

You can only set a custom variable in one place. So, you can't set it with both a `WixVariable` element and on the command line.

Building an installer without Visual Studio

Now that you've been shown Candle and Light, it may help to see a complete example of compiling and linking a WiX project to get an MSI. First off, create a new directory for your project and call it `PracticeWix`. Next, add a text file to it called `InstallMe.txt`. This will give us something to install. Then, create a file with the `.wxs` extension and call it `PracticeWix.wxs`.

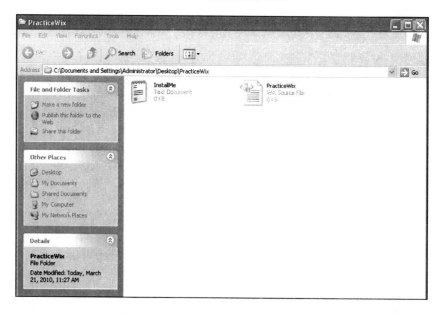

Open `PracticeWix.wxs` with a text editor like Notepad and the following markup. It will install the text file to a directory called `PracticeWix`. We'll add one of the built-in WiX dialogs too.

```xml
<?xml version="1.0"?>
<Wix xmlns="http://schemas.microsoft.com/wix/2006/wi">
    <Product
        Id="*"
        Name="PracticeWix"
        Language="1033"
        Version="1.0.0.0"
        Manufacturer="Myself"
        UpgradeCode="B9B82C37-34EC-4F50-9D0E-0DF8F06F1F64">

        <Package Compressed="yes" />
        <Media Id="1" Cabinet="media1.cab" EmbedCab="yes" />

        <Directory Id="TARGETDIR" Name="SourceDir">
```

```
                <Directory Id="ProgramFilesFolder">
                    <Directory Id="INSTALLLOCATION"
                        Name="PracticeWix" />
                </Directory>
            </Directory>

            <DirectoryRef Id="INSTALLLOCATION">
                <Component Id="cmp_InstallMeTXT"
                    Guid="825F0C9A-AACC-4E37-B8A2-30A452EB58F9">
                    <File Id="InstallMe.txt" Source="InstallMe.txt"
                        KeyPath="yes" />
                </Component>
            </DirectoryRef>

            <Feature Id="PracticeWix" Title="PracticeWix" Level="1">
                <ComponentRef Id="cmp_InstallMeTXT" />
            </Feature>

            <UIRef Id="WixUI_Minimal" />
        </Product>
    </Wix>
```

Now, to compile it, open a command prompt window and navigate to the `PracticeWix` folder. Assuming you've added the WiX `bin` directory to your `PATH` environment variable, the following command will call Candle to build our one `.wxs` file:

```
candle.exe -v -arch x86 -ext "WixUIExtension.dll" -out "PracticeWix.
wixobj" PracticeWix.wxs
```

This should create a new file in the `PracticeWix` folder called `PracticeWix.wixobj`. Next, use Light to turn that into an MSI.

```
light.exe -v -ext "WixUIExtension.dll" -out "PracticeWix.msi"
PracticeWix.wixobj
```

You should see a fairly long log of the linking process, including the ICE validation checks. In the end, this should create the MSI file. Go ahead an double-click on it to launch the installer.

Summary

In this section, we discussed the command line tools Candle, the WiX compiler, and Light, the linker. Although Visual Studio uses them for you, you can use them from the command prompt without using Visual Studio at all. In the next chapter, we'll switch gears and cover something completely different: how to read and write to the Windows Registry at install time.

10
Accessing the Windows Registry

Applications often need to save configuration data about themselves. This might include the install directory path, the location of a remote server, or whether or not certain functionality is turned on. Companies often choose to store this information in the Windows Registry. To that end, Windows Installer lets you read and write to the Registry at install time.

In this chapter, we'll discuss the following topics:

- Reading data stored in the Registry
- Writing to the Registry
- Performing miscellaneous tasks in the Registry such as setting user permissions for registry keys

Reading from the Registry

To read data stored in the Registry, you'll use the RegistrySearch element. If the value you're looking for exists, it will be saved into a property you'll have placed as a parent element to the RegistrySearch. Here's an example that looks for the "myValue" value stored in HKEY_CURRENT_USER\Software\MyCompany and stores it in a property called REGISTRY_RESULT. Whichever property you decide to use, make sure that it is public (uppercase). The example follows:

```
<Property Id="REGISTRY_RESULT">
  <RegistrySearch Id="MyRegistrySearch"
                  Root="HKCU"
                  Key="Software\MyCompany"
                  Name="myValue"
                  Type="raw"  />
</Property>
```

By placing the `RegistrySearch` element inside a `Property` element, we're saying that we want the registry value to be stored in that property. The attributes on the `RegistrySearch` element mostly tell Windows Installer where to look for the value. `Id` just gives the search a unique identity in the MSI database and can be set to whatever you like.

The `Root` attribute sets which top-level node, or "hive", in the Registry to look under. Your options are:

- HKLM: for HKEY_LOCAL_MACHINE
- HKCR: for HKEY_CLASSES_ROOT
- HKCU: for HKEY_CURRENT_USER
- HKU: for HKEY_USERS

The `Key` attribute sets what registry key to look for and `Name` sets the value to read inside that key. So, in the last example, we want to read the `myvalue` value in the `MyCompany` key. The `Type` attribute tells the installer what sort of data is stored in `myValue`. Most of the time, you'll set this to `raw`.

Setting `Type` to `raw`, as opposed to `file` or `directory`, which we'll discuss next, means that the data you get back will contain extra characters to help you distinguish what kind of data it is. If you've worked with the Registry before, you know that there are several types of data you can store: DWORD, REG_BINARY, REG_SZ, and so on. Following is a table that explains which special characters are added to the value once you've retrieved it:

Type of data	Characters added to value
DWORD	A # sign is added to the beginning, which may be followed by a + or -
REG_BINARY	A #x is added to the beginning and each hexadecimal digit is shown as an ASCII character prefixed with another #x
REG_EXPAND_SZ	A #% is added to the beginning
REG_MULTI_SZ	A [~] is added to the beginning
REG_SZ	No extra characters are added. Any # signs in the value, however, will be escaped by turning them into two # signs

Setting `Type` to either `file` or `directory` is used when the value is the actual path to a file or directory on the local machine. Use it when you want to add a check to see if the file or directory specified actually exists. For example, this would check that the file path stored in the value "pathToFile" really exists:

```
<Property Id="MY_PROPERTY">
  <RegistrySearch Id="myRegSearch"
                  Root="HKLM"
                  Key="Software\WIXTEST"
                  Name="PathToFile"
                  Type="file">
    <FileSearch Id="myFileSearch" Name="[MY_PROPERTY]" />
  </RegistrySearch>
</Property>
```

If the path doesn't exist, the property won't be set. Notice that we have to add a `FileSearch` element to do the checking. Simply set its `Name` attribute to the `Id` of your property in brackets. You can also check if a directory exists, as in the next example, by setting `Type` to `directory` and adding a `DirectorySearch` element:

```
<Property Id="MY_PROPERTY">
  <RegistrySearch Id="myRegSearch"
                  Root="HKLM"
                  Key="Software\WIXTEST"
                  Name="PathToDirectory"
                  Type="directory">

    <DirectorySearch Id="myDirSearch"
                     Path="[MY_PROPERTY]" />
  </RegistrySearch>
</Property>
```

Here, if the directory can't be found, the property MY_PROPERTY won't be set.

Another attribute that you can add to the `RegistrySearch` element is `Win64`. When set to `yes`, your installer will read from the 64-bit portion of the Registry on a 64-bit system. Most of the time, WiX handles this for you, setting this flag if you've built your project to target a 64-bit platform. Setting it manually allows you to explicitly choose where to search. For example, you may set it to `no` to search the 32-bit portion on a 64-bit system.

Using this built-in Registry search functionality saves you the trouble of writing it yourself in, say, C# code. When does the installer do the search? During the *AppSearch* action in the UI sequence.

Writing to the Registry

To write to the Registry, you'll use the `RegistryValue` element by itself or paired with a `RegistryKey` element. By itself, `RegistryValue` can perform simple writes. Writing multiple things to the same place is easier when you use `RegistryKey`. We'll discuss both of these in the next sections. Writing occurs during the "deferred" stage of the Execute sequence during an action called `WriteRegistryValues`.

RegistryValue

Writing to the Registry is sort of like installing something on the end user's computer. So, you'll have to place your `RegistryValue` element inside a `Component`. This is actually a good thing as it gives you the opportunity to set component-level conditions on the action. You could use this to only write to the Registry if a certain condition is met. Refer back to *Chapter 4* for a discussion on component-level conditions.

Just like when you're installing a file, you must mark something inside the component as the KeyPath item. In this case, we can mark the `RegistryValue` itself. Here's an example that writes to a value called "myValue" in the HKLM\Software\WixTest\Test key:

```
<DirectoryRef Id="INSTALLLOCATION">
  <Component Id="CMP_WriteToRegistry"
            Guid="DA01C245-8633-4147-92F0-C063003DB493">

    <RegistryValue Id="myRegistryValue"
                KeyPath="yes"
                Action="write"
                Root="HKLM"
                Key="Software\WixTest\Test"
                Name="myValue"
                Value="my value"
                Type="string" />
  </Component>
</DirectoryRef>
```

Because the element is packaged inside a `Component`, it will be removed for us during an uninstall, freeing us from that responsibility. The `RegistryValue` element's `Id` attribute simply serves to uniquely identify it in the MSI database. We use the `KeyPath` attribute to mark it as the KeyPath for the component.

The `Action` attribute can take one of three values: `append`, `prepend`, or `write`. You'd use append or prepend when the type of data you're storing is `REG_MULTI_SZ` and you aren't creating a new value, but rather updating an existing one. `REG_MULTI_SZ` is a type that contains multiple items of data in a single value. If you use either of these and there isn't an existing value, one will be created. Setting `Action` to `write` tells the installer to overwrite any existing value or to otherwise create a new one.

The `Root`, `Key`, and `Name` attributes set the path in the Registry to write to. `Root` can be set to any of the values available to `RegistrySearch` with one addition—`HKMU`. This is a Registry hive that's only related to installs. It means that if this is a per-user install, the value will be written under `HKEY_CURRENT_USER`. If it's a per-machine install, it will be written under `HKEY_LOCAL_MACHINE`.

Set the `Value` attribute to the value to store in the specified Registry value. You'll specify what type of data it is with the `Type` attribute, which can be one of the following:

- `string`: meaning a `REG_SZ` type
- `integer`: meaning a `REG_DWORD` type
- `binary`: meaning a `REG_BINARY` type
- `expandable`: meaning a `REG_EXPAND_SZ` type
- `multiString`: meaning a `REG_MULTI_SZ` type

When writing more than one value to the same Registry key, it's easier to use the `RegistryKey` element, which we'll cover next.

RegistryKey

With the `RegistryKey` element, you can set the key you want to write to once and then nest several `RegistryValue` elements inside. Use its `Root` and `Key` attributes to set the key, as in this example:

```
<Component ...>
  <RegistryKey Root="HKCU"
               Key="Software\MyCompany">
    <RegistryValue Name="myValue"
                   Action="write"
                   Value="myValue"
                   Type="string"
                   KeyPath="yes" />
  </RegistryKey>
</Component>
```

Here, we've set the `RegistryKey` element to write to the `HKCU\Software\MyCompany` key. The child `RegistryValue` element specifies what to set the `myValue` value to. Now, to write to more values in the same key, just add more `RegistryValue` elements. Notice that we've set the `RegistryValue` in the previous example as the KeyPath item. If you add more values, you should set their `KeyPath` attributes to `no`. Also notice that neither element requires an `Id` attribute.

The `RegistryKey` element has an optional attribute called `Action` that sets how the values should be removed during an uninstall. Most of the time, you should just omit this attribute. However, if you set it to `createAndRemoveOnUninstall`, during an uninstall, not only will the values you've set be removed, but also everything else in that key and all subkeys that you didn't create. This is probably not the desired behavior in most cases, but might come in handy under special circumstances. Note that if you specify this attribute, you must give the `RegistryKey` and `RegistryValue` elements `Id` attributes.

Another use for `RegistryKey` is to set a `REG_MULTI_SZ` value. Remember, this type of value can hold multiple items of data. This technique looks just like the last example except that the `Name` attribute of each `RegistryValue` stays the same to signify that they're writing data to the same place. Here's an example that writes two values to `myValue`:

```
<Component ... >
  <RegistryKey Action="create"
               Id="myRegKey"
               Root="HKLM"
               Key="SOFTWARE\WixTest\Test" >

    <RegistryValue Id="myRegistryValue"
                   Name="myValue"
                   Value="first value"
                   Type="multiString"
                   KeyPath="yes" />


    <RegistryValue Id="myRegistryValue2"
                   Name="myValue"
                   Action="append"
                   Value="second value"
                   Type="multiString"
                   KeyPath="no" />
  </RegistryKey>
</Component>
```

In this example, both `RegistryValue` elements have their `Type` attributes set to `multiString` to show that they are writing to a `REG_MULTI_SZ` value. Notice that the second one has an `Action` of `append`. You could set this on both elements, but for the first it isn't necessary. You can also use `prepend` to add a value to the beginning of the value.

Setting NeverOverwrite

When writing to the Registry, you have the option of specifying that you only want to create the key or value if it doesn't already exist. For this, you'll add the `NeverOverwrite` attribute to the parent `Component` element. The next example only adds the registry value "myValue" if it doesn't exist:

```
<Component Id="CMP_regvalue"
           Guid="7088AC98-898E-4FB4-98A6-6549AD3495E8"
           NeverOverwrite="yes">

  <RegistryValue Id="myRegistryValue"
                 Root="HKLM"
                 Key="Software\WixTest\Test"
                 Name="myValue"
                 Value="a new value"
                 Type="string"
                 Action="write"
                 KeyPath="yes"/>
</Component>
```

Removing Registry values

When it comes to uninstalling your product, you don't need to worry too much about the registry keys you've created. Windows Installer will make sure that all components, including registry keys, are cleaned up. However, in case you want to remove items from the Registry that you didn't create—perhaps they were created by one of your other products—WiX provides a way to do it.

Two elements are used to remove data from the Registry: `RemoveRegistryKey` and `RemoveRegistryValue`. We'll cover both in the following sections.

RemoveRegistryKey

You'll use the RemoveRegistryKey element when you want to remove a key from the Registry and all of its subkeys. It must be placed inside a Component element, as in this example:

```
<DirectoryRef Id="INSTALLLOCATION">
  <Component Id="CMP_RemoveRegistryKey"
             Guid="3B0C6FD9-D73A-4CE9-8053-BBBB2BE8716B"
             KeyPath="yes">
  <RemoveRegistryKey Id="MyRemoveRegistryKey"
                     Root="HKLM"
                     Key="Software\WixTest\myKey"
                    Action="removeOnInstall" />
  </Component>
</DirectoryRef>
```

Here, the Component element is marked as the KeyPath, since you cannot do this with the RemoveRegistryKey element.

The RemoveRegistryKey element's Id attribute sets the unique key for this entry in the MSI database. Root specifies the hive where the key we're removing is and Key lists the path to it. You can, via the Action attribute, specify when to remove this key. It can be set to either removeOnInstall or removeOnUninstall.

RemoveRegistryValue

Whereas RemoveRegistryKey removes a key and all of its subkeys, the RemoveRegistryValue element is more targeted. It allows you to remove a specific value inside a particular key. It should be placed inside a Component element, like so:

```
<DirectoryRef Id="INSTALLLOCATION">
  <Component Id="CMP_RemoveRegistryValue"
             Guid="A07AEF74-C9A9-4D61-8852-A4EC3F9E13F9"
             KeyPath="yes">
    <RemoveRegistryValue Id="MyRemoveRegistryValue"
                         Root="HKLM"
                         Key="Software\WixTest\MyKey"
                         Name="myValue" />
  </Component>
</DirectoryRef>
```

The syntax of `RemoveRegistryValue` is very similar to `RemoveRegistryKey` except that it adds a `Name` attribute to specify the value to remove from the key. Notice that there's no `Action` attribute because you don't have the option of removing a value during an uninstall.

Copying Registry values

WiX doesn't provide a specific element for copying data from one registry value to another. However, you can accomplish this task by pairing a `RegistrySearch` element with a `RegistryValue`. First, you'll store the value in a property by using a `RegistrySearch`. Then, you'll reference that property in the `Value` attribute of the `RegistryValue` element. Here's an example:

```
<Property Id="MY_REG_VALUE">
   <RegistrySearch Id="MyRegistrySearch"
                   Root="HKLM"
                   Key="Software\MyCompany\MyKey"
                   Name="MyDWORDValue"
                   Type="raw" />
</Property>

<DirectoryRef Id="INSTALLLOCATION">
   <Component Id="CMP_CopyRegValue"
              Guid="747965AA-90F4-4262-BE55-3C1F4F7F65B4">
      <RegistryValue Id="MyRegistryValue"
                     KeyPath="yes"
                     Root="HKLM"
                     Key="Software\MyCompany\MyKey"
                     Name="MyCopiedValue"
                     Value="[MY_REG_VALUE]"
                     Action="write"
                     Type="string" />
   </Component>
</DirectoryRef>
```

The first thing we did was use a `RegistrySearch` element to look up `MyDWORDValue` stored in the `HKLM\Software\MyCompany\MyKey` key. Its value is then stored in a property called `MY_REG_VALUE`.

Next, we create a new component and add a `RegistryValue` element to it. It specifies that it will create a new registry value under the same key as the original, but called `MyCopiedValue`. We set its value with the `Value` attribute, which references the `MY_REG_VALUE` property in square brackets.

Notice that we can set the `Type` to `string` here even though the value we're copying is actually of type DWORD. Because the value stored in the property is retrieved using the `raw` type, it will contain special characters to denote its datatype. When we copy it to our new value, Windows will infer the datatype by this. So, in essence, it doesn't matter what you put for the `RegistryValue` element's `Type` attribute. Windows can figure out on its own what type it should be.

Registry permissions

Every key in the Registry has a set of permissions saved to it that affects which users can read or alter it. You can see this in the Registry Editor by going to **Run | regedit**, right-clicking on a key and selecting **Permissions**. WiX allows you to change these permissions with its `PermissionEx` element.

`PermissionEx` isn't in the default WiX namespace, but rather in the *Util* extension. So, you'll need to add a reference in your project to `WixUtilExtension.dll`, found in the WiX `bin` directory, and add the `UtilExtension` namespace to your `Wix` element. Here's an altered `Wix` element:

```
<Wix xmlns="http://schemas.microsoft.com/wix/2006/wi"
xmlns:util="http://schemas.microsoft.com/wix/UtilExtension">
```

Here, we've assigned the Util namespace to the prefix `util`. Now, when we create a registry key with a `RegistryKey` element, we'll nest a `PermissionEx` element inside it to set its permissions. The next example sets the permissions of a key called `MyKey` so that a user named "nickramirez" has all permissions to it:

```
<DirectoryRef Id="INSTALLLOCATION">
<Component Id="CMP_WriteToRegistry"
          Guid="DA01C245-8633-4147-92F0-C063003DB493">

  <RegistryKey Id="MyRegistryKey"
              Root="HKLM"
              Key="Software\MyCompany\MyKey">

    <RegistryValue ... />

      <util:PermissionEx User="nickramirez"
                          GenericAll="yes" />
  </RegistryKey>
</Component>
</DirectoryRef>
```

Use the `User` attribute to set the name of the Windows user account to apply permissions to it. Here, we've given them the `GenericAll` permission. The following table lists all of your options:

Attribute	As seen on the key	What it does
GenericAll	Full Control	Gives user all permissions.
GenericRead	Read	Grants `QueryValue`, `EnumerateSubkeys`, `Notify`, and `ReadControl`. Must have at least one other permission specified.
GenericExecute	n/a	Same privileges as `GenericRead`, but it can be specified alone.
GenericWrite	n/a	Grants `SetValue`, `CreateSubkey`, and `ReadControl`.
ChangePermission	Write DAC	Allows the user to read the discretionary access control list for the key.
CreateLink	Create Link	Allows the user to create symbolic links to the key.
CreateSubkeys	Create Subkey	Allows the user to create new subkeys inside the key.
Delete	Delete	Allows the user to delete the key
EnumerateSubkeys	Enumerate Subkeys	Allows the user to identify all of the subkeys in the key.
Notify	Notify	Allows the user to receive audit message about the key.
Read	Query Value	Allows the user to read the values in the registry key.
ReadPermission	Read Control	Allows the user to read the information in the key's access control list (ACL).
Synchronize	n/a	Sets whether to wait to access the key until another thread has finished accessing it.
TakeOwnership	Write Owner	Makes the user the owner of the key.
Write	Set Value	Allows the user to set the values of the registry key.

You can nest several `PermissionEx` elements inside a single `RegistryKey` to set access levels for various users. Be sure not to be so restrictive that no user has enough rights to remove the key. That would cause problems during an uninstall. You can also nest a `PermissionEx` inside a `RegistryValue` element to apply rights to that value's parent key.

Summary

In this chapter, we discussed how to read from and write to the Windows Registry at install time. Reading makes use of *AppSearch* functionality that occurs early on in the UI sequence. The value is stored in a property that you can then use elsewhere in your markup.

Writing is done with `RegistryKey` and `RegistryValue` elements, the former being used for writing multiple values and the latter for writing a single value. You have the option of setting permissions on these values and specifying whether or not to replace existing data. In the next chapter, we'll cover how to install, start, stop, and uninstall Windows services.

Controlling Windows Services

11

A Windows service is an application that runs continuously in the background and doesn't interact with the user of the computer. They typically start up when the computer is booted. You can see a list of installed services by selecting **Run** from your Start menu and entering `services.msc`.

During an installation, your MSI package may need to interact with services that already exist on the end user's computer or even install and configure its own. In this chapter, we'll cover the WiX elements that allow you to do this. Specifically, we'll cover the following topics:

- Creating a simple Windows service
- Registering and configuring services with the `sc.exe` utility
- Installing a service with the `ServiceInstall` element
- Using `ServiceControl` to start, stop, and remove a service
- Setting a user account, dependencies, and recovery options

Creating a simple Windows service

A Windows service always maps back to an executable file that's stored on the local hard drive. Although that executable could host a sophisticated program like a Windows Communication Foundation service, here we'll create one that's much simpler. Our service will simply write to a log file periodically.

Visual Studio provides a project template for creating a Windows service. Go to **File | New | Project | Windows | Windows Service**.

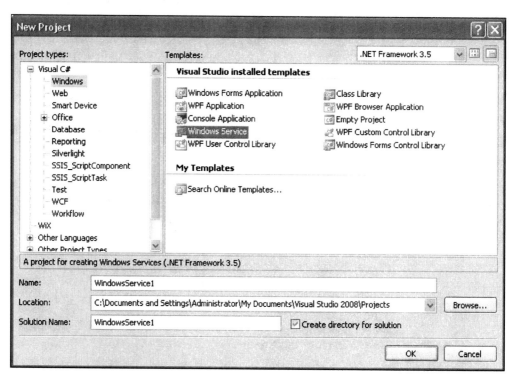

Once you've created this new project, right-click on the `Service1.cs` file in the **Solution Explorer** and select **View Code**. The C# code that you'll see displays a class, here named `Service1` that is derived from `System.ServiceProcess.ServiceBase`. It overrides the `OnStart` and `OnStop` methods.

These are the methods that every Windows service must implement so that they can be started and stopped by the **Service Control Manager (SCM)**. The SCM is a process that tracks which services are installed and monitors their individual status. Later on, we'll cover how to issue some basic commands to the SCM from the command line.

The following code in `Service1.cs` adds the functionality necessary to write to a log file every five seconds.

```
namespace WindowsService1
{
    using System;
    using System.IO;
    using System.ServiceProcess;
```

```
using System.Threading;

public partial class Service1 : ServiceBase
{
    private Thread thread;

    public Service1()
    {
        InitializeComponent();
    }

    protected override void OnStart(string[] args)
    {
        ThreadStart job = new ThreadStart(this.WriteToLog);
        this.thread = new Thread(job);
        this.thread.Start();
    }

    protected override void OnStop()
    {
        this.thread.Abort();
    }

    protected void WriteToLog()
    {
        while (true)
        {
            string appDataDir = Environment.GetFolderPath(
            Environment.SpecialFolder.CommonApplicationData);

            string logDir = Path.Combine(appDataDir,
                "TestInstallerLogs");

            if (!Directory.Exists(logDir))
            {
                Directory.CreateDirectory(logDir);
            }

            string logFile = Path.Combine(logDir,
                "serviceLog.txt");
            FileStream fs = new FileStream(logFile,
                FileMode.Append);
            StreamWriter sw = new StreamWriter(fs);
            sw.Write("Log entry at " + DateTime.Now + "\r\n");
```

```
            sw.Close();
            fs.Close();
            Thread.Sleep(5000);
        }
    }
  }
}
```

As you can see, we spin up a new thread in the `OnStart` method. This begins the writing. The `OnStop` method uses the `Abort` method to close the thread. A private method called `WriteToLog` handles the actual logic. We separate the job into its own thread so that the service can start in a timely manner without getting hung up.

Compile the project to get the executable file for our service. Next, we'll see how to use the SCM to register and configure it.

Using sc.exe

To communicate with the Service Control Manager, you can use a command-line tool called `sc.exe`. To register our executable as a service, we'll use its `create` command. Every service gets a behind-the-scenes short name such as `testsvc`. Specify the new name as the first parameter to `create`. The `binPath` parameter sets the path to the executable. Be sure that the equal sign has no spaces before it and one after it. Follow this convention with all `sc.exe` parameters that use an equal sign.

```
sc create testsvc binPath= "C:\WindowsService1.exe"
```

After running this command, you'll see the new service in the services management console (`services.msc`) amongst the other installed services. Yours will show up as `testsvc`. It won't be started yet for you. You'll have to start it manually, either through the services management console or with `sc.exe`'s `start` command.

```
sc start testsvc
```

You'll always have to start your service the first time. However, you can change how it starts from then on. For example, you could have it start up each time the computer is turned on. To do that, add the `start` argument to the `create` command, as shown in the following code snippet:

```
sc create testsvc binPath= "C:\WindowsService1.exe" start= auto
```

The following table lists the possible values for the start argument:

Start value	Meaning
demand	This is the default. Service must be started manually.
auto	Starts the service each time the computer is restarted.
boot	Mostly used for device drivers. Starts the service at boot time.
system	Mostly used for device drivers. Starts the service at kernel initialization.
disabled	The service cannot be started.

Something more that the `create` command can do is set a more user-friendly name to be displayed in the services management console. So, if you'd rather have users see `Test Service` instead of `testsvc`, you can add the `DisplayName` argument to the `create` command.

```
sc create testsvc binPath= "C:\WindowsService1.exe" start= auto
DisplayName= "Test Service"
```

If you need to stop the service, you can use the `stop` command. Here is an example:

```
sc stop testsvc
```

To delete the service, use the `delete` command:

```
sc delete testsvc
```

Notice that even if you've assigned the service a `DisplayName`, you still have to reference the `testsvc` name when issuing commands. You can find the service name of any installed service by right-clicking on it in the services management console and selecting **Properties**. You can also find it with `sc.exe`'s `GetKeyName` command which takes the `DisplayName` as a value and returns the service name—among other information. The following example looks up the service name for the `Test Service` service, returning the result `testsvc`.

```
sc GetKeyName "Test Service"
```

Another thing to look at is how to set dependencies for your services. You'd use this if your service required other services to be running before it could be started. As an example, suppose `testsvc` couldn't start unless `dependencySvc` was already running. You could specify that by adding the `depend` argument:

```
sc create testsvc binPath= "C:\WindowsService1.exe" depend= dependencySvc
```

You can specify more than one dependency by separating each name with a forward slash (/). Windows will make sure that each service is started up in the correct order if it depends upon another.

One final thing to look at is setting the error logging level of your service. By default, this is set to normal, meaning that when the computer is powered on, if there is an error while trying to start the service, it will be logged and a messagebox will be displayed to the user. You may decide to change this to either ignore, in which case the error is logged but the user doesn't see a messagebox, or critical, meaning that if the service can't be started, the computer will try to restart with the last known good configuration. This is set with the create command's error argument.

```
sc create testsvc binPath= "C:\WindowsService1.exe" error= ignore
```

Using WiX to install a service

Now that you know how to install a service from the command line, let's look at how to do it with an installer. WiX has an element called ServiceInstall that you can use to add a new service to the services management console. This assumes that you've already created the executable file that will become the endpoint for your service, as discussed earlier.

First of all, we'll use the familiar Component and File elements to install the .exe to the install directory on the target machine. Add the following code to your WiX project:

```
<DirectoryRef Id="INSTALLLOCATION">
    <Component
        Id="CMP_WindowsService1"
        Guid="3D3DE5C1-7154-4c61-9816-248A85F6DEBF">

        <File
            Id="WindowsService1.exe"
            Name="WindowsService1.exe"
            KeyPath="yes"
            Source=".\WindowsService1.exe" />
    </Component>
</DirectoryRef>
```

Next, add a ServiceInstall element to the same component to register the WindowsService1.exe file as a service. Notice that a lot of the functionality from sc.exe is present here such as setting the DisplayName, the startup type, and error logging level.

```
<DirectoryRef Id="INSTALLLOCATION">
    <Component
        Id="CMP_WindowsService1"
        Guid="3D3DE5C1-7154-4c61-9816-248A85F6DEBF">
```

```
<File
    Id="WindowsService1.exe"
    Name="WindowsService1.exe"
    KeyPath="yes"
    Source=".\WindowsService1.exe" />

<ServiceInstall
    Id="InstallWindowsService1"
    Name="testsvc"
    DisplayName="Test Service"
    Start="auto"
    ErrorControl="normal"
    Type="ownProcess" />
    </Component>
</DirectoryRef>
```

When `Type` is set to "`ownProcess`", it means that the service will execute in its own Windows process. When set to "`shareProcess`", it can be grouped into the same process as other services running in the same executable. If you choose `shareProcess`, then if even one of the services in the process fails, all of the services in that process will fail. It is safer to separate services into their own processes, if possible.

There are several other optional attributes available, some of which we'll discuss in more detail later in the chapter. They are:

Attribute name	Description
Arguments	Specify any command-line arguments required to run the service.
Account	The account under which to start the service, valid only when `ServiceType` is `ownProcess`.
Password	The password for the account, valid only when the account has a password.
Description	The text that will be under the `Description` label for your service in the services management console.
Vital	Either `yes` or `no`, the overall installation should fail if this service can't be installed.
LoadOrderGroup	A group of services that your service can join (or create) to be started when the computer starts up.

Starting, stopping, and uninstalling a service

The ServiceInstall elements works well for installing a service, but doesn't provide a way to start, stop, or uninstall one. For that, you'll use the ServiceControl element. It can be added to the same component as the ServiceInstall element thereby sending signals to the testsvc you're installing.

The following example starts the service during install and stops and removes it during uninstall. These actions happen during the deferred stage of the Execute sequence.

```
<DirectoryRef Id="INSTALLLOCATION">
    <Component ... >

        <File ... />

        <ServiceInstall ... />

        <ServiceControl
            Id="sc_WindowsService1"
            Name="testsvc"
            Start="install"
            Stop="both"
            Remove="uninstall"
            Wait="yes" />
    </Component>
</DirectoryRef>
```

The Name attribute specifies the service that you want to control. Start, Stop, and Remove can each be set to one of the following values: install, uninstall, or both. In this example, we've set Stop to both so that if our service is already installed (from a previous install), we'll stop it before installing the new version and starting it up again.

WiX schedules these actions during the Execute sequence in the following order:

- StopServices
- DeleteServices
- RemoveFiles
- InstallFiles
- InstallServices
- StartServices

Notice that other actions that deal with installing and removing files are performed after services have been stopped and deleted and before services are installed and started. That way, those processes are freed up before the underlying executable files are modified.

Getting back to the previous example, the Wait attribute tells the installer whether it should pause and wait for each action to complete before moving on. If the rest of your install depends on your service being in a certain state, then you should set Wait to yes.

The ServiceControl element isn't limited to sending signals to services you're installing. It can do the same for any service that's installed on the end user's computer. All you have to do is change the Name attribute. For example, if we wanted to stop the DHCP Client service (named Dhcp) before installing files and start it up again afterwards, we could do so by adding a ServiceControl element with a Name attribute of Dhcp.

```
<Directory ... >
    <Component ... >
        <File ... />

        <ServiceControl
            Id="startAndStopDhcp"
            Name="Dhcp"
            Start="both"
            Stop="both"
            Wait="yes" />
    </Component>
</Directory>
```

Notice that we don't have to include a ServiceInstall element to use ServiceControl. Also, ServiceControl here doesn't use the Remove attribute, which tells the installer when to uninstall the service. We should leave the DHCP Client service after our application has been uninstalled.

Setting the service's user account

Ordinarily, when you install a service, it runs under the *LocalSystem* account. You can see this by opening the services management console, right-clicking on a service, selecting **Properties** and choosing the **Log On tab**. LocalSystem is a special account used by the SCM which gives service-wide ranging privileges to interact with the computer. If you'd like to give your service more limited access, you can assign it to another user account.

Two accounts that you might consider are *LocalService* and *NetworkService*. These accounts have fewer privileges than LocalSystem, but are still built-in and ready to use. To set a new user account for your service, add the `Account` and `Password` attributes to `ServiceInstall`. If the account doesn't have a password, which is the case with LocalService and NetworkService, you can omit the `Password` attribute. Here's an example:

```
<DirectoryRef Id="INSTALLLOCATION">
    <Component
        Id="CMP_WindowsService1"
        Guid="3D3DE5C1-7154-4c61-9816-248A85F6DEBF">

        <File
            Id="WindowsService1.exe"
            Name="WindowsService1.exe"
            KeyPath="yes"
            Source=".\WindowsService1.exe" />

        <ServiceInstall
            Id="InstallWindowsService1"
            Name="testsvc"
            DisplayName="Test Service"
            Description="Test service for WiX"
            Start="auto"
            ErrorControl="normal"
            Type="ownProcess"
            Account="NT AUTHORITY\LocalService" />

        <ServiceControl
            Id="sc_WindowsService1"
            Name="testsvc"
            Start="install"
            Stop="both"
            Remove="uninstall"
            Wait="yes" />
    </Component>
</DirectoryRef>
```

Here, we've added the `Account` attribute to the `ServiceInstall` element and set it to `NT AUTHORITY\LocalService`. You'll be able to see this after installing the package by opening the services management console, right-clicking on the new service, selecting *Properties* and clicking the *Log On* tab.

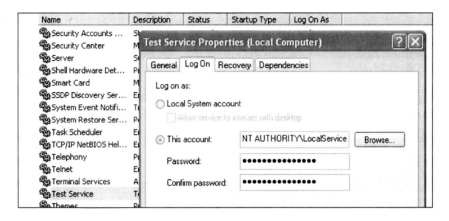

Hardcoding NT AUTHORITY\LocalService or NT AUTHORITY\NetworkService won't work on non-English operating systems, as the names won't translate. So, you should instead use WiX properties that will be translated into the proper user account names at install time. The WiX Util extension offers these properties. You can find a list at http://wix.sourceforge.net/manual-wix3/osinfo.htm.

Here's an example that uses the WIX_ACCOUNT_LOCALSERVICE property in place of NT AUTHORITY\LocalService. You must first add a PropertyRef element to reference the property in your project.

```
<PropertyRef Id="WIX_ACCOUNT_LOCALSERVICE"/>

<DirectoryRef Id="INSTALLLOCATION">
    <Component ...>
        <File ... />

        <ServiceInstall
            Id="InstallWindowsService1"
            Name="testsvc"
            DisplayName="Test Service"
            Description="Test service for WiX"
            Start="auto"
            ErrorControl="normal"
            Type="ownProcess"
            Account="[WIX_ACCOUNT_LOCALSERVICE]" />

        <ServiceControl ... />
    </Component>
</DirectoryRef>
```

You can also set the account to a local user or domain user. Be sure to always include the domain name or computer name, such as `DomainName\UserName`. For the next example, we'll create a new user during the course of the install and then assign that account to the service.

To create a new local user, use the `User` element from the WiX `Util` extension. After adding a reference in your project to `WixUtilExtension.dll`, add the following namespace to you Wix element:

```
<Wix xmlns="http://schemas.microsoft.com/wix/2006/wi"
   xmlns:util=
      "http://schemas.microsoft.com/wix/UtilExtension">
```

Now, you can use the `User` element in your markup. This new component will add a new user named `JoeUser`:

```
<Property Id="MY_PASSWORD" Hidden="yes" Value="password" />


<DirectoryRef Id="INSTALLLOCATION">
   <Component
      Id="CMP_NewUser"
      Guid="29019429-AA87-401C-AF87-5BA4798EE6F1"
      KeyPath="yes">

      <util:User
         Id="addNewUser"
         LogonAsService="yes"
         CreateUser="yes"
         Name="JoeUser"
         UpdateIfExists="yes"
         Password="[MY_PASSWORD]"
         PasswordNeverExpires="yes"
         RemoveOnUninstall="yes" />
   </Component>
</DirectoryRef>
```

In order to start a Windows service that starts automatically, the assigned user account must have the "Logon As a Service" right from the computer's local security policy. You can give the new account this by setting the `User` element's `LogonAsService` attribute to `yes`.

The `CreateUser` attribute tells the installer to create this user account if it doesn't exist. `Name` sets the account's name. `UpdateIfExists` tells the installer to only update the account's settings if it *does* already exist. `Password` sets the password for the account. Here, we're using a hardcoded property, but in practice you'd probably get this from the user. The `PasswordNeverExpires` attribute prevents the password from ever expiring and `RemoveOnUninstall` ensures that the account will be deleted when the product is uninstalled.

Now, we can use this account in the `ServiceInstall` element:

```
<DirectoryRef Id="INSTALLLOCATION">
  <Component
      Id="CMP_WindowsService1"
      Guid="3D3DE5C1-7154-4c61-9816-248A85F6DEBF">

    <File
        Id="WindowsService1.exe"
        Name="WindowsService1.exe"
        KeyPath="yes"
        Source=".\WindowsService1.exe" />

    <ServiceInstall
        Id="InstallWindowsService1"
        Name="testsvc"
        DisplayName="Test Service"
        Description="Test service for WiX"
        Start="auto"
        ErrorControl="normal"
        Type="ownProcess"
        Account=".\JoeUser"
        Password=[MY_PASSWORD] />

    <ServiceControl
        Id="sc_WindowsService1"
        Name="testsvc"
        Start="install"
        Stop="both"
        Remove="uninstall"
        Wait="yes" />
  </Component>
</DirectoryRef>
```

You can use `.\` before the account name to reference the local computer name, if you don't know it. You can also specify a domain account here by prefixing the name with the domain name. You should also know that a local user account can only start a service if the `ServiceInstall` element has an `Interactive` attribute set to `no`, which is the default, and a `Type` set to `ownProcess`.

Adding service dependencies

If your service requires that other services be started before it can function properly, you can use the `ServiceDependency` element to add those services as dependencies. You'll place it inside the `ServiceInstall` element. Here's an example that states that the DNS Client service, named `Dnscache`, must be started before starting our Test Service:

```
<ServiceInstall
    Id="InstallWindowsService1"
    Name="testsvc"
    DisplayName="Test Service"
    Description="Test service for WiX"
    Start="auto"
    ErrorControl="normal"
    Type="ownProcess">

    <ServiceDependency Id="Dnscache" />
</ServiceInstall>
```

The ServiceDependency element's `Id` attribute sets the name of the service to depend on. Now, Windows will make sure that the DNS Client service is started before the Test Service. You can add more `ServiceDependency` elements for additional dependencies.

You can also set `Id` to the Name of another `ServiceInstall` element. That way, if you're installing two services, you can specify that one should be started before the other. Here's an example:

```
<DirectoryRef Id="INSTALLLOCATION">
    <Component ... >
        <File ... />

        <ServiceInstall
            Id="InstallWindowsService1"
            Name="testsvc1"
            DisplayName="Test Service 1"
            Start="auto"
            ErrorControl="normal"
            Type="ownProcess" />

        <ServiceControl ... />
    </Component>

    <Component ... >
```

```
        <File ... />

        <ServiceInstall
            Id="InstallWindowsService2"
            Name="testsvc2"
            DisplayName="Test Service 2"
            Start="auto"
            ErrorControl="normal"
            Type="ownProcess">

            <ServiceDependency Id="testsvc1" />
        </ServiceInstall>

        <ServiceControl ... />
    </Component>
</DirectoryRef>
```

Here, the service called `Test Service 2` will be started after `Test Service1` has been started.

Another thing you can do is add one of your services to a "load order group" and then start that entire group before starting one of your other services. A load order group is simply a category under which several services are grouped. You can use the `ServiceInstall` element's `LoadOrderGroup` attribute to join an existing group. If that group name doesn't exist, it will be created for you. The next example joins the `Test Service 1` service to the `TestGroup` group:

```
<ServiceInstall
    Id="InstallWindowsService1"
    Name="testsvc1"
    DisplayName="Test Service 1"
    Start="auto"
    ErrorControl="normal"
    Type="ownProcess"
    LoadOrderGroup="TestGroup" />
```

If we then had another service, we could specify, via the `ServiceDependency` element, that all services in `TestGroup` should be started first. You'd add the `Group` attribute, set to `yes`, to signify that the `Id` in the `ServiceDependency` refers to a group name.

```
<ServiceInstall
    Id="InstallWindowsService2"
    Name="testsvc2"
    DisplayName="Test Service 2"
```

```
    Start="auto"
    ErrorControl="normal"
    Type="ownProcess">

    <ServiceDependency Id="TestGroup" Group="yes" />
  </ServiceInstall>
```

When you set a dependency for a service, be aware that if the dependency can't be started, an error will occur. You can tell Windows what to do when this happens with the `ServiceConfig` element.

Service recovery with Util:ServiceConfig

Windows allows you to set actions to be taken if your service fails at some point while it's running. Your three options are: try to restart the service, run an executable file or script, or reboot the machine. You can see these settings in the services management console by viewing the **Properties** of your service and clicking the **Recovery** tab.

First, let's alter the original Windows service that we created by changing the `WriteToLog` function so that it throws an error the third time it prints a message. As this error is uncaught, it will cause the service to stop running. This will give the failure recovery actions a chance to kick in. Here is the new code for `WriteToLog`:

```
protected void WriteToLog()
{
    int count = 0;

    while (true)
    {
        count++;

        if (count >= 3)
        {
            throw new Exception("Service failed.");
        }

        string appDataDir = Environment.GetFolderPath(
            Environment.SpecialFolder.CommonApplicationData);

        string logDir = Path.Combine(appDataDir,
            "TestInstallerLogs");

        if (!Directory.Exists(logDir))
        {
            Directory.CreateDirectory(logDir);
        }

        string logFile = Path.Combine(logDir, "serviceLog.txt");
        FileStream fs = new FileStream(logFile,
            FileMode.Append);
        StreamWriter sw = new StreamWriter(fs);
        sw.Write("Log entry at " + DateTime.Now + "\r\n");
        sw.Close();
        fs.Close();
        Thread.Sleep(5000);
    }
}
```

Now, the service will fail after writing to the log twice. Going back to our WiX project, let's add a project reference to the WiX `Util` extension, if it's not already there. Be sure to add the `UtilExtension` namespace:

```
<Wix xmlns="http://schemas.microsoft.com/wix/2006/wi"
    xmlns:util=
        "http://schemas.microsoft.com/wix/UtilExtension">
```

This allows us to use the ServiceConfig element through which we can set the failure recovery options. If you want to set the options for a service that's already installed, place the ServiceConfig inside its own Component element. If, however, you want to set the options of a new service you're installing, place it inside that ServiceInstall element, as in this example:

```
<ServiceInstall
    Id="InstallWindowsService1"
    Name="testsvc"
    DisplayName="Test Service"
    Description="Test service for WiX"
    Start="auto"
    ErrorControl="normal"
    Type="ownProcess">

    <util:ServiceConfig
        ServiceName="testsvc"
        FirstFailureActionType="restart"
        SecondFailureActionType="restart"
        ThirdFailureActionType="runCommand"
        RestartServiceDelayInSeconds="5"
        ProgramCommandLine=
            "C:\Program Files\TestInstaller\PrintError.cmd"
        ResetPeriodInDays="1" />
</ServiceInstall>
```

Here, we've set recovery actions for the testsvc service. The first time it fails, the action specified by the FirstFailureActionType will be performed. The second time, it will be the action in SecondFailureActionType and then ThirdFailureActionType the third time. Each should be set to one of three values: restart, runCommand, or reboot.

Specifying restart means that Windows will attempt to restart the service after a delay time of seconds specified by the RestartServiceDelayInSeconds attribute. Here, we've set it up so that the service will restart five seconds after it fails.

Notice that we've set both the first and second action types to restart, meaning that the service will try to restart itself twice before running the command specified by the ProgramCommandLine attribute. Unfortunately, you can't use a WiX property here to reference the directory where the batch script, executable, VBScript, or whatever type of program you're running is located. Also, it doesn't interpret environment variables or network shares. So, you're stuck specifying the full path to the program to execute and it must be on the local drive.

You can also set an action to `reboot` in which case the computer will reboot. You can add the `RebootMessage` attribute, set to a string, to show a custom message to the user telling them that the system will restart. Or, you can omit it to keep the default. Many times, however, this message isn't shown. It's all up to the operating system.

We've set the `ResetPeriodInDays` to `1`, meaning that it will be one full day before the error count is reset to zero. This, unfortunately, doesn't give you the fine-grained control that you get with `sc.exe`, which lets you specify the value in seconds. If the error count goes higher than three, it just keeps executing the action specified by the `ThirdFailureActionType` attribute. Resetting the count brings you back to the `FirstFailureActionType`.

Summary

In this section, we discussed Windows Services both from the standpoint of working with them via the command line with the `sc.exe` utility and with WiX. WiX lets you add a new service to the services management console and configure its startup, error logging level, and user account. Services can also be configured so that they depend on other services and have failure recovery. Having all of this functionality built in can really simplify things. In the next chapter, we will discuss how to localize an install package for different languages.

12
Localizing Your Installer

Localization is the process of making a piece of software, or in this case an installer, suitable for the region and culture it will be used in. This can include changing the language of displayed text, making sure that images and colors are culturally appropriate, and adjusting the size of UI elements to fit longer or shorter words.

In this chapter, we'll cover the following aspects of localization:

- Setting the language and code page attributes of your `Product` and `Package` elements
- Adding WiX localization files
- How to use Light.exe to localize an MSI
- Translating built-in error messages and the end user license agreement
- Creating a single multi-language installer

Setting language and code page attributes

The `Product` and `Package` elements, which appear in your main WiX source file, both utilize attributes that specify language codes (LCIDs) and code pages. A **language code** is a numeric ID used to classify a particular language and the region where it's spoken. Being able to codify these things, as opposed to always having to spell out "English as spoken in the United States", makes for much easier processing. Now, you can simply say "1033", which is the equivalent in LCID terms.

A full chart of LCIDs can be found at Microsoft's MSDN web site by searching for "locale Id". The URL is:

```
http://msdn.microsoft.com/en-us/library/0h88fahh(VS.85).aspx
```

Although that page also provides LCIDs in hexadecimal form, you should always use the decimal form in WiX.

A **code page** is set of extra printable characters that aren't covered in the basic ASCII set. ASCII covers all of the English alphabet and common punctuation marks. You can see a chart displaying ASCII at:

```
http://msdn.microsoft.com/en-us/library/60ecse8t%28VS.80%29.aspx
```

However, it doesn't cover Chinese or Japanese characters, or characters found in European languages, for example. For that, you'll need to reference a code page that defines their shape. Without it, your installer won't know how to render the characters you want.

A full list of code pages can be found at Microsoft's MSDN web site:

```
http://msdn.microsoft.com/en-us/library/dd317756
```

As an example, you could specify a code page of "950" to make Traditional Chinese characters available. In the following sections, we'll see how the `Product` and `Package` elements make use of LCIDs and code pages.

Package element

First, let's look at the `Package` element. Its job is to sum up details about the installer such as who the author is and what platform it supports. Another important bit of information it publishes is the language used. An MSI package only ever lists one supported language and it does so by setting the `Package` element's `Languages` attribute. Here's an example that sets the supported language to `1033`, English - United States:

```
<Package Compressed="yes"
         InstallerVersion="301"
         Platform="x86"
         Manufacturer="Awesome Company"
         Description="Installs Awesome Software"
         Languages="1033" />
```

When the end user launches the installer, their computer looks to the `Package` element to find out what the supported language is. If that language isn't installed locally, an error will be displayed telling the user so. Windows Installer stores the supported language in something called the **Template Summary** property. You can find more information about it at:

```
http://msdn.microsoft.com/en-us/library/Aa372070
```

It's possible, and in fact preferable, to set the Languages attribute to 0, which sets the supported language to "neutral". This means, essentially, that you can set the true language later, at link time. We'll discuss exactly how when we get to WiX localization files. This next example simply omits the Languages attribute:

```
<Package Compressed="yes"
         InstallerVersion="301"
         Platform="x86"
         Manufacturer="Awesome Company"
         Description="Installs Awesome Software" />
```

The Package element also has an attribute called SummaryCodepage that's used to set the code page for the summary properties. Summary properties are the details shown when you right-click on an MSI file and view its **Properties**. If any of these use characters outside of the ASCII set, they'll need a code page to display them.

You could set a hardcoded value, as in this example:

```
<Package Compressed="yes"
         InstallerVersion="301"
         Platform="x86"
         Manufacturer="Awesome Company"
         Description="Installs Awesome Software"
         SummaryCodepage="1252" />
```

Here, we've specified that the code page to use is "1252", which is the code page that contains characters for English. You might explicitly set this if you use extended characters such as the copyright symbol. If we'd used Chinese characters in, for example, the Description attribute, we'd have had to specify a code page such as "950".

WiX provides a way to set the SummaryCodepage at link time. Instead of hardcoding the code page value, use a placeholder called a **localization variable**. It looks like this:

```
<Package Compressed="yes"
         InstallerVersion="301"
         Platform="x86"
         Manufacturer="Awesome Company"
         Description="Installs Awesome Software"
         SummaryCodepage="!(loc.SummaryCodepage)" />
```

This means that you can swap the code page for whichever language you decide to use without having to change your WiX markup. We'll cover localization variables later on when we get to WiX localization files. That's where you'll set the variable to a different value for each language.

Product element

While the `Package` element publishes the summary properties for the MSI, the `Product` element contains its actual content. As such, setting *its* language and code page properties affects the characters stored in the installer and the messages it produces.

The `Product` element has an attribute called `Language` that's used when displaying error and progress messages. Unlike the `Package` element's `Languages` attribute, which can be omitted, you must always set the `Product` element's `Language` attribute. Here's an example that sets `Language` to "1033":

```
<Product Id="3E786878-358D-43AD-82D1-1435ADF9F6EA"
         Name="Awesome Software"
         Language="1033"
         Version="1.0.0.0"
         Manufacturer="Awesome Company"
         UpgradeCode="B414C827-8D81-4B4A-B3B6-338C06DE3A11">
```

To make life easy when localizing your package for more than one language, use a localization variable which we can then define later:

```
<Product Id="3E786878-358D-43AD-82D1-1435ADF9F6EA"
         Name="Awesome Software"
         Language="!(loc.LanguageId)"
         Version="1.0.0.0"
         Manufacturer="Awesome Company"
         UpgradeCode="B414C827-8D81-4B4A-B3B6-338C06DE3A11">
```

The `Product` element is also responsible for setting the code page for the characters used throughout the MSI database. You can set its `Codepage` attribute, as in this example:

```
<Product Id="3E786878-358D-43AD-82D1-1435ADF9F6EA"
         Name="Awesome Software"
         Language="!(loc.LanguageId)"
         Codepage="1252"
         Version="1.0.0.0"
         Manufacturer="Awesome Company"
         UpgradeCode="B414C827-8D81-4B4A-B3B6-338C06DE3A11">
```

A more flexible approach is to simply set `Codepage` to "0". This specifies that the code page is neutral. You can then set it with a WiX localization file, which contains elements for doing so. Here's an example:

```
<Product Id="3E786878-358D-43AD-82D1-1435ADF9F6EA"
         Name="Awesome Software"
```

```
Language="!(loc.Language)"
Codepage="0"
Version="1.0.0.0"
Manufacturer="Awesome Company"
UpgradeCode="B414C827-8D81-4B4A-B3B6-338C06DE3A11">
```

Now, the decision about the code page can be made at link time. Localization files have a code page attribute too and this will override the "0" code page set here.

WiX localization files

Suppose, to create an MSI for each language, you had to maintain separate Visual Studio projects or WiX source files for each one. That would become a hassle pretty quickly. With WiX localization files (.wxl), you can reuse the same WiX markup, but swap out the text for each language you build. Light, the WiX linker, lets you specify a **WiX localization file** (.wxl) file to use.

A .wxl file contains strings for a particular language. These can be swapped with placeholders (localization variables) when Light runs, creating an MSI with language-specific text. To create a new .wxl file, right-click on your WiX project in Visual Studio's **Solution Explorer** and select **Add | New Item | WiX Localization File**.

The convention is to name each .wxl file the same as the language short string — such as en-us.wxl — of the strings it contains. Following is an example .wxl file that contains several strings localized for English; the fill will be named as en-us.wxl:

```xml
<?xml version="1.0" encoding="utf-8"?>
<WixLocalization Culture="en-us"
                 Codepage="1252"
                 xmlns=
                 "http://schemas.microsoft.com/wix/2006/localization">

    <String Id="SummaryCodepage">1252</String>
    <String Id="LanguageID">1033</String>
    <String Id="Comments">This is in English</String>
    <String Id="Description">Also in English</String>
    <String Id="InstallButtonText">Install</String>
</WixLocalization>
```

Your localized strings are held inside a WixLocalization element. Its Culture attribute labels what the language of those strings is. Instead of using an LCID, you'll use a language short string, such as "en-us". A list of possible values can be found at:

```
http://msdn.microsoft.com/en-us/library/0h88fahh(VS.85).aspx
```

The `Codepage` attribute sets the code page for the MSI. This is what overrides the `Product` element's code page, if you've set it to "0". Notice also that we must reference a new namespace for this file:

```
http://schemas.microsoft.com/wix/2006/localization
```

Inside the `WixLocalization` element are `String` elements that define the text you want to localize. Each will become a localization variable that you can then use in your WiX markup. For example, the first `String` element, which has an `Id` of `SummaryCodepage` and a value of `1252`, can be used in your `Package` element like so:

```
<Package
    . . .
    SummaryCodepage="!(loc.SummaryCodepage)" />
```

Everywhere that you want to localize text—UI controls, feature titles and descriptions, directory names—you can use localization variables. Then, simply by switching the .wxl file you reference, the values of those variables change.

The `String` element has two optional attributes: `Localizable` and `Overridable`. `Localizable` is purely for documentation purposes. You might set it to `no` on `String` elements that don't contain actual words, but non-words like GUIDs. You might, for example, store a different GUID for a component based on the language, if the file that's contained in that component changes depending upon the language.

Setting `Overridable` to `yes` lets you to set two `String` elements with the same `Id`. Ordinarily, doing so would cause an error. However, if one of the `String` elements is `Overridable`, then it will be overwritten by the other. For example, suppose you have two `.wxl` files, both specifying the same culture, that each define a `String` element with an `Id` of `MyString`. If one has the `Overridable` attribute set to `yes` and the other doesn't, the element that doesn't will be used. The UI dialog sets that come with the WiX toolset define `.wxl` files for several languages and they set the `Overridable` attribute on all of their strings. This allows you to replace the default strings with your own by adding your own `.wxl` files.

The standard dialogs from the `WixUIExtension` use localization variables extensively. Here's some of the markup they use for the `WelcomeDlg` dialog. You can see several localization variables:

```
<Dialog Id="WelcomeDlg"
        Width="370"
        Height="270"
        Title="!(loc.WelcomeDlg_Title)">

    <Control Id="Next"
             Type="PushButton"
```

```
                    X="236"
                    Y="243"
                    Width="56"
                    Height="17"
                    Default="yes"
                    Text="!(loc.WixUINext)" />

        <Control Id="Cancel"
                    Type="PushButton"
                    X="304"
                    Y="243"
                    Width="56"
                    Height="17"
                    Cancel="yes"
                    Text="!(loc.WixUICancel)">
            <Publish Event="SpawnDialog"
                    Value="CancelDlg">1</Publish>
        </Control>

        <Control Id="Bitmap"
                    Type="Bitmap"
                    X="0"
                    Y="0"
                    Width="370"
                    Height="234"
                    TabSkip="no"
                    Text="!(loc.WelcomeDlgBitmap)" />
```

The WiX source code contains the .wxl files that define these variables. Here's a sample from the Spanish version:

```
<String Id="WelcomeDlgTitle"
        Overridable="yes">
          {\WixUI_Font_Bigger}
          Le damos la bienvenida a la Instalación de
          [ProductName].
</String>

<String Id="WixUINext"
        Overridable="yes">&amp;Siguiente</String>

<String Id="WixUICancel"
        Overridable="yes">Cancelar</String>

<String Id="WelcomeDlgBitmap"
        Overridable="yes">WixUI_Bmp_Dialog</String>
```

WiX provides `.wxl` files for more than ten languages including Spanish, German, French, Hungarian, Polish, Japanese, and Russian. Remember, you can override these strings by creating your own `.wxl` files and adding `String` elements with `Id` attributes that match those defined by WiX. You can also make your own UI and localize it with completely new strings.

The role of Light.exe

Light is the tool that links your `.wxl` files with the `.wixobj` files created by Candle. During its processing, it will look for `-loc` and `-cultures` flags given to it on the command line. You can specify more than one `-loc` flag, each pointing to a `.wxl` file. The `-cultures` flag tells WiX *which* `.wxl` file — or files — to use. Any that have a matching `Cultures` attribute in their `WixLocalization` element will be used. Here's an example:

```
Light.exe -loc en-us.wxl -loc en-us2.wxl -loc de-de.wxl
 -cultures:en-us "*.wixobj" -out myInstaller.msi
```

Here, we've specified that we want to build our MSI using the `en-us` culture. Assuming that `en-us.wxl` and `en-us2.wxl` both have that culture, both will be used. The `de-de.wxl` file will be ignored. You can specify more than one culture by separating each with a semi colon. This will set the first culture as the primary one to use and those that follow it as the fallback in case a particular string isn't defined in the first.

The next example builds the installer using German strings ("de-de"), but falls back to English strings if a localization variable isn't defined. If neither defines it, then an error will occur.

```
Light.exe -loc en-us.wxl -loc de-de.wxl -cultures:de-de;en-us
 "*.wixobj" -out myInstaller.msi
```

You can also specify an "invariant" culture by setting the `-cultures` flag to "neutral". Here's an example:

```
Light.exe -cultures:neutral "*.wixobj" -out myInstaller.msi
```

This will use the `.wxl` file that has a `WixLocalization` element with a `Culture` set to an empty string. Invariant-culture `.wxl` files are usually localized for English and are used as the "base" MSI package when creating a multi-language installer with language transforms. We'll cover how to create a multi-language MSI later in the chapter.

Something else to be aware of is that Visual Studio has its own **Cultures to build** text field on the **Build** page of a WiX project's **Properties**. You can set one or more language short strings here, but they mean something different than when setting them with Light's `-cultures` flag. Visual Studio will build a separate installer for each language you specify. It does this by calling Light multiple times.

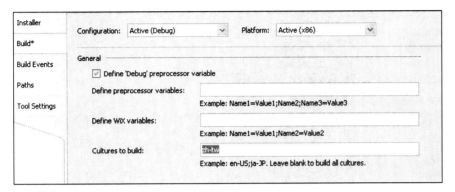

You can set more than one language by separating them with semicolons. If you leave this field blank, Visual Studio will build an MSI for every `.wxl` file you have in the project.

Localizing error messages

Windows Installer responds to certain errors by displaying a messagebox with text about what went wrong. You can see a list of these errors at:

`http://msdn.microsoft.com/en-us/library/aa372835(VS.85).aspx`

Unfortunately, they're always in English. You can see an example of this by triggering the **Source not found** error. Follow these steps:

1. Create a simple `.wxs` file, but set the `EmbedCab` attribute on the `Media` element to `no`. This means that the installer won't embed the CAB file in the MSI and will look for it in the same directory as the installer. The `Media` element will look like this:

   `<Media Id="1" Cabinet="media1.cab" EmbedCab="no" />`

2. Add a project reference to the `WixUIExtension` and add one of the standard dialog sets, such as `WixUI_Minimal`:

   `<UIRef Id="WixUI_Minimal" />`

3. On the **Build** page of the project's **Properties**, set the **Cultures to build** to "es-es".

4. Compile the `.wxs` file into an MSI and then remove the CAB file from the output directory.

5. Launch the installer, accept the license agreement and **Instalar**.

You'll see a message like this:

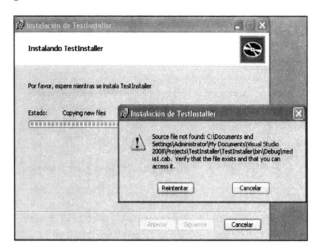

By setting the **Cultures to build** to "es-es", we've said that we want to use the Spanish `.wxl` files from the `WixUIExtension`. This means that most of the text in the UI will be translated for us. However, the error message, which comes from the underlying Windows Installer, isn't.

To correct this problem, we'll have to replace the default error message with a localized one. Each message is identified by a number. For the **Source not found**, it's 1311. To override the message, add an `Error` element inside a UI element in your `.wxs` file. Set its `Id` to the error number and the inner text to the localized message. Here's an example:

```
<UI>
  <Error Id="1311">
  Archivo no encontrado: [2].Compruebe que el archivo existe y que
  puedes acceder a él.
  </Error>
</UI>
```

Trusting that Google Translate knows its stuff, this should be the Spanish translation of the original message. Rebuild the MSI, delete the CAB file, and try to install. You should see the new message:

Notice that we used [2] as a placeholder for the missing file's path. Windows Installer fills in the information for us. Refer to the MSDN site for the template to use for each error.

There's one thing left to do. We've hardcoded the Spanish translation for the message. What we really should do is place that into a Spanish .wxl file and use a localization variable inside the Error element. That way, we can have translations for all of the languages we support. Follow this example:

```
<?xml version="1.0" encoding="utf-8"?>
<WixLocalization Culture="es-es"
          xmlns="http://schemas.microsoft.com/wix/2006/localization">

  <String Id="Error_1311">
  Archivo no encontrado: [2]. Compruebe que el archivo existe y que
  puedes acceder a él.
  </String>
</WixLocalization>
```

Now we can use a localization variable:

```
<UI>
  <Error Id="1311">!(loc.Error_1311)</Error>
</UI>
```

This variable can be replaced for each different language.

Localizing the EULA

All of the dialogs sets from the `WixUIExtension` display an End User's License Agreement (EULA). It's always in English, defaulting to an RTF file called `License.rtf` in the `WixUIExtension` source files. You'll want to replace this with your own agreement and at the same time localize it. Luckily, all you have to do is specify a path to your own RTF file with the link-time variable `WixUILicenseRtf`. The following line, which you can place in your main `.wxs` file, replaces the default license agreement with a custom one:

```
<WixVariable Id="WixUILicenseRtf"
            Value="CustomAgreement.rtf" />
```

You can also set this value from the command line when calling Light via the `-d` flag:

```
Light.exe -dWixUILicenseRtf=CustomAgreement.rtf -loc es_es.wxl
 -cultures:es-es -ext WixUIExtension.dll
 -out "es-es\AwesomeSoftware.msi" .\*.wixobj
```

Another option is to set it from within Visual Studio. Right-click on the project, select **Properties**, and add the variable in the text field labeled **Define WiX variables**.

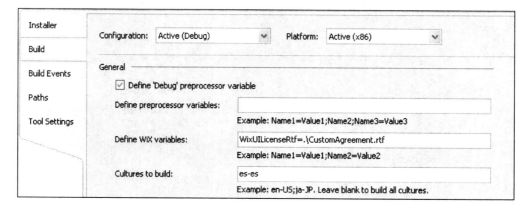

Once you've pointed this variable to the new file, you'll see your RTF text for the license agreement:

You can use this technique to create a language-specific EULA for each localized MSI. Another way of localizing the EULA is to create a custom dialog that displays the license agreement and then use a localization variable for the license content. That way, you can store your RTF text in a .wxl file. This gives you more control than using the `WixVariable`. Here's an example of a `ScrollableText` control that uses a localization variable to display a localized license agreement:

```
<Control Id="LicenseText"
         Type="ScrollableText"
         X="20"
         Y="60"
         Width="330"
         Height="140"
         Sunken="yes"
         TabSkip="no">
    <Text>!(loc.LicenseText)</Text>
</Control>
```

Now you can create a new `String` element in your .wxl file that contains the RTF text, as shown:

```
<String Id="LicenseText">
<![CDATA[
  {\rtf1\ansi\ansicpg1252\deff0\deflang1033
    {\fonttbl{\f0\fswiss\fcharset0 Arial;}}
  {\*\generator Msftedit 5.41.21.2500;}
  \viewkind4\uc1\pard\f0\fs20 Custom License Agreement\par}]]>
</String>
```

Creating a multi-language MSI

In addition to being able to create multiple separate MSIs for each language, it's also possible to create a single MSI that shows a different language depending on the end user's language settings. The process is automatic for the user. They don't need to choose the language.

 Note that the procedure you'll learn here isn't supported by Microsoft, but is widely used.

To get started, build separate MSIs for each language. For a simple example, add a project reference to the `WixUIExtension`, add a `UIRef` element to your markup to reference one of the standard dialog sets, and set the **Cultures to Build** in Visual Studio to **es-es;en-us;de-de**. This will build Spanish, English, and German installers using the `.wxl` files that are embedded in that extension.

Visual Studio, by default, sends the output of each localized MSI to its own folder.

Each folder contains an MSI for a different language. To merge these installers into one, you'll need to verify that your main `.wxs` file has the following:

- The `Product` element has a `Codepage` attribute set to `0`
- The `Product` element has a `Language` attribute set to a localized variable such as `!(loc.ProductLanguage)`
- Add `.wxl` files to your project for each language and add the `ProductLanguage` string, setting it to the LCID that matches that language
- If needed, add a `Codepage` localization variable to be used in the `Package` element's `SummaryCodepage` attribute; this is a must for Oriental languages

Rebuild if necessary. Now, we're ready to merge the various MSIs into one. Basically, we're going to create **transform files** that we'll embed inside a single MSI. A transform file (`.mst`) contains a comparison between two MSIs. Often they're used when building patches. However, they work for our needs too.

We'll compare each language's MSI against the English version (our "base") to produce a transform file that contains the differences between the two languages. We'll then bundle all of the transform files inside the English MSI and when the end user launches it, it will dynamically choose which transform file to apply. The transform will alter the MSI (sort of like a patch) then and there *at install time* so that the language of the transform replaces all of the current strings.

To make the comparison between English and each other language and make our transform files, we'll use a tool that ships with WiX called **Torch**. Torch takes an input file, an `updatedInput` file to compare it to, and an output file as parameters. Here is the general syntax:

```
torch.exe [-?] [options] targetInput updatedInput -out outputFile
[@responseFile]
```

Here's an example that compares the English and Spanish versions and creates a transform file called "es-es.mst":

```
torch.exe -t language "en-us\TestInstaller.msi"
"es-es\TestInstaller.msi" -out "transforms\es-es.mst"
```

It's a good idea to name your `.mst` files so that it's obvious which language they contain. Include the `-t` flag, set to `language`. The `-t` stands for "template" and without it you won't be able to compare MSIs that have different code pages. In this example, we're storing the output in a folder called `transforms`. Make sure that this folder exists before you call Torch.

The next step is to embed all of the transforms inside the English MSI. WiX doesn't have a tool to do this, so we'll have to look elsewhere. The Windows SDK comes with several VBScript files that perform various MSI-related tasks. You may need to download the SDK from the MSDN website. You can find more information at:

```
http://msdn.microsoft.com/en-us/library/aa372865%28VS.85%29.aspx
```

The VBScript file we're interested in is called `WiSubStg.vbs` and can usually be found in the `Samples` directory of the Windows SDK. On my computer, it's located at `C:\Program Files\Microsoft SDKs\Windows\v7.0\Samples\sysmgmt\msi\scripts`. Once you've found it, copy it to your project's directory and execute the following command:

```
WiSubStg.vbs "en-us\TestInstaller.msi" "transforms\es-es.mst" 1034
```

The first argument is the path to the English version MSI. The second is the path to one of the transform files. You'll need to repeat this call for each one. The third parameter gives a name to the transform for when it's embedded inside the MSI. The convention is to name it the LCID of the language, such as "1034" for Spanish. This process embeds all of the transform files inside the English MSI.

The next step is to set the value of the Languages attribute on the Package element so that it publishes all of the languages that the MSI now supports. We don't have to alter the MSI directly. We can use another tool from the Windows SDK called WiLangId.vbs. Copy this file to your project's directory. The following command will set the Languages attribute to the three languages we've embedded inside the MSI: 1033 (English), 1034 (Spanish), and 1031 (German). You'll need to add other LCIDs if you've added other languages.

```
WiLangId.vbs "en-us\TestInstaller.msi" Package 1033,1034,1031
```

That's it. The MSI is now a multi-language MSI. To test it out, change the language settings of your user profile to Spanish. Go to **Control Panel | Regional and Language Options**, select the **Regional Options** tab and select Spanish as your language. The MSI will then display its content in Spanish.

Launch the MSI and it should be the Spanish version. If you change your language back to English, the MSI should then display itself in English. If the user's preferred language is not one of the languages supported by your MSI, it will default to showing English since that was the base MSI without any transforms applied to it. The downside, however, is that the **Summary Properties** will always be in English since the transform is applied when the MSI is launched. Right-clicking on the installer and viewing its properties won't activate the transform.

Summary

In this chapter, we discussed how to localize a WiX installer. Localization files (.wxl) make this task much simpler and faster. You can use Light to select a language to build, saving you from having to recompile each time. Furthermore, with a few more steps, you can create a single installer that can handle multiple languages.

In the next chapter, we'll cover how to plan for software upgrades and how to perform them with WiX markup.

13
Upgrading and Patching

In this chapter, we'll discuss planning for and authoring updates for your software. Windows Installer offers an impressive set of functionality in this area and it pays to learn your options early on, before the first version of your software is released into the wild. As you'll learn, building your initial MSI with updates in mind will help make your job much easier when it finally comes to sending out changes.

We'll cover the following topics:

- Planning for updates, including choosing the type of update to perform
- Authoring a major upgrade
- Deploying a minor upgrade or small update with a patch

Planning for updates

In the Windows Installer world, people tend to categorize updates into three groups: *major upgrades*, *minor upgrades*, and *small updates*. The primary distinction between these groups is the size of the update, or in other words, the number of changes that will take place. Speaking at a high level, a major upgrade completely replaces the existing software with a new set of files, registry keys, and so on. By contrast, minor upgrades and small updates only replace some of the files and leave the rest as they are.

In this section, we'll discuss how to plan for an update. It's beneficial to do this from the start before you actually need to author an update. In some cases, if you haven't authored your original installer in a way that supports updates, you'll find the task much harder later on.

Choosing an update type

A **major upgrade** is the simplest type of update to set up. It's really a complete MSI, just like any other you've created previously, with all of the components of your software included just like the original install. The difference is that if it detects an older version, it removes it.

You should use a major upgrade if any of the following are true:

- Enough of the product has changed to warrant completely replacing it.
- You've removed a feature from the install or moved it in the feature hierarchy—for example, made it a child to another feature.
- You've moved a component from one feature to another or deleted one.
- You simply want to keep things simple. Major upgrades are easier to implement than any other option.

A major upgrade changes the installer's `ProductCode` property (the Product element's ID) to indicate that this is a completely new product. However, as it's still the same type of product—as in, you're replacing one calculator with another calculator—you'll keep the installer's `UpgradeCode` the same. For the lifetime of a product, through all of its incarnations, the `UpgradeCode` should *never* change. You'll also increment the `Product` element's `Version` attribute.

A **minor upgrade** updates existing files without uninstalling the original product. It can be used to fix bugs or add features and components. Instead of changing the `ProductCode`, you'll only increment the product's version number. That way, you're saying that this is still the same product, but with changes. It can be distributed as a patch file (`.msp`) or, like a major upgrade, as an MSI. Although you can add new features and components with a minor upgrade, you should not reorganize the feature-component tree.

A **small update** is distributed as a patch. It's smaller in scope than a minor upgrade, typically only changing a few files. It has so few changes that you won't even bother to change the version number.

The following table sums up when you'll need to change the Product element's `Version` and `Id` attributes:

Update type	Change Product Version?	Change Product ID?
Major Upgrade	Yes	Yes
Minor Upgrade	Yes	No
Small Update	No	No

Per-user or per-machine

When your update is going to remove a previous version of your software, such as during a major upgrade, Windows searches the Registry to find information about the previous product such as its ProductCode and the location of its features and components. If your original install was installed as "per-machine", meaning not for a specific user, then your update will have to do the same. Otherwise, the installer may look in the wrong section of the Registry, the part belonging to the current user, and not find the product.

```xml
<Property Id="ALLUSERS" Value="1" />
```

To keep things consistent, you should always set the ALLUSERS property—even in your very first installer. When set to 1, the install is per-machine. When set to an empty string, it uses the per-user context. If set to a 2, the context will be per-machine if the user has administrative rights, otherwise it will be per-user. However, this isn't a hard and fast rule and changes depending on the operating system. View the MSI documentation for more information, http://msdn.microsoft.com/en-us/library/aa367559%28VS.85%29.aspx.

You can also use the Package element's InstallScope attribute to the same effect. Behind the scenes it will set the ALLUSERS property for you. You can set it to perMachine or perUser. If you go this route, be sure to remove any markup that sets ALLUSERS directly.

Major upgrade

A major upgrade is a full installation package that removes any older versions of the same product. To create one, you'll need to do the following:

- Change the Product element's Id to a new GUID
- Increment the Product element's Version
- Add an Upgrade element that defines which older versions to remove
- Add the RemoveExistingProducts standard action to the InstallExecuteSequence

We'll go over each step. Before we get to that, let's make an MSI that will install the "old" software—the software to update. You can use the following markup in a new WiX project, which you can call "OldInstaller". Notice that the Product element's Version is "1.0.0.0". Also, take notice of the Product's Id and UpgradeCode, as these will come into play later.

You may recall that you can use an asterisk (*) for `Id` and WiX will choose a new GUID for you each time you compile the project. You can do that here, if you choose to. You would not want to do that, because later on when we're creating a minor upgrade or small update the `ProductCode` should not be changed. We'll use a hardcoded GUID here to illustrate that it *is* changed during a major upgrade.

```xml
<?xml version="1.0" encoding="UTF-8"?>
<Wix xmlns="http://schemas.microsoft.com/wix/2006/wi">

    <Product
        Id="3E786878-358D-43AD-82D1-1435ADF9F6EA"
        Name="Awesome Software"
        Language="1033"
        Version="1.0.0.0"
        Manufacturer="Awesome Company"
        UpgradeCode="B414C827-8D81-4B4A-B3B6-338C06DE3A11">

        <Package InstallerVersion="301" Compressed="yes" />
        <Media Id="1" Cabinet="media1.cab" EmbedCab="yes" />

        <Property Id="ALLUSERS" Value="1" />

        <!--Directory structure-->
        <Directory Id="TARGETDIR" Name="SourceDir">
            <Directory Id="ProgramFilesFolder">
                <Directory Id="INSTALLLOCATION"
                                        Name="Awesome Software" />
            </Directory>
        </Directory>

        <!--Components-->
        <DirectoryRef Id="INSTALLLOCATION">
            <Component
                Id="CMP_InstallMeTXT"
                Guid="E8A58B7B-F031-4548-9BDD-7A6796C8460D">
                <File
                    Id="FILE_InstallMeTXT"
                    Source="InstallMe.txt" KeyPath="yes" />
            </Component>
        </DirectoryRef>

        <!--Features-->
        <Feature Id="ProductFeature" Title="Main Product"
                    Level="1">
```

```
            <ComponentRef Id="CMP_InstallMeTXT" />
        </Feature>

    </Product>
</Wix>
```

This installs a text file called `InstallMe.txt`, so be sure to add one to your project. To show that this is the old version, you could write some text in it like "This file comes from the old version". During the upgrade, we'll replace this file with a new one.

Build this example and install it. Later on, when we have the upgraded version, we'll have this older version to uninstall. Next, create a new WiX project and call it `NewInstaller`. You can reuse most of the markup from the previous example, except for `Product` element's `Id` and `Version` which needs to be changed.

```
<Product
    Id="B55596A8-93E3-47EB-84C4-D7FE07D0CAF4"
    Name="Awesome Software"
    Language="1033"
    Version="2.0.0.0"
    Manufacturer="Awesome Company"
    UpgradeCode="B414C827-8D81-4B4A-B3B6-338C06DE3A11">
```

By changing the `Id`, we're setting up a major upgrade. We'll be replacing the old product with a new one. We've also changed the `Version` attribute to show that this is the newer product. Windows Installer ignores the fourth digit during upgrade scenarios, so you should only rely on the first three when detecting an earlier version.

Next, change the text inside the `InstallMe.txt` file to say something like "This file comes from the new version". The component's GUID should stay the same. If you wanted to, you could add or remove components, but in this example we're replacing an existing one. At this point, if we installed both the old and the new package, the old would not be removed. You'd be able to see both in Add/Remove Programs.

We can remove the older version before installing the new one by adding an `Upgrade` element as a child to the `Product` element. Here's an example that shows adding an `Upgrade` element to the `NewInstaller.wxs`. As you can see, it has an `Id` attribute that's set to the GUID used in the `UpgradeCode` attribute of the `Product` element. This tells Windows where to find the older version's information in the Registry.

```xml
<?xml version="1.0" encoding="UTF-8"?>
<Wix xmlns="http://schemas.microsoft.com/wix/2006/wi">

    <Product
        Id="B55596A8-93E3-47EB-84C4-D7FE07D0CAF4"
        Name="Awesome Software"
        Language="1033"
        Version="2.0.0.0"
        Manufacturer="Awesome Company"
        UpgradeCode="B414C827-8D81-4B4A-B3B6-338C06DE3A11">

        <Package InstallerVersion="301" Compressed="yes" />
        <Media Id="1" Cabinet="media1.cab" EmbedCab="yes" />

        <Property Id="ALLUSERS" Value="1" />

        <Upgrade Id="B414C827-8D81-4B4A-B3B6-338C06DE3A11">

        </Upgrade>
```

The `UpgradeCode` doesn't change between the old and new version. Now Windows will be able to find products that have that `UpgradeCode`. To fine-tune the search, add an `UpgradeVersion` element.

```xml
<Upgrade Id="B414C827-8D81-4B4A-B3B6-338C06DE3A11">
    <UpgradeVersion
        Property="OLD_VERSION_FOUND"
        Minimum="1.0.0.0"
        Maximum="2.0.0.0"
        IncludeMinimum="yes"
        IncludeMaximum="no"
        OnlyDetect="no"
        IgnoreRemoveFailure="yes"
        MigrateFeatures="yes"
        Language="1033" />
</Upgrade>
```

The `Property` attribute is required, but we won't have a use for it yet. Later on, it will come into play when we try to detect if a *newer* version than the one we're installing is already installed. Be sure to make this property public (all uppercase).

The `Minimum` and `Maximum` attributes set the range of versions to look for. These work hand-in-hand with the `IncludeMinimum` and `IncludeMaximum` attributes, which set whether `Minimum` and `Maximum` should be inclusive. Here, we've set `Minimum` to `"1.0.0.0"` and `IncludeMinimum` to yes, which means that the search will look for all prior versions including `"1.0.0.0"`. We've set the `Maximum` to `"2.0.0.0"`, but set `IncludeMaximum` to `"no"`. This means that the search will look for versions up to the version just before this one, which could be as high as 1.255.65535.65535.

Setting `OnlyDetect` to `"no"` means that when we find an older version, we'll go ahead and remove it. We won't stop at just detecting it. This is another attribute that will take on more significance when we try to detect if a newer version is already present.

`IgnoreRemoveFailure` sets whether the installer should fail if the older version can't be removed. Here we've set it to `yes` to ignore these sorts of failures and allow the install of the newer product to continue. If you're more comfortable with aborting the process if the older version can't be uninstalled, you should set this to `no`. The `MigrateFeatures` attribute, when set to `yes`, will install the same features that the end user had selected before in the old install. Of course, if you have a UI, they'll still get a chance to make changes.

The `Language` attribute is another filter and specifies the language of the products you want to detect. It accepts an LCID, such as "1033". You can omit this attribute to detect all languages or set it to a list of LCIDs, separated by commas.

The last thing to do is add the `RemoveExistingProducts` action to the `InstallExecuteSequence` table. This is defined by Windows Installer and will remove any of the products that have been detected by the Upgrade element.

```
<InstallExecuteSequence>
    <RemoveExistingProducts After="InstallFinalize" />
</InstallExecuteSequence>
```

I've scheduled this action to run after `InstallFinalize`, but you have several alternatives.

Scheduled when	Effect
After `InstallInitialize`	Installer removes the old version completely before installing the new one. If the install fails, a rollback will cause the old version to be brought back. This should not be used if you're installing files to the GAC or the WinSxS folder, as there is a bug: `http://support.microsoft.com/kb/905238`. To use this sequence, you must also schedule `InstallExecute` after `RemoveExistingProducts`.
Before `InstallInitialize`	Installer removes the old version completely before installing the new one. If the install of the new fails, the old version will not be brought back.
Before `InstallFinalize`	The new version is installed and then the old version is removed. If the install fails, a rollback will bring the old version back (it may not have even been removed at that point). This is more efficient because files that haven't changed don't need to be replaced. To use this sequence, you must also schedule `InstallExecute` before `RemoveExistingProducts`.
After `InstallFinalize`	The new version is installed and then the old version is removed. If the uninstall of the old fails, the new version remains and the old version is also kept. On the other hand, if the install of the new fails, only the old will remain.

If you schedule `RemoveExistingProducts` after `InstallInitialize`, you must also schedule the `InstallExecute` action to run after it. Here's an example:

```
<InstallExecuteSequence>
    <RemoveExistingProducts After="InstallInitialize" />
    <InstallExecute After="RemoveExistingProducts" />
</InstallExecuteSequence>
```

Similarly, if you schedule `RemoveExistingProducts` before `InstallFinalize`, you must schedule the `InstallExecute` action to run before it. Here's an example:

```
<InstallExecuteSequence>
    <InstallExecute Before="RemoveExistingProducts" />
    <RemoveExistingProducts Before="InstallFinalize" />
</InstallExecuteSequence>
```

Now you're ready to build the `NewInstaller` project and install. It should remove the older version. You'll notice that there are no dialogs that tell the user that the old version is being removed. From their perspective, it's a seamless process.

So, what happens if a newer version is already installed? Typically in that situation, you'll want to display a message to the user telling them that a newer version is already present and then abort the current install.

To do so, we'll add a second `UpgradeVersion` element. This time, we'll make use of the `Property` and `OnlyDetect` attributes. By setting `OnlyDetect` to `yes`, the software *won't* be automatically uninstalled if found.

```
<Upgrade Id="B414C827-8D81-4B4A-B3B6-338C06DE3A11">
    <UpgradeVersion
          Property="OLD_VERSION_FOUND"
          Minimum="1.0.0.0"
          Maximum="2.0.0.0"
          IncludeMinimum="yes"
          IncludeMaximum="no"
          OnlyDetect="no"
          IgnoreRemoveFailure="yes"
          MigrateFeatures="yes"
          Language="1033"/>

    <UpgradeVersion
          Property="NEWER_VERSION_FOUND"
          Minimum="2.0.0.0"
          IncludeMinimum="no"
          OnlyDetect="yes"
          Language="1033" />
</Upgrade>
```

This `UpgradeVersion` element will detect any version starting with a number higher than "`2.0.0.0`" and extending to "`255.255.65535.65535`" as we didn't include a maximum. If it finds one, the `NEWER_VERSION_FOUND` property will be set, which we can then use in a launch condition:

```
<Condition Message="A newer version of [ProductName] is
    already installed. Exiting installation.">
    <![CDATA[Installed OR NOT NEWER_VERSION_FOUND]]>
</Condition>
```

Here's the full markup for our new installer:

```
<?xml version="1.0" encoding="UTF-8"?>
<Wix xmlns="http://schemas.microsoft.com/wix/2006/wi">

<Product
    Id="B55596A8-93E3-47EB-84C4-D7FE07D0CAF4"
        Name="Awesome Software"
```

```
Language="1033"
Version="2.0.0.0"
Manufacturer="Awesome Company"
UpgradeCode="B414C827-8D81-4B4A-B3B6-338C06DE3A11">

<Package InstallerVersion="301" Compressed="yes" />
<Media Id="1" Cabinet="media1.cab" EmbedCab="yes" />

<Property Id="ALLUSERS" Value="1" />

<Condition Message="A newer version of [ProductName] is
    already installed. Exiting installation.">
    <![CDATA[Installed OR NOT NEWER_VERSION_FOUND]]>
</Condition>

<!--Directory structure-->
<Directory Id="TARGETDIR" Name="SourceDir">
    <Directory Id="ProgramFilesFolder">
        <Directory Id="INSTALLLOCATION"
            Name="Awesome Software" />
    </Directory>
</Directory>

<!--Components-->
<DirectoryRef Id="INSTALLLOCATION">
    <Component
        Id="CMP_InstallMeTXT"
        Guid="E8A58B7B-F031-4548-9BDD-7A6796C8460D">
        <File
            Id="FILE_InstallMeTXT"
            Source="InstallMe.txt" KeyPath="yes" />
    </Component>
</DirectoryRef>

<!--Features-->
<Feature Id="ProductFeature" Title="Main Product"
    Level="1">
    <ComponentRef Id="CMP_InstallMeTXT" />
</Feature>

<!--Upgrade element-->
<Upgrade Id="B414C827-8D81-4B4A-B3B6-338C06DE3A11">
    <UpgradeVersion
        Property="OLD_VERSION_FOUND"
```

```
          Minimum="1.0.0.0"
          Maximum="2.0.0.0"
          IncludeMinimum="yes"
          IncludeMaximum="no"
          OnlyDetect="no"
          IgnoreRemoveFailure="yes"
          MigrateFeatures="yes"
          Language="1033" />

      <UpgradeVersion
          Property="NEWER_VERSION_FOUND"
          Minimum="2.0.0.0"
          IncludeMinimum="no"
          OnlyDetect="yes"
          Language="1033" />

    </Upgrade>

    <InstallExecuteSequence>
        <RemoveExistingProducts After="InstallFinalize" />
    </InstallExecuteSequence>
  </Product>
</Wix>
```

Minor upgrade

Although a minor upgrade, like a major upgrade, can be distributed as a full MSI, in this chapter we'll focus on the more efficient method of distributing it as a patch file (.msp). In this case, a minor upgrade doesn't uninstall the previous version. It only replaces some existing files or adds new ones. We can use the same OldInstaller project that we did for a major upgrade for our product to update. Here's what its Product element should look like:

```
<Product
    Id="3E786878-358D-43AD-82D1-1435ADF9F6EA"
    Name="Awesome Software"
    Language="1033"
    Version="1.0.0.0"
    Manufacturer="Awesome Company"
    UpgradeCode="B414C827-8D81-4B4A-B3B6-338C06DE3A11">
```

Create a new WiX project and call it `MinorUpgradeInstaller`. You can reuse the markup from the old installer, but change the `Product` element's `Version` attribute. Leave its `Id` the same.

```
<Product
    Id="3E786878-358D-43AD-82D1-1435ADF9F6EA"
    Name="Awesome Software"
    Language="1033"
    Version="1.0.1.0"
    Manufacturer="Awesome Company"
    UpgradeCode="B414C827-8D81-4B4A-B3B6-338C06DE3A11">
```

In the upgrade installer, we've changed the `Version` from `1.0.0.0` to `1.0.1.0`. This indicates that this is a minor upgrade. You can, if you wish, design your own numbering system. Remember that Windows Installer ignores the fourth digit.

Feel free to change the contents of the `InstallMe.txt` file to say something like "This file comes from a minor upgrade". Build both the old and new installer. Next, we'll discuss how to create the patch.

Authoring a patch file

To create a patch file, we need to make a new WiX source file that will define the patch's characteristics. Create a new `.wxs` and call it `Patch.wxs`. Don't add it to your project. It should exist on its own outside of your installer. Here's the markup to add to it:

```
<?xml version="1.0" encoding="UTF-8"?>
<Wix xmlns="http://schemas.microsoft.com/wix/2006/wi">
    <Patch
        AllowRemoval="yes"
        Classification="Update"
        Comments="Patch for Awesome Software v. 1.0.0.0"
        Description="Updates Awesome Software to v. 1.0.1.0"
        DisplayName="Awesome Software Patch 2010-05-01"
        Manufacturer="Acme Products"
        MoreInfoURL="http://www.mysite.com/patchinfo.html"
        TargetProductName="Awesome Software">

        <Media Id="1000" Cabinet="MyPatch.cab">
            <PatchBaseline Id="MyPatch" />
        </Media>

        <PatchFamily
            Id="MyPatchFamily"
```

```
            Version="1.0.1.0"
            ProductCode="3E786878-358D-43AD-82D1-1435ADF9F6EA"
            Supersede="yes">

            <ComponentRef Id="CMP_InstallMeTXT" />
        </PatchFamily>
    </Patch>
</Wix>
```

The `Patch` element is the root element in this file. Its `AllowRemoval` attribute configures the patch so that it can be removed after it's been applied without having to uninstall the entire product. So you know, you can uninstall a patch file from the command line by setting the `MSIPATCHREMOVE` property to the path of the patch file. You use `msiexec`:

msiexec /i MyInstaller.msi MSIPATCHREMOVE=C:\MyPatch.msp

Classification contains the category for the patch. It's up to you what to set this to, but your options are: *Critical Update, Hotfix, Security Rollup, Security Update, Service Pack, Update,* and *Update Rollup.*

The `Comments` and `Description` attributes let you add additional information about the patch and will be displayed in the file's Properties. `DisplayName` also appears in the Properties and should be set to a user-friendly name for the file. `Manufacturer` should be set to the name of your company.

You can use the `MoreInfoURL` attribute, which is also displayed in the file's Properties, to provide a website address where customers can get more information about the patch. The `TargetProductName` attribute can be set to the name of the software that this patch applies to. If this `.wxs` file contains characters that rely on a code page, you can set the optional `CodePage` attribute.

Next, inside the `Patch` element, add a `Media` element with a child `PatchBaseline` element.

```
    <Media Id="1000" Cabinet="MyPatch.cab">
        <PatchBaseline Id="MyPatch" />
    </Media>
```

The `Media` element's `Id` should be higher than any Media element used in the MSI package you want to update. So, it's safer to use a high number like `1000`. You can give the CAB file any name you like using the `Cabinet` attribute.

The `PatchBaseline` element is used to define a name that we can reference later as we're building the patch file. I've given it the same name as the CAB file.

The last thing to do in this file is add a `PatchFamily` element. This will define the product that this patch applies to and whether or not earlier patches should be overwritten.

```
<PatchFamily
    Id="MyPatchFamily"
    Version="1.0.1.0"
    ProductCode="3E786878-358D-43AD-82D1-1435ADF9F6EA"
    Supersede="yes">

    <ComponentRef Id="CMP_InstallMeTXT" />
</PatchFamily>
```

The `Id` attribute gives your new `PatchFamily` a name. A `PatchFamily` contains the updates of your patch. The `Version` attribute is used to sequence the install order of your changes and can be set to the version number of your `Product` element. You can use the `ProductCode` attribute to target a specific product to patch. `Supersede`, when set to `yes`, signals that this patch should override other earlier patches.

Inside the `PatchFamily` element, nest `ComponentRef` elements to pull in the files that you want to update. Note that, like when working with `Fragment` elements, pulling in one component will pull in all neighboring components in the parent Fragment or Product. So, you don't need to reference every file that you're updating if they exist in the same `.wxs` file under the same root element.

We're now ready to build our patch, which we'll have to do from the command line. We'll discuss this in the next section.

Building the patch on the command line

You should now have two MSI files, one for the old version of your product and one for the new, and two `.wixpdb` files to go with them. When you build WiX projects in Visual Studio, a separate `.wixpdb` file is automatically created. This file contains the data held in the MSI, but in XML format. You should also have a `.wxs` file that defines the patch. We've called this file `Patch.wxs`.

Open a command prompt and navigate to your project's directory. The following commands will compile and link the `Patch.wxs` file. First, call Candle to create a `.wixobj` file.

candle.exe Patch.wxs

Next, call Light to create a `.wixmsp` file from the `.wixobj`.

light.exe Patch.wixobj

Now, let's switch gears and compare the two .wixpdb files and store the differences between them. This will create a transform file in XML format (.wixmst).

```
torch.exe -p -xi OldInstaller.wixpdb MinorUpgradeInstaller.wixpdb -out
Patch.wixmst
```

It's time to merge everything together into a patch file. We can use Pyro.exe to consolidate the .wixmsp and .wixmst files into an .msp file.

```
pyro.exe Patch.wixmsp -t MyPatch Patch.wixmst -out Patch.msp
```

The first argument is the .wixmsp file that was created by Light. The -t argument accepts the Id we gave to the PatchBaseline element in our Patch.wxs file. This is followed by the name of the .wixmst file created by Torch. The -out argument allows us to name the resulting .msp file.

After this, you'll have Patch.msp—a file that looks like an MSI, can be read with Orca, and that the end user can double-click to install. It's smaller than an MSI though. It only contains the differences between our old version product and the new version. When the customer uses it, it will simply apply the changes. This is our "minor upgrade".

Patch.msp

You can also apply this patch from the command line:

```
msiexec /p Patch.msp
```

Small update

A small update is like a minor upgrade except that it's usually smaller in scope. You might use it when only a few files have changed and you don't intend to change the Product's version number.

The steps to create it are mostly the same as when creating a minor upgrade patch.

1. Create a new WiX project with the modified files. Do not change the Product element's Id or Version.

2. Build the old and new versions of the product, storing the .wixpdb files that get created.

3. Create a patch `.wxs` file that defines the contents of the patch.

4. From the command line, build the `.wxs` file with Candle and link it with Light to produce a `.wixmsp` file.

5. Use Torch to generate a `.wixmst` file of the differences between the old and new `.wixpdb` files.

6. Use Pyro to merge the `.wixmsp` and `.wixmst` files to create an `.msp` file.

This gives you a patch file that when used will update files, but won't change the software's `ProductCode` or version.

Summary

In this chapter, we talked about the three types of updates. Major upgrades are the easiest to do, but are the least efficient for small sets of changes. They perform a complete uninstall of any older versions before or after installing the new files. One of the perks of this is that it gives you a clean slate. You don't have to worry so much about testing functionality with older components. Many times, such as when you've changed existing features, you'll have to use a major upgrade.

Minor upgrades and small updates are delivered as patch files and are typically much smaller. They only replace some of the existing files and add new features. These can be an ideal way of keeping customers up-to-date on bug fixes.

Index

Symbols

-ag argument 52
-ai flag 238
-arch flag 224
-bcgg flag 242
-bf flag 238, 242
-b flag 238
-binder flag 238
-cc flag 242
-cg <ComponentGroup> argument 55
-cg <ComponentGroupName> argument 52
-ct flag 243
-cub flag 243
-cultures flag 239, 290
-dcl flag 243
-d flag 224, 239, 247, 294
-dr <DirectoryName> argument 52, 55
-dut flag 239
-eav flag 243
-ext <extension> argument 52
-ext flag 224, 239
-fips flag 225
-fv flag 243
-g1 argument 52, 55
-gg argument 52, 55
-? | -help argument 52
-ice flag 243
.ico file 179
-I flag 225
-indent <N> argument 52
-ke argument 52
-loc flag 239
-nologo argument 52
-nologo flag 225, 239
-notidy flag 240

-o flag 225, 240
< operator 100
<= operator 100
<> operator 100
= operator 100
> operator 100
>= operator 100
-out argument 52
-out flag 54, 225, 240
-pdbout flag 244
-pedantic flag 225, 240
-p flag 225
-pog:<group> argument 52
-reusecab flag 242, 244
-sacl flag 244
-sadmin flag 240
-sadv flag 240
-sa flag 244
-scom argument 52
-sfdvital flag 226
-sf flag 245
-sfrag argument 52, 55
-sh flag 245
-sice flag 245
-sl flag 245
-sloc flag 240
-sma flag 240
-spdb flag 245
-srd argument 52, 55
-ss flag 226, 241
-sts flag 241
-suid argument 52
-sui flag 241
-sval flag 245
-svb6 argument 52
-sv flag 241

P

package element, WiX project
about 18, 284
example 285
InstallerVersion attribute 18
Password attribute 180, 269
patch
building, on command line 314, 315
PatchBaseline element 313
Patch element 313
patch file
authoring 312, 313
PathEdit control
example 182, 197, 198
PATH environment variable 223
PermissionEx element 260
attributes 66
PermissionEx element, attributes
Append 66
ChangePermission 66
Delete 66
Execute 66
GenericAll 66
GenericExecute 66
GenericRead 66
GenericWrite 66
Read 66
ReadPermission 66
Synchronize 66
TakeOwnership 66
Write 66
permissions, Registry 260, 261
POWERSHELLVERSION property 103
preprocessor extension 229-234
preprocessor variable 42
Privileged property 105
ProcessComponents action 120
product element, WiX project
about 16
Codepage attribute 17
Id attribute 17
Language attribute 17
Manufacturer attribute 18
Name attribute 17
UpgradeCode attribute 18
Version attribute 17

ProgressBar control
about 201
example 201-204
ProgressBlocks attribute 201
progress dialog
adding 158-161
ProjectAggregator2 12
project templates, WiX 12, 13
properties
about 71
acessing, in deferred stage 132, 134
declaring 72, 73
publishing 215
referencing 73, 74
setting 72, 73
Property attribute 172, 179, 189
property element, WiX
about 72
Id attribute 72
Value attribute 72
Publish element
about 172, 205
events 206-214
example 205, 208
nesting, inside Control element 205, 206
versus Subscribe element 209
Publish element, events
AddLocal 206-212
AddSource 206
CheckExistingTargetPath 206
CheckTargetPath 206
DirectoryListNew 206
DirectoryListOpen 206
DirectoryListUp 206
DoAction 207, 212, 213
EnableRollback 207
EndDialog 207-214
NewDialog 207, 214
Reinstall 207
ReinstallMode 207
Remove 207
Reset 207
SelectionBrowse 207
SetInstallLevel 207
SetTargetPath 207
SpawnDialog 207
SpawnWaitDialog 207

Thank you for buying
WiX: A Developer's Guide to Windows Installer XML

About Packt Publishing

Packt, pronounced 'packed', published its first book "*Mastering phpMyAdmin for Effective MySQL Management*" in April 2004 and subsequently continued to specialize in publishing highly focused books on specific technologies and solutions.

Our books and publications share the experiences of your fellow IT professionals in adapting and customizing today's systems, applications, and frameworks. Our solution based books give you the knowledge and power to customize the software and technologies you're using to get the job done. Packt books are more specific and less general than the IT books you have seen in the past. Our unique business model allows us to bring you more focused information, giving you more of what you need to know, and less of what you don't.

Packt is a modern, yet unique publishing company, which focuses on producing quality, cutting-edge books for communities of developers, administrators, and newbies alike. For more information, please visit our website: www.packtpub.com.

About Packt Open Source

In 2010, Packt launched two new brands, Packt Open Source and Packt Enterprise, in order to continue its focus on specialization. This book is part of the Packt Open Source brand, home to books published on software built around Open Source licences, and offering information to anybody from advanced developers to budding web designers. The Open Source brand also runs Packt's Open Source Royalty Scheme, by which Packt gives a royalty to each Open Source project about whose software a book is sold.

Writing for Packt

We welcome all inquiries from people who are interested in authoring. Book proposals should be sent to author@packtpub.com. If your book idea is still at an early stage and you would like to discuss it first before writing a formal book proposal, contact us; one of our commissioning editors will get in touch with you.

We're not just looking for published authors; if you have strong technical skills but no writing experience, our experienced editors can help you develop a writing career, or simply get some additional reward for your expertise.

open source*
community experience distilled

[PACKT]
PUBLISHING

IBM Lotus Notes and Domino 8.5.1

The Upgrader's Guide

Upgrade your system and embrace the exciting new features of the Lotus Notes and Domino 8.5.1 platform

Tim Speed   Barry Rosen   Joseph Anderson   David Byrd
Brad Schauf   Dennis Gibson   Dick McCarrick   PACKT

IBM Lotus Notes and Domino 8.5.1

ISBN: 978-1-847199-28-7   Paperback: 336 pages

Upgrade your system and embrace the exciting new features of the Lotus Notes and Domino 8.5.1 platform

1. Upgrade to the latest version of Lotus Notes and Domino

2. Understand the new features and put them to work in your business

3. Thoroughly covers Domino Attachment Object Service (DAOS), Domino Configuration Tuner (DCT), and iNotes

IBM Lotus Notes 8.5 User Guide

A practical hands-on user guide with time saving tips and comprehensive instructions for using Lotus Notes effectively and efficiently

Foreword by Ed Brill
Director, Product Management, IBM Lotus Software

Karen Hooper   [PACKT] enterprise

IBM Lotus Notes 8.5 User Guide

ISBN: 978-1-849680-20-2   Paperback: 296 pages

A practical hands-on user guide with time saving tips and comprehensive instructions for using Lotus Notes effectively and efficiently

1. Understand and master the features of Lotus Notes and put them to work in your business quickly

2. Contains comprehensive coverage of new Lotus Notes 8.5 features

3. Includes easy-to-follow real-world examples with plenty of screenshots to clearly demonstrate how to get the most out of Lotus Notes

Please check **www.PacktPub.com** for information on our titles

Lotus Notes Domino 8: Upgrader's Guide

ISBN: 978-1-847192-74-5   Paperback: 276 pages

What's new in the latest Lotus Notes Domino Platform

1. Upgrade to the latest version of Lotus Notes and Domino.

2. Understand the new features and put them to work in your business

3. Appreciate the implications of changes and new features

IBM Cognos 8 Planning

ISBN: 978-1-847196-84-2   Paperback: 424 pages

Engineer a clear-cut strategy for achieving best-in-class results

1. Build and deploy effective planning models using Cognos 8 Planning

2. Filled with ideas and techniques for designing planning models

3. Ample screenshots and clear explanations to facilitate learning.

4. Written for first-time developers focusing on what is important to the beginner

Please check **www.PacktPub.com** for information on our titles

CPSIA information can be obtained at www.ICGtesting.com
Printed in the USA
LVOW111325311012

304946LV00008B/1/P